Y0-CAI-421

BETWEEN THE FLAG
AND THE BANNER

SUNY Series in Israeli Studies
Russell Stone, editor

BETWEEN THE FLAG AND THE BANNER

Women in Israeli Politics

by

Yael Yishai

State University of New York Press

Published by
State University of New York Press, Albany

© 1997 State University of New York

All rights reserved

Printed in the United States of America

No part of this book may be used or reproduced in any manner
whatsoever without written permission. No part of this book may
be stored in a retrieval system or transmitted in any form or by
any means including electronic, electrostatic, magnetic tape, me-
chanical, photocopying, recording, or otherwise without the prior
permission in writing of the publisher.

For information, address State University of New York Press,
State University Plaza, Albany, N.Y., 12246

Production by Marilyn P. Semerad
Marketing by Nancy Farrell

Library of Congress Cataloging-in-Publication Data
Yishai, Yael, 1993–
    Between the flag and the banner : women in Israeli politics / by
Yael Yishai.
        p.   cm. — (SUNY series in Israeli studies)
    Includes bibliographical references (p.   ) and index.
    ISBN 0-7914-3127-4. — ISBN 0-7914-3128-2 (pbk.)
    1. Women in politics—Israel.   2. Women—Government policy–
–Israel.   I. Title.   II. Series.
HQ1236.5.I75Y57   1996
320.9'0082—dc20   97-1515
                                                              CIP

                    10 9 8 7 6 5 4 3 2 1

CONTENTS

v

For Ori — an equal partner

LIST OF TABLES
AND ILLUSTRATIONS

Tables

PREFACE

During a flight to the United States on my way to sabbatical leave, I noticed something strange in my Israeli passport: on page 3, my picture was pasted beside an empty space, under which I found written: "The wife's picture." When I looked closely at the official document, I found, to my amazement, on page 2 "Name" and "Accompanied by his wife"; not *spouse* but *wife*. As I have no wife, the space left for her picture and for writing her name remained empty. The passport was not issued in the pre-suffragist era, when men did most of the travelling, but in 1994, when women's equality in Western democracies had become a truism. Obviously, I was not detained at the airport due to the empty provisions designated for my "wife," but I had this strange sense of being unequal to the "husband" with whom I was supposed to accompany, and whose picture was to have been pasted next to mine. Why is the "wife" an appendage to the husband? Why is the nuptial bond so important as to be included in a passport? Why is it inserted in an official document of a state which subscribed to women's equality earlier, and in legislation more extensively, than many other Western societies?

While spending my sabbatical year at the Institute for the Research of Women and Gender at Stanford University, I had time to ponder these questions. Having been engaged for a lengthy period in a study of Israel's particular, and paradoxical, democracy, I tried to add the case of women in Israel to some of the broader questions confronting the Jewish state: how to reconcile particular group (or, for that matter, gender) interests with larger national objectives; how to integrate into the collective society without blurring one's special needs; how to avoid tradition without being torn from a perpetual heritage. Women in Israel have faced these problems, which have affected their political organization, behavior, and identity. These will be discussed in this book.

The status of women in Israel has been studied from sociological and psychological perspectives. The subject, however, eluded the attention of political scientists, preoccupied with "more important issues," such as the Arab-Israeli conflict and the state's electoral reform. This book is aimed at filling this lacuna by providing an analysis of the place of women in Israeli politics. Although it centers on women and their political mobilization, public policy regarding gender equality cannot be overlooked. The ways and means by which the state has promoted women's equality in the public and private domains are also examined.

One of the major questions probed in this study is the interaction between women and the state. The feminist attitude toward the state has been highly equivocal. Some scholars regard the state as a patriarchal institution taking an active part in oppressing women, and contend that women have replaced their dependence on individual men by dependence on the state—a shift that has not nourished their power. A different view does not charge the state with the subordination of women, whose position, it is stated, has largely been a "nonissue" left to social forces. The state has thus been a silent observer of socioeconomic developments, or even blind to the actual transformations taking place. The main argument of this book is that in Israel both approaches appear to hold true. Women are dependent on state agencies not only because they are consumers of welfare rights but because the state is the major, for many citizens perhaps the sole, source of identification. At the same time, however, women's affairs remained a "nonissue" as long as they were not elaborated in terms congruent with traditional roles. Safeguarding the privileges involved in custody over the *flag* of the national cause, the state stood by women's side as long as they were willing to forego the *banner* of gender equality.

In writing this book I received invaluable financial and moral support from several sources. I acknowledge with gratitude the essential financial support provided by a grant from the Israel Foundation trustees, which enabled me to gather and analyze the data, and the Jewish-Arab Center at the University of Haifa, which funded the study of Arab women. I heartily thank my editor, Murray Rosovsky, who with efficiency and competence turned my manuscript into readable English. I am very grateful to my friends and colleagues at the Institute for the Study of Gender and Politics, without whose inspiration and encouragement I would have continued in the rough waters of political science without noticing that women have their own vessel. Many thanks are extended to the activists of the women's movement in Israel, who patiently and often enthusiastically responded to my probing questions. A final expression of thanks is extended to my family members: my husband, daughters, sons, and their daughters and sons—not only for having endured my indulgence in the study of women's politics but for enabling me to experience (and enjoy) the blessings of gender equality.

CHAPTER 1

Between the Flag and the Banner: Dilemmas in the Political Life of Israeli Women

The political lives of women in Israel have been shaped by an acute dilemma, a choice between their desire to foster national progress and their quest for feminist self-fulfillment. Women who wanted to play an equal part in building the new homeland rejected sex as a basis for political mobilization and interest aggregation; but those subject to gender discrimination found themselves shut out of the national effort. The perplexing choice for women was between participation in collective efforts at the expense of their particular interests, and adopting a feminist position that would guarantee their rights as women. The first option implied subscribing to overarching collective goals and acting from "within"; the second involved adherence to feminism and mobilizing from "without." This book is about the dilemma before Israeli women, the means they have selected to resolve it, and how their actions have affected the status of women in society.

The account is of women's politics in one particular country, but it may be valid for other societies too. The dilemma women in Israel face may well be that of women in emerging nations, especially during periods of social and political upheaval. At such times participants are subject to heavy demands, and the call for loyalty to the common goal is great. Identification with a national movement may impose constraints on the development of partial mobilization centering on issues such as the cause of women. These constraints, their origins, and their consequences for women in Israel are the major themes of this book.

The underlying argument is that carrying the double burden of predominating common values as well as submission to particular and partial interests obstructs both effective mobilization and influence. Vacillation between two contrasting loyalties weakens effectivity of action and hinders social change. The dilemma is real in that giving up collective values may exact its price in foresaken social rewards; conceding particular interests may take its toll in personal integrity. When a choice is made, however, either because collective (national) demands ease off, or because the group under question is willing to pay the price entailed in breaching established norms, change is more likely to occur. The origins and nature of the quandary of Israeli women and its consequences for political power and influence are discussed in what follows.

Israel as a Case Study of Women and Politics

As we approach the mid-1990s, the literature on the place of women in political life abounds with case studies of various countries. Although these studies ask similar questions (How do women fare in the power game? What are their beliefs? To what extent are they represented in decision-making bodies? Is their political behavior different from that of men? How intense is their mobilization to political life? What shape has this mobilization taken?) and use similar conceptual frameworks (theories of mobilization, theories of patriarchy), the countries where the studies were done may be differentiated by two parameters, which need not be mutually exclusive: rate of political development and type of political regime.

The majority of case studies on women and politics have been conducted, to date, in Western industrialized countries. These cover the United States (Kirpatrick 1974), Canada (Bashevkin 1985), Europe (Lovenduski 1986), New Zealand (Catt and McLeay 1993), and the Nordic states (Haavio-Mannila et al. 1985). Studies have focused on the partisan arena (Lovenduski and Norris 1993), and on women's movements (Mansbridge 1986;

Costain 1992). The subject attracting primary attention among scholars of women and politics is females' share in the political elite, and the processes enabling them to enter decision-making institutions, that is, national and local elections (e.g., Epstein and Coser 1981). Public policy regarding women has also been subject to academic treatment (Gelb and Palley 1987; Gelb 1989; Boneparth and Stoper 1989). With the expansion of feminism, however, instructive case studies have been published on the political life of women in developing countries in Asia and Africa. Good examples are Egypt (Sullivan 1986), Turkey (Arat 1989), India (Panda 1990), Pakistan (Mumtaz and Shanheed 1987), and Malayzia (Danez 1987).

The studies on women and politics in these two types of country have generally reached diverse conclusions. Scholars in the developed industrialized world usually lamented women's minor share in the country's political resources and their disproportionately small contribution in shaping their national life. Even where women have secured impressive political gains, such as in the Scandinavian countries, they were still perceived as being subject to patriarchal norms and structures (Haavio-Mannila and Skard 1985; Siim 1991). By contrast, writers focusing on the role of women in developing countries that have failed to attain the economic standards of the West, generally claim that women have contributed their share in national development, albeit in their own unique way. In Egypt, for example, women were found to play legitimate and important roles in public life. They were described as "agents of change, helping to transform social customs as well as laws and, through work, contributing to increasing production." This was done by concentration in such fields as health, education, and welfare, which are associated with women's traditional interests (Sullivan 1986, 164). In Taiwan, owing to the mandatory reserved-seat system, "women have made significant strides in their political participation and representation over the last several decades that rival the progress that took nearly a century in the United States and Western Europe" (Bih-er, Clark, and Clark 1990, 193).

The second category of country dealt with in these case studies may be distinguished by the characteristics of the political regime. Most studies have focused on women in democratic societies, which also happen to be economically developed. In conditions of democracy, women's rights are enshrined in constitutional guarantees. Although their participation in political life may be hindered by informal and undeclared male discrimination, they nevertheless enjoy freedom of association and civil liberties. These circumstances have fostered the emergence of a gender consciousness, deemed a necessary condition for promoting gender equality (Rinehart 1992). It is generally agreed by students of women's politics in democratic countries that feminism is on the rise, that increasingly more women tend to participate in politics, and that the gender gap emanating from women's lesser role in political life has gradually been closing.

Studies of women, however, are no longer confined to the democratic, developed world but have been extended to states governed by authoritarian elites, or those that are undergoing processes of democratization. Prominent among the first type is the former USSR (Lapidus 1978; Browning 1987), where women's inequality stood in sharp contrast to the professed egalitarian principles of the Communist regime. According to Soviet theorists, women's interests were adequately represented in the political institutions by male politicians. Feminists, however, attributed women's vulnerability to the glaring absence of women's consciousness. The predominance of class struggle over other forms of social activity had attenuated women's awareness of gender interests. Their omission from positions of power seriously affected their ability to challenge their subordination in all its forms.

Among the nondemocratic regimes are former colonies, where struggles for national liberation had taken place. In the past many studies of nationality ignored sex as a significant issue (e.g., Gellner 1983; Smith 1986). The forces that spawn nationalism appeared so sweeping and all-encompassing as to dwarf problems associated with gender. Women's equality tends to remain a nonissue as long as national redemption has not been attained. Diminution of gender as a basis for women's mobilization is particularly evident when nationalism cannot readily assert itself but requires the investment of major human resources. Under these circumstances gender problems are simply ignored. In recent years more attention has been devoted to the issue (e.g., Walby 1991). The possible clash between national objectives and feminist interests, however, has not received much attention. In Israel this clash has played a decisive role in the shaping of women's politics.

Serious scholarly attention has been given to women's roles in countries undergoing processes of democratization, particularly in Latin America (e.g., Molyneaux 1985; Alvarez 1990). It has been argued that Latin America's democratic transitions, by all accounts the region's salient political trend in the 1980s, cannot be properly understood without consideration of the role played by women and by feminists; conversely, the changing role of women cannot be assessed outside the context of transition politics. The transition from military authoritarian rule to democracy happened to coincide with the reemergence of feminist movements and the rapid growth of organizations among poor urban women throughout Latin America. As noted by Alvarez (1989, 18) Brazilians witnessed the emergence and development of perhaps the largest, most varied, most radical, and most successful women's movement in contemporary Latin America.

The countries covered by the two sets of case studies—democracies and authoritarian or democratizing nations—leave a lacuna which is filled by Israel. On the one hand, Israel is a vigorous democracy where a variety of interests compete and clash; yet it differs greatly from the Western world in its strong national vision. It is a democracy sustained by the rule of law and the guarantee of civil justice, but it is a "mobilized democracy" where the elite exerts tremendous power over the people. Israel has been placed by the World Bank in the category of high-income economies (World Development Report 1991). With a per capita GNP of nearly $13,000 in 1992, it can hardly be considered a developing society. Yet the composition of its population, a substantial proportion of which originated in traditional societies in Asia and Africa, and its ongoing war with its Arab neighbors have blurred its image as an affluent country. Furthermore, Israel is a young-ancient nation. It was established in 1948, in the huge post–World War II wave of struggles for independence that swept many countries in Asia and Africa. At the same time, the state was founded on an ancient biblical heritage. It is mostly a secular society, with less than 30 percent observing religious tenets, but the great majority of the population subscribes to basic principles of the Jewish faith. Finally, Israel is a sovereign state, a member in numerous international organizations. At the same time, it constantly nurtures its relations with the Jewish communities in other countries. Recently a proposal was raised to extend Israeli citizenship to Jews living outside the country (Karmon 1994).

All these paradoxes place Israel in a unique situation, passed over by scholars of women's politics in other corners of the world. Being both a democracy and a mobilized state, an affluent society with marked attributes of "development," the case merits special attention. How do women fit into this myriad and compounded environment? Why do they have to choose between adherence to the (national) flag and the (feminist) banner?

Making Choices:
Between the Flag and the Banner

The title of this book intimates that the national flag and the feminist banner were incompatible, if not mutually exclusive. A short review of the discrepancies between the two is in order to demonstrate the reasons for this incongruence.

Democracies can be placed on a continuum extending from a "service state" to a "visionary state." In the first, government is content to provide services and reconcile conflicting interests among different groups and individuals. This pattern prevails in most industrialized states, where the authorities may be concerned with the affluence and welfare of their citizens but they are not guided by, or committed to, a transcendent mission. In the classical description of the Western state, these authorities respond to the public mood and assuage grassroots pressures in order to stay in power. By contrast, in a visionary state, there is more emphasis on mobilization and socialization (Apter 1965, 25). Here "the government has a predetermined vision or goal, and its primary function is to educate and mobilize on its behalf" (Liebman and Don-Yehiya 1987). Where vision prevails, a highly articulated system of symbols and myths defining the community socializes the population and mobilizes them for the realization of national goals. In a visionary democracy there is constant tension between the collective imperatives of society and particularistic needs of subgroups within it, including women.

Vision is likely to develop in democracies facing intransigent opposition from without and/or rapid social change within. In such circumstances the vision centers on a strong national identity, defined in terms of allegiance to one's nation-state (Gellner 1983, 3). The purpose of national identity is to deepen individual commitment and loyalty to the regime, to increase solidarity among society's members, and to provide them with a sense of a community (Seton-Watson 1977). A "community" in this regard does not consist only of "common institutions and a single code of rights and duties for all the members" (Smith 1991, 9) but also of a strong sense of belonging. Where allegiance to the "vision" pervades, sustained by a comprehensive socialization structure, particularistic groups, including women, may be reluctant to carry their own banner. The sweeping force of national goals obstructs the crystallization of their own needs.

In Israel the two pillars that both necessitate and sustain the national vision are the state's precarious security and its mission of ingathering the exiles. Pursuing goals associated with feminism might conceivably have hindered the realization of these goals.

Women and Security

Surrounded as it was by hostile neighbors, Israel had to cope with external threats and incessant belligerency. These factors have had decisive effects on the country's polity, economy, and value system. The problem of national security has dominated the political agenda, displacing almost every other item. Despite the inception of the peace process, media headlines, government discussion, and public attention still reflect the primacy of security in Israeli life. That questions of survival rank first is evident also from the structure of the national budget. Israel expends far more on its security than other Western nations. Annual military expenditures have usually exceeded 20 percent of the GNP. The country's well-known defense burden has contributed to a dominance of the economy by the government to a degree hardly known in other democracies. It has been noted that "Israeli policymakers have economic responsibilities that resemble those of Eastern Europe, in the context of aggressive political parties, labor organizations, and other features of the democratic West" (Sharkansky 1988, 5). The impact of security on public life has been accentuated by the lengthy service of Israelis in the armed forces. Every young man has compulsory service in the military for at least three years. Many serve for five years, and continue to do so in reserve units about one month a year, until they are in their fifties.

Living in a state of siege has not been easy for Israeli women, because the host of norms, values, and attitudes that sustain military might have excluded women and driven them to the margins of society. The halo sparkling around the military generated a positive attitude toward the use of force. The image of the Sabra (native-born Israeli) is of a youngster characterized by strength, courage, and action. A general unease with emotion is masked by an ethos of heroism. Emotionalism, a typical feminine characteristic, has been rejected as a form of weakness that is both incompatible with the norm of the pioneer-warrior and ineffective in times of danger. Only recently a heated public debate took place when a senior army commander condemned the display of soldiers weeping over their dead comrade, killed in battle, disapproving such an outlet of emotion.

To this may be added women's lesser contribution to the country's security. Although women recruits march in parades after basic training, and are often shown on television screens abroad carrying their rifles on their shoulders, for the army they are wearing "paper khaki" (Hazleton 1977, 138). In 1949 the Defense Service Law was enacted. After heated discussion in the Knesset, fueled by religious opposition to recruitment of women, it was decided to conscript women for a shorter period than men and to exempt two categories of women: married and/or religiously observant. It was also decided to establish a women's corps entirely separate from other units in the Israel Defense Forces (IDF). As women have always been considered a burden by military authorities, exemption from duty has been easily obtained: A woman merely has to declare herself religious to be excused from army service. Over the years the Defense Service Law has been amended several times but the principles underlying military service by women have remained intact. A Commission on the Status of Women pointed out that:

> When the IDF was first established, the state recognized the right of the women to serve in all jobs on a voluntary basis. As time elapsed equality has disappeared. The only considerations are army efficiency and economic ones. Jobs are opened and closed to women on this basis. As a result, the IDF lags behind other armies which are more resourceful in absorbing women. (1978; quoted by Bloom 1991, 135).

At present women serve only twenty-two months in the military; they are not allowed to join combat units. Some progress has been made regarding women's status in the armed forces as increasingly more enter occupations previously closed to them. By and large, however, women soldiers are still the secretaries, the clerks, the telephonists, the nurses, the teachers, and the social workers of the IDF. There are no women pilots, tank crews, or paratroopers. Women do not serve in artillery units nor are they found on battleships. One woman, the commander of the Women's Corps (Chen), takes part in the meetings of the IDF's General Staff, but her rank is lower than that of her male colleagues. Thus, despite the many myths concerning the role of women as soldiers (Yuval-Davis 1985), they serve mostly in subordinate and supportive roles, unless in welfare occupations traditionally held by women. The woman soldier's life, concludes Bloom (1991, 137), "remains sufficiently circumscribed to allow her both to do national service and to return to society understanding her role as a woman." The seeds of duality are sown in the preeminent institution of Israeli society, the armed forces.

The exclusion of women from active service has confined them to nurturing roles and has hindered their entrance to the power arena. Women were expected to contribute to the national effort by sticking to their traditional female roles. The male-dominated society could be benevolent to women as long as they conformed, in their attitudes and activities, to established patterns of female behavior. As they could not demonstrate bravery in the battlefield, women had to excel in the kitchen to prove their patriotism. Waintrater (1991, 118) describes how women channeled their anxiety during the October War (1973) "into the things they do best": baking cakes. Their massive engagement in this endeavor resulted in a flour shortage. The women were baking too many cakes, and continued to do so even when the shortage became publicly known. Women were expected to make life easier for the men at the home front, to nurture, to care, and to love. Scores of women volunteers have always swamped the country whenever war has broken out, ministering to wounded soldiers and providing them with goodies to lift their spirits. The normative constraints on women's equality generated by the siege mentality have been summed up by a woman legislator as follows: "The Israeli woman is an organic part of the family of the Jewish people and the female constitutes a practical symbol of that. But she is a wife and a mother in Israel, and therefore it is of her nature to be a soldier, a wife of a soldier, a sister of a soldier, a grandmother of a soldier " (quoted by Hazleton 1977, 141).

When asked, "How do you live in the military milieu, in a society based on the supremacy of men?," the wife of the chief of staff described in a nutshell the impact of the defense requirement on women's status. She said: "It is obvious that we, the women, are 'helpmates' and the husbands, members of the armed forces, can function only owing to the support given to them at home."[1] Breaking the caring tradition would have breached a fundamental norm: doing one's best for the country's survival. Hence women had to choose between the national imperative, relegating themselves to domestic commitments and responsibilities, and a feminist advocacy, which would relieve them of this constriction.

Women and Immigration

Immigration has played a profound role in the process of nation-building: as stated, ingathering of the exiles has been one of the major functions of the Jewish state. Since its creation the state of

Israel has absorbed over two million Jewish immigrants, four times the size of its population when it won independence. The Law of Return, giving the right to all Jews to immigrate to Israel and to automatically acquire citizenship on arrival, highlights the national commitment. Immigration is widely discussed in the media and documented by official sources since its scale is deemed as a major indicator of the nation's strength and the fulfillment of ultimate Zionist ideals. The immigrants are of varied backgrounds and from numerous countries of origin. In the early days of statehood most were either European Jews, Holocaust survivors, or Jews from Arabic-speaking countries in the Middle East and North Africa. The most recent large-scale immigration (some half a million people) are from the countries of the former Soviet Union, which have opened their gates to let Jews out after a long period of severe restrictions. From another corner of the world have come black Ethiopian Jews.

In the country's formative period the hardships involved in immigrant absorption underlined the difficulties in Israel's process of modernization. The majority of immigrants arriving after the establishment of the state came from countries that were relatively deprived and underdeveloped socially and economically (between 1948 and 1954 immigrants from Arabic-speaking countries constituted 51.7 percent). Most of them found it extremely hard to adjust to the advanced economy of the fledgling state, populated mainly by Jews from the developed world. From the perspective of the Israeli authorities, however, there was "no choice" but to "drag these 'backward' immigrants into the modern age—as they saw it, for the (mostly economic) good of the State of Israel as well as the good of the immigrants themselves" (Lehman-Wilzig 1990, 29). While the plight of these immigrants was particularly severe, Israel as a whole suffered its worst economic situation ever. Data reveal that from 1951 to 1953 the per capita national income plummeted by 14.3 percent, and real income fell by 10.6 percent in 1952 alone.

The grave constraints on resources militated against women's economic equality. During the first seven years of statehood, over 400,000 new immigrants came to Israel, swelling the population by approximately one-third. The economy could not absorb such a large number of newcomers into the labor force.

Government employment policy was directed at creating jobs primarily for men, not women, who were left out of the labor market owing to the national imperative of immigrant absorption (Izraeli 1991, 166). With the expansion of the state's economy in subsequent years, increasingly more women joined the labor force. Men's employment needs, however, took precedence over women's. Consequently, unemployment rates have always been higher for women than for men. Furthermore, women were channeled into low-paying and/or "feminine" jobs that would not interfere with the work done by men and would not encroach on the successful absorption of the new immigrants.

Another byproduct of immigration causing women's economic inequality was a growing demand for volunteer service. Although the state guaranteed the basic needs for the immigrants' absorption, the burden of defense and the economic hardships weighed heavily on government agencies and left much to voluntary activity. Women were expected to contribute to the national effort of immigration absorption not through the power of their productive labor, but rather by enfolding the newcomers in their compassion. As we shall see, women's voluntarism was channeled through party institutions, and was not a product of community or grassroots activity. It therefore posed no threat to state authorities nor did it challenge widely endorsed values. Women conformed to these norms by rallying to the flag and dutifully pitching in. They were encouraged to undertake social work among immigrants, to settle them into their new surroundings, and to accustom them to their new environment. Their contribution to immigrants absorption has been vividly described by Pope (1991, 227):

> During the first years after independence, the Council of Women Workers served the interests of the state by focusing on the problem of immigrant absorption. Hundreds of female volunteers were encouraged to undertake social work among immigrants, who were temporarily housed in transit camps. In addition to food distribution and relief work, the Council held Hebrew language courses among women, which helped to foster their new Israeli identity. Together with the Histadrut's Agricul-

tural Center, it encouraged auxiliary farming on small plots in immigrant housing developments, and initiated basic vocational training to enable women to join the workforce.

By channeling their efforts into volunteer activity, women have accepted a secondary role in the country's economy. In Israel volunteer work has a well-established status as a legitimate form of participation in public affairs. Being outside the competitive systems of the labor market and party politics, it is considered, however, a marginal public activity, especially suitable for women (Bar-Yosef and Padan-Eisenstrak 1993). Admittedly, women's movements took pains to prod women to enter the workforce, albeit on two conditions: that work and domestic commitments be in harmony and that the work contribute to the national effort. A woman choosing a feminist course, putting her own needs for fulfillment above the exigencies of the country, jeopardized a fundamental, highly imposing, national norm.

To sum up, it was unusual for Israeli women to turn their backs to the security needs of the country and its mission of ingathering the exiles, even though adherence to these goals was incompatible with gender equality.

The Conceptual Framework

The conceptual framework for this book draws upon a major theme in feminist literature: women's vacillation between operating outside or inside the political establishment; between mobilizing their own resources or those of the male-dominated political elite.

The first option—working from without—is predicated on women's mobilization capacities, their ability to recruit and activate members, to solicit financial resources, and to establish a stable and effective organizational structure. Most important, however, is the enhancement of prospective members' consciousness and identification with the group's cause. It has been widely acknowledged that movements are most readily mobilized around common interests. On the face of it, women do share interests as much as any other group that attempts to wield political influence. Confronted with widespread stereotyping and inequality in the workforce and in political life, they act to promote equality (Sears and Huddy 1990). A precondition for women's successful mobilization, however, is their awareness of their gender interests (Katzenstein 1987; Rhodes 1990). It has been assumed that when women's consciousness is raised a distinct pattern of feminine attitudes and behavior will follow, manifesting itself in a gender gap. Most research to date on the women's movement in the United States has adopted the mobilization perspective (Freeman 1975; Conover 1984; Mansbridge 1986; Gelb and Palley 1987).

Effective mobilization for the feminist cause involves organization as well as attitude. When women act from without they usually adhere to values not shared by men. They are also inclined to be organizationally detached from mainstream political institutions, being either self-sufficient or relying on the women's constituency at large for human and financial resources. When leaning toward "mobilization," women are expected to cut through the partisan arena and act in concert with other women. They are likely to coordinate their strategies and cooperate within the feminist arena in their efforts to influence policy. In short, when women embark on the course of mobilization, they opt out of mainstream politics, and they tend to let the feminist voice ring out.

The other option noted above—acting from within—implies integration or association with existing centers of power, adherence to widely accepted norms, and concentration on conventional political processes (Klein 1984; Costain 1992). It has been suggested in the literature that links to political parties and elites are indispensable for political influence (Klandermans 1990, 127). Alliance with the establishment provides women with extensive communication and recruitment networks. Studies have shown that influence of nongovernmental actors on policy-making depended not only on consciousness enhancement, but on the extent to which organizations could activate allies with substantial political resources. Ties with the party system and government institutions could thus increase group impact in political life (Costain and Costain 1987). The implications of the integration theory for women's consciousness and organizational behavior are self-evident: instead of joining women's associations, women make use of existing women's sections and subunits within the roof-organization of political parties and trade unions or any other established political organ, and work in cooperation with its predominantly male elite. Women's promotion of welfare legislation within social-democratic parties or trade unions in the Scandinavian countries is a good example of acting from within (Siim 1988). The integration model thus presumes a low level of feminist identification, organizational links with male-dominated political groups, and alliance with establishment associations rather than with other women's groups.

To sum up, the mobilization theory concentrates on the uniqueness of female interests and the need to confront the male-dominated polity through organizational and ideological means. It assumes that women are fundamentally different from men, and that the difference should be acknowledged and utilized as a political resource. The integration theory, on the other hand, centers on cooperation and alliance with men, assuming that female interests are not exclusively "feminine" and may be shared by men as well. Each of these option has its pitfalls and hazards. Excessive reliance on mobilization may hinder effectiveness. This was the case of the women's movement in the United States struggling to ratify the ERA, as related by Mansbridge (1986). Intemperate resort to integration may be hindered by patriarchy, by men's attempt to monopolize, cajole, and direct women's politics. This was the case in the Scandinavian countries, as we are told by Hernes (1989).

The two-pronged choice—mobilization or integration—has been linked to another major feminist dilemma: private or public. A large body of scholarship has accumulated demonstrating women's inequality in political life and their rarity in policy-making institutions. That women are still "second-class citizens," at least in this respect, has become a truism. A major pretext for the gender bias in politics has been propounded in the distinction between "private life" where women predominate and "public life" where men are most evident (Elshtain 1981). Some scholars have emphasized the significance of the historical, gender-differentiated separation between the public and the private in the writings of the great political theorists of the past (Okin 1979, 1989; Pateman 1989). Researchers have also focused on more mundane life styles, in which responsibilities are not evenly divided between men and women. The sexual division of labor in the economy and in the home, so it has been asserted, operates to keep women at bay regarding political activity. How to defeat this inhibiting distinction is subject to controversy.

One school of thought argues that the solution lies in freeing women from "biological tyranny" and dismantling all social and cultural structures that are erected upon this tyranny, including the family. The most radical version of this solution calls for test-tube babies to replace biological reproduction (Firestone 1972). More moderate accounts, however, regard women as victims of male subordination, sustained by women's domestic chains. Women's private family roles in marriage, motherhood, and homemaking are the main culprits, impairing their full integration in political life (Sapiro 1983). Increasingly, demands have been pressed to establish women as sovereign rulers over the representation of their lives (Jones 1993, 193), rather than to mold them in norms forged by a male-dominated world.

According to another school, the isolation and debasement of women under the terms of male-dominated structures must be fought, but not the functions associated with "private" life. Instead of excluding the private life from the public scene, integration between the two should be sought. Instead of eradicating values associated with the private world, women should entertain their own morality of nurturing and caring and share it with men. They "must take care to preserve the sphere that makes such a morality of responsibility possible and extend its imperative to men as well" (Gilligan 1977, quoted by Elshtain 1981, 336). Instead of declaring war on men, the proponents of the private world have urged the expansion of the underlying principles governing its practices. Women's "different voice" in social interactions—a voice that stresses cooperation rather than conflict, maintaining relationships rather than achieving abstract justice, should be sounded in public. Pitted against each other are, therefore, two feminist theories. The first propagates an intelligible, visible, and clear-cut separation between the female and the male world, arguing that this move is a precondition for the eradication of patriarchy and its associated gender inequality. The second postulates that the public and private arenas should be integrated in way beneficial to both. Turning the personal into the political is likely to eliminate women's disadvantage.

The two theories—mobilization/integration and private/public—could be linked together. Those favoring mobilization endorse self-sufficiency and a concomitant separation between men and women. The proponents of integration may accept the need for cooperation and the benefits attached to a joint activity. Needless to say, a clear choice between these two options—mobilization or integration—exists on paper only, as women more often than not opt for the two strategies at one and the same time. Yet the undeniable tension between autonomous activity and reliance on partisan resources has been seen to limit women's exercise of effective political power (Bashevkin 1985). In Israel this tension is more acute owing to the disparity between the national imperative and feminist interests. Mobilization would have meant women placing their unique needs at the fore, activating the women's constituency, and forging alliances within the women's arena—in short, rallying around the banner. Integration would have implied heavy reliance on establishment political parties and national institutions and adamant adherence to norms associated with these institutions. To track the choices women in Israel have made, three specific research questions were under consideration in this study:

1. *What is the scope and the type of women's organization for political action?* If mobilized for action outside the conventional political structure, women will concentrate on grassroots activity, removed from the partisan arena. If integration is the way chosen, the presence of women will be felt in state agencies and nationally elected institutions.

2. *What are the sources for the emergence of women's voice?* In the mobilization model, women themselves are the source for political power. Enlisting wide constituencies of women

to the feminist cause is a precondition for an effective activity outside the political establishment. Integration could be carried out on the elite level by women activists who derive their power from political parties, regardless of women's consciousness or willingness to take part in public life.

3. *What are the outcomes of women's political activity?* When acting in politics, women attempt to influence public policy. Discerning how much the government responds to outside pressure and how much to internally generated initiatives on women's issues is not an easy task. But when mobilization underlies women's politics, their influence on policy decisions is expected to be clear. Conversely, when integration is the dominant feature, women may gain from the achievements of other actors, not necessarily associated with the women's movement.

Landmarks on the Path to Equality

Historical developments have set the stage for women's politics in Israel. The most notable characteristic in this country is the sharp contrast between legislation on women's equality and reality, between formal regulation and daily life. By any account, Israel is numbered among the few in the world termed "first-wave countries" (Pharr 1981, 173). These are ranked by the rate of advancement in them of women's political rights as this occurred across the world in the last century. Suffrage was granted in pre-state Israel by the British mandate authorities in the early years of the century, some twenty years before the establishment of the state. Although the Jewish population in the country numbered just a few thousand people who were coping with enormous difficulties, the small community granted its women the right to vote at about the same time as the United States and Sweden. When judged by the "threshold of activism," Israel again is in good company, together with the Anglo-American and Scandinavian countries. Women have held high political office; women have organized for political activity; a gamut of legislation upheld women's rights.

Equality between men and women in Israeli society was inscribed in the state's birth certificate, the Declaration of Independence. This document—one of the first of its kind to include sex as a group classification for the purpose of equal social and political rights—specified that "The State of Israel will maintain equal social and political rights for all citizens, irrespective of religion, race or sex." Although the principles of equality spelled out in this document are not endowed with constitutional force, they have been applied as constitutional principles in court. Next, the major steps to make women equal to men were taken in four consecutive phases, corresponding to economic and political changes.

The first phase was in 1951, being the passing of the Women's Equal Rights Law entitling women to legal equality and equal rights to carry out legal transactions. Regulation of personal matters, however, was left untouched under the authority of religious jurisdiction. The law was adopted in one of Israel's most difficult times. The country was still licking its wounds from the devastating war of independence; it was plagued by one of the severest economic crises ever, and it was preoccupied by the absorption of mass immigration. Added to this was governmental instability caused by a deep rift between the central governing party Mapai and the religious bloc on the one hand, and left-wing Mapam on the other. Technically, controversy with the orthodox parties centered on educational facilities for the new immigrants, but the real rivalry was over mobilization of the new constituencies. The government came under severe criticism from the left too, for adopting a pro-U.S. stance when that power was engaged in the Korean War. With the approach of elections to the Second Knesset, which took place in 1951, two years before they were due, what the government needed most was legitimacy. The Women's Equal Rights Law served as the perfect means for buttressing the governing party: it proved that the government did not yield to religious pressures while upholding religious control over matters of women's (and men's) personal status; it catered to the interests of women while not violating those of men. Israeli women took pride in the new law, largely overlooking the paragraphs detrimental to women's status.

The second phase came in the wake of the International Year for Women (1975), when an ad hoc Commission on the Status of Women was appointed by Prime Minister Yitzhak Rabin. It is true that the creation of the commission was linked with Israel's international standing at the time. Still shocked by the exhausting effects of the Yom Kippur War of October 1973, what Israel needed most in the mid-1970s was international support. The government had to cope with external threats as well as with internal difficulties. In 1975 Israel was subject to a sweeping denunciation by the United Nations General Assembly, which adopted a resolution equating Zionism with racism. Israeli zealots of Gush Emunim, the pro-territories movement, staged demonstrations in areas densely populated by Arabs. In short, the government was in dire need of proving that Israel was a legitimate member of the international community. Establishing a commission to further the women's cause served this end.[2]

The commission's main function was to act as a fact-finding body. Its comprehensive recommendations, however, served as a blueprint for women's equality. The women's movement applauded the establishment of the commission, which was headed by one of its members. But it rejected any attempt to forge women's interests apart from the national collective ones. Instead, it stressed that the commission should define local circumstances and adjust them to the special needs of the state and its women citizens. It further demanded that intensive dialogue between men and women should be maintained and partnership in rights and duties required by the Israeli reality should be emphasized.[3] Women thereby evinced antagonism toward a feminist message. Still, the commission's work generated campaigns identified with the Western feminist movement. Assertiveness-training groups for women were started nationwide and counseling centers for victims of domestic violence were opened.

The commission presented its report and recommendations in February 1978 and these led to the institutionalization of concern for women within the government system. Consequently, the third phase of women's equalization was characterized by large-scale bureaucratization. Israel witnessed a turnover in government when the perennial opposition—the Likud—replaced the long-time party in government, the Labor Party. The establishment of the National Unity Government revealed that the rifts sundering Israeli society were not as deep as perceived. The state appeared to have entered a new phase, when power was gradually shifting from the political parties to the bureaucracy. Ideological contentions still permeated the Knesset and the public arena, but issues were settled mostly on the administrative level. Women's equality was quietly placed on the bureaucratic agenda as the commission's recommendations gradually penetrated state agencies. In 1984 a National Council for the Advancement of Women was established, whose members were nominated by the prime minister. Its function was to advise the prime minister on all issues pertaining to women. Various governmental units were set up whose sole function was to promote women's equality. Among these are the bureau of the Advisor to the Prime Minister on Women's Status, charged with taking the lead in promoting equality; the Department of Women's Employment in the Ministry of Labor and Social Affairs; and advisors on women's status in most government ministries.

The fourth and so far the final step toward gender equality was taken in the 1990s, when women's issues were relocated high on the legislative agenda. The introduction of primaries as a means for selecting parliamentary candidates sharpened politicians' sensitivity to the public mood. Although, as will be shown, there is no gender gap evident in the Israeli electorate, and women's issues do not loom large in ballot choices, catering to women's interests nevertheless appears promising from the electoral perspective, at least as viewed by prospective candidates. Consequently, unprecedented Knesset activity on behalf of women has been taking place. In April 1994 a sub-committee on the status of women was established, whose chairmanship has rotated between Labor and Likud representatives. Legislative measures promoting women's status have already been initiated in the short time-span of the subcommittee's existence.

To sum up, when judged by institutional arrangements, Israel shows an egalitarian facade, corresponding to its phases of development. Initially, the state wooed women in order to gain legitimacy; in the second phase promoting gender equality appears to have been a part of an adaptation process to winds blowing in other Western societies. In the third phase, women's rights were elaborated in the bureaucratic arena. In the current fourth phase, more legislative measures are again being undertaken. Now, however, it is not the party that seeks legitimacy but each legislator, adjusting to altered political circumstances. The foregoing discussion indicates that while women's equality has received adequate attention, this has been confined to the institutional level rather than converted into action. This shortcoming, as the major argument of this book suggests, is both a product and a cause of the duality faced by women in society and political life.

The Plan of the Book

The following chapters are grouped into three parts, the first of which looks into women's share in the country's power structure. Chapter 2 describes the women in the institutional political elite. It explores women's representation in the national uni-cameral legislature (the Knesset), government, local government, the senior civil service, and the political parties. Golda Meir notwithstanding, this chapter demonstrates the meager share of Israeli women in the governing elite, a share that has remained fairly stable throughout the existence of the state. Chapter 3 probes women's activity in political institutions, that is, women's associations and political parties. The analysis follows the development of the women's movement in Israel from the early days of Jewish settlement in Palestine to the present. It demonstrates the weakness of the feminist movement as a grassroots association on the one hand and the absorption of feminist ideas and strategies by the conventional women's associations on the other.

The second part of the book moves on from the analysis of women activists to look at ordinary women. Chapter 4 examines women's political participation. It analyzes their interest in politics, their views about political issues, including the Arab-Israeli conflict, and what they do to influence policy-makers. The use of data compiled specifically for this study, and their comparison with data from 1972 adds a developmental perspective. Findings from a study in an Arab town makes it possible to compare Jewish and non-Jewish women in Israel. In the fifth chapter, women's gender identity is studied. How do Israeli women (Jewish and non-Jewish) relate to major issues of feminism? What social and economic determinants contribute to the development of their gender identity? How does gender identity affect political participation and political orientations? These are the major questions addressed by this chapter.

The third part of the book explores public policy on women, especially the influence of women's association on its formulation and implementation. Chapter 6 focuses on economic policy. Analysis of women's status in the economy precedes the discussion, which continues with an account of legislative measures taken to introduce gender economic equality. The chapter concludes with the description of women's contribution to the formulation of economic policy. Chapter 7 looks into three aspects of family policy: personal status (marriage and divorce), women as family heads, and violence against women. The discussion sets forth the obstacles before Israeli women who attempt to mitigate the pervasive religious influence over personal matters. It shows that when women adhere to their inferior image they enjoy wide political support. In the eighth chapter the analysis focuses on body politics in Israel, more specifically, on the regulation of abortion. How, why and to what extent, have state authorities approved termination of pregnancy, and what has been women's contribution to this liberalization, are the major questions addressed.

The ninth and final chapter assembles the findings of this discussion of women and politics in Israel as a whole by summarizing integration versus mobilization. It opens with an assessment of the progress women have made in political life. How has the need to choose between the flag and the banner affected women's status? The chapter then explores the possible causes for both women's advancement as well as their failure to attain equality. These causes, it is argued, are founded in the "golden family cage" from which women cannot, nor do they wish to, escape. Finally, conclusions are drawn from the case of women regarding the Israeli polity at large.

PART I

Women in Political Institutions
and Associations

CHAPTER 2

Women in the Elite

Discussion of women in the Israeli elite brings to mind the late prime minister Golda Meir, a woman of worldwide renown. Meir was helped neither by the tutelage of a political father nor by a politician husband, but rose through arduous and long party work. But the woman prime minister was a glaring exception. In Israel, as in most other societies, women are grossly underrepresented in the elites where political power is concentrated (Norris 1987; Randall 1987). As political elites distribute scarce national resources and determine public policies, it is critical for women to enter their ranks to further their interests. If women are underrepresented in decision-making bodies, they will probably have little influence on how gender issues are settled. This chapter discusses women's presence in the legislature, the government, the bureaucracy, political parties, and civic organizations. In all these, women are manifestly underrepresented and have far less access to power than men. Whether this insufficiency is linked to women's ambivalence in the political domain or is caused by factors beyond their control has remained a moot question, which is probed in this chapter.

Women in the Legislature

Women's underrepresentation in national legislatures has been widely documented (Lovenduski and Woodall 1987; Oakes and

Almquist 1993). Data gathered by the Inter-Parliamentary Union reflect how the number of women in parliaments had evolved over the years, both in individual countries and on the regional and world levels. As noted in the opening of the union's survey: The Figures speak for themselves" (Distribution of Seats 1991, 1). The world average for women's representation in popular chambers was 11.0 percent in 1991. In some regions in Asia and Europe the percentage was higher—about 12.5. This figure obviously conceals a wide variety among countries: in Finland and Sweden women have reached a peak representation of some 38 percent, whereas in Turkey—a Muslim though secular country—women have constituted only 1.3 percent of the parliament members. In the Arab states the average proportion of women legislators is the lowest in the world—a mere 3.7 percent. How does Israel fare compared with other countries?

Bearing in mind that Israel is located in the Middle East, a region imbued with traditional mores, the proportion of women representatives is impressive, ranging between 7.5 percent and 10 percent. Figure 2.1 shows women's representation in the Knesset across time, from the First Knesset (1949) to the Thirteenth Knesset (1992). When the First Knesset convened immediately after the state won independence, there were 11 women among the 120 MKs (Members of the Knesset), among them members of Labor and Herut parties and one delegate of a Women's Party (discussed below).[1] The Women's Party was short-lived, disappearing from the political arena before the elections to the Second Knesset, held only two years after the convening of the first. But the number of women delegates remained the same, as it did until 1959, when it dropped to nine. Between 1959 and 1984 the number of women elected to the parliament fluctuated between eight and ten. In 1988 (in the elections to the Twelfth Knesset) women were shocked to learn that the number of women legislators reached a record low of seven (i.e., 5.8 percent of the total). In 1992, however, the situation was rectified as the number climbed back to eleven, the same number as forty-four years earlier in the formative years of statehood.

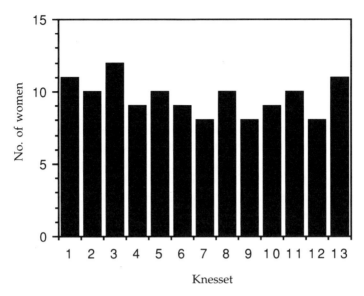

Figure 2.1 Women in the Knesset, 1949–1992

Source: *Government Yearbooks* 1950–1993.

A review of female representation across parties reveals that Israel confirms the general rule postulating an advantage for women in left-wing parties. So far, fifty-two women have served at least one term in the Knesset. Among these, some 77 percent belonged to left-wing parties (the Labor Party, previously known by the names Mapai and the Alignment; Achdut Haavoda, Mapam, the Civil Rights Movement, Meretz, the Communist Party); only two women belonging to the National Religious Party were elected to the Knesset, and only ten (19.2 percent) affiliated with right-wing parties (General Zionists, Liberals, Herut, Likud, Hatehiya, Tzomet). This distribution is no longer valid, as in the last elections in 1992, two women Likud members have entered the Legislature, constituting 18 percent of total women's representation in the Thirteenth Knesset.

Comparative data reveal that the turnover of women legislators tends to be proportionately higher compared with their male counterparts (Randall 1987, 104). This has not been the case in the

Knesset, where the turnover of women is rather low. Once in a position of power, a woman is likely to remain there. Exceptions do occur, as is particularly evident in the Thirteenth Knesset. In 1992, the ranks of legislators were joined by eleven women, of whom eight had been elected for the first time. Those serving many-term incumbencies usually found it difficult to cope with being outside the legislative arena. When Beba Idelson, a well-known women's leader, for example, found out, on the eve of the elections to the Sixth Knesset (1965) that party leadership did not intend to put her on the slate, she said that it was about time she quit, letting younger people (not women!) "contribute their share to the national effort." Shortly thereafter Idelson published articles in the monthly bulletin of the Women Workers' Movement imbued with feminist ideas, calling for the establishment of an all-women parliament (discussed in chapter 3).

That women have remained in positions of power for relatively long periods does not mean that they actually wielded power. Quite a few women served as Deputy Speakers. In all but four Knessets (First, Eighth, Tenth, and Twelfth), a woman, and on two occasions two women, served in this prestigious, though powerless, position of Deputy Speaker. Like his/her British counterpart, the Knesset Speaker is expected to remain politically neutral and to administer the business of the House rather than to exert influence on policy-making. The two most powerful Knesset committees are the Foreign and Security Affairs Committee and the Finance Committee, the former because of the crucial matters it deals with, the latter because of its influence over the distribution of national resources. Up to the present Knesset, a woman has hardly ever belonged to either of these two esteemed bodies. Women could barely be found on the Knesset Interior Committee, focusing on local government, or on the Knesset Committee, responsible for formulating the House rules. Only in 1984 did one woman succeed in being assigned to the twenty-one-member Foreign Affairs and Security Committee, and another to the Finance Committee. In contrast, four women were appointed to the Labor and Social Welfare Committee (Buber-Agassi 1991, 207). As in other states, women have tended to cluster in committees responsible for matters associated with traditional women's interests, such as education, welfare, and the services in general. Table 2.1 shows the distribution of women MKs on the Knesset committees. It is seen that changes have taken place in recent years. For example in the current Knesset there are two women members of the Foreign and Security Affairs Committee, a significant rise over the past.[2] Yet data also manifest the political vulnerability of women, who failed to enter the legislature in any notable way, and even when they did they were doled out marginal positions in its power structure.

As noted, the Thirteenth Knesset has witnessed an innovation in the creation of a specific Subcommittee on Women's Affairs, with its chair alternating between Labor and Likud. It comprises all eleven female MKs and deals with women's issues. Its deliberations, legislative proposals, and public activity, display an unabashedly feminist spirit. The women in the present Knesset, while not exempting themselves from interest in and responsibility for general affairs of state, are acting in their legislative capacity as representatives of women.

Table 2.1 Women on Knesset Committees, 1949–1992

	Committee									
Knesset	a	b	c	d	e	f	g	h	i	j
1	2	0	1	0	5	2	4	3	–	0
2	2	0	0	0	3	1	4	2	–	0
3	2	0	0	0	6	0	5	2	–	1
4	2	2	1	0	3	1	4	3	–	0
5	3	0	1	0	4	0	4	3	–	2
6	4	0	0	2	5	1	6	2	–	0
7	1	0	0	0	1	0	4	3	–	1
8	1	0	0	1	3	2	4	2	–	0
9	1	0	0	1	3	2	–	3	1	0
10	2	1	0	2	1	1	–	3	1	0
11	2	1	1	1	2	2	–	4	2	0
12	2	2	1	1	1	1	–	3	1	2
13	1	0	2	3	3	0	–	4	2	1

a = Knesset Committee; b = Finance Committee; c = Foreign and Security Affairs Committee; d = Interior Committee; e = Education and Culture Committee; f = Constitution, Law, and Justice Committee; g = Public Services Committee; h = Labor Committee; i = Immigration Committee; j = Economic Committee.

Source: *Government Annual*, vols. 1950–1993.

Underrepresentation of women in the Knesset, however, does not imply that their voice has remained silent or unheard. A study of the performance of women in the Israeli legislature (Goldberg 1982) reveals that women have been more active than their male peers, and have been not less but sometimes even more successful in their legislative efforts. Women were found to introduce more bills than men, and more of their bills have been enacted. At the time the research was conducted, in the early 1980s, women did not form an institutionalized parliamentary group. Their concerted activity was dogged by disagreement on both national and gender issues. The bridging of the gap dividing women's interests furnishes evidence on the growing importance of the feminist "banner" in the lives of Israeli women legislators.

Women in the Government

When Sara Doron, one of the very few women who served as a minister, was not elected by her party members to serve another term in the Knesset, Prime Minister Yitzhak Shamir made a warm farewell speech in her honor, in which he said: "Because Doron was so successful in her job, we did not feel we missed other women." Token representation of women in the government has been an entrenched norm. The most illustrious woman serving in the cabinet was Golda Meir, who headed this paramount forum. Prior to her incumbency as a premier, Meir was the first female in the government, serving as minister of labor and social security (1949–51), minister of labor (1951–56), and minister of foreign affairs (during the years 1956 and 1966), a highly prestigious position, second only to the prime minister.[3] The next woman minister was Shulamit Aloni, serving as a minister without portfolio for six months (between 3 June 1974 and 30 October 1974). Her resignation from the government came about through the inclusion in the coalition of the National Religious Party (NRP), whose members refused to serve with Aloni in the same cabinet not only because she was a woman but primarily because her party (the Civil Rights Movement) espoused separation between state and religion. During the Likud's term in power there was one women minister—Sara Doron—also serving as minister without portfolio and for a relatively short period. In the late 1980s Israel had a record-size cabinet of twenty-six ministers, five of them without portfolio, but not a single woman was numbered among them. This was true even when the government was controlled by the Labor Party in the framework of the National Unity Government. Since 1992, however, the situation has changed, as two women (Shulamit Aloni, Meretz, and Ora Namir, Labor), were appointed ministers. Their inclusion in the government may be the harbinger of a brighter future for Israeli female politicians.

Who Are the Women Representatives?

As in other Western countries, legislators, including women, tend to be recruited from the more privileged social sectors. The law of unequal proportion, stating that the higher the political position, the lower the affinity with the broad social strata, is valid in the Israeli context too. Review of the demographic characteristics of the fifty-two women legislators (including those serving in the present Knesset), reveal that an overwhelming majority (86.3 percent) originated in Europe and America; only five women were born in Arabic-speaking countries. These figures stand in stark contrast with the demographic composition of the Israeli Jewish population, approximately 40 percent of which (on average) in the period under consideration immigrated from Asia and Africa. Data on male legislators also demonstrate underrepresentation for Sephardim (Jews from Arabic-speaking countries); but the proportion of men is still higher than that of women (Yishai 1984). Immigration from Asia and Africa has dwindled in the past two decades; at the same time, the proportion of native-born Israelis has steadily increased. These demographic factors are reflected in the Knesset's female composition. As noted, in 1992 eight women entered the Knesset for the first time. All were born in Israel (only one of them is from a Sephardi family). Not a single Arab woman has ever been a member of the Israeli Knesset.

The second prominent characteristic is the women representatives' length of residence in the country (year of immigration).
Of the thirty-two women MKs born abroad, a large majority
(about 80 percent) arrived in the country before the 1930s. They
were therefore veterans, well integrated into the power circles
of the country. The proportion of new immigrants was scant.
One good example is Marcia Freedman, who immigrated from
the United States in 1968 and only five years later (in 1973) was
elected to the Knesset. Haika Grossman, a famous veteran of
the struggle against the Nazis in Poland and a surviving hero-
ine of the Warsaw Ghetto, arrived in Israel in 1948; she had to
wait twenty-five years before she entered her party's Knesset
faction. Until the present Knesset, women legislators reached
the prime of their lives before they became legislators. Golda
Meir, for example, was fifty before she was elected (to the First
Knesset); Ora Namir, the incumbent minister of labor and welfare, was forty-seven years old when first elected. In the Twelfth
Knesset, where thirty-four male MKs (over a quarter of the total) were under forty-five; none of the women MKs was under
forty-five. In 1992 only one woman was younger than forty. By
comparison, fifteen men belonged to this age group when elected
to the Thirteenth Knesset.

Women representatives are distinct from men not only in
their demographic characteristics but also in their self-images.
In the past, women legislators used to shy away from power
politics. Over and over again they emphasized that what they
want is "to contribute." "Power does not interest me," said Tamar
Eshel on her election to the Knesset (1977). "All I want is to aid
in the recovery of my party, and to see it leads the nation and
the state again."[4] This image was sustained by male politicians
as well. When interviewed by the correspondent of the women's
movement journal, one of them stated the following: "The cruel
reality of political life inhibits women, who often do not use
their elbows for pushing themselves forward." The metaphor
was repeated by a left-wing minister who asserted that "it seems
that women do not have a talent for using elbows."[5] A spirit of
modesty among women was evident also in the 1980s. An incoming MK, placed in the prestigious second place on her party
(Labor) list, said in a press interview: "If I had time to consider,

if they had asked me, I would have objected [to being placed second] . . . I decided to keep quiet because I thought that everybody would say, 'Look at her, she's putting on a show.' I would have felt much more comfortable if I had been placed, say, eighth on the list." Why was she willing to forgo the advantages of seniority in her party? The answer she gave was clear-cut: "I am not after prestige, I do not possess elbows, I never engage in political conspiracies."[6] The image of the woman politician, characterized by unselfish, "clean" motives, clearly emerges from this description.

Women MKs also took pains to emphasize that their political career was geared to national ends. When a woman candidate was asked why she had embarked on "this crazy race to the Knesset," she replied that "this is a mission . . . I am not a feminist, but I support women's advancement—for their own sake and for the sake of society. There is tremendous waste in the fact that women do not contribute what they can. We lose a human resource."[7] This brief statement concisely summarizes the self-image of the Israeli woman Knesset member.

Have Women Represented Women?

Women's representation in the legislature was found to be critical in order to satisfy the principles of representative democracy (Mosher 1968). But it remains an open question if women parliamentarians indeed promote women's interests by their legislative activity. Recalling what Golda Meir, the symbol of women's equality in Israel, had to say, the answer to this question in the Israeli context tends to be negative. Upon receiving a distinguished award, Golda Meir enumerated all the events in her life that had made her happy. Expressing herself as if answering the question, "What else does a person need?" she noted that Israelis, unlike their brothers in exile, were safe and secure in their own country; that Jews cultivated their own land and enjoyed autonomy and freedom; that Jews had realized their dream, to live and thrive under their vineyard and under their fig-tree; and primarily, "if a Jewish woman . . . enjoys the privilege of having a daughter and grandchildren in a society that surpasses all other societies in its pursuance of justice and integrity, equality and human value—what else should a Jewish-Israeli woman desire?"[8] This long list of accomplishments and gratification includes not a single reference to the role and status of women in society, other than that extolling the happiness enshrined in being a mother and a grandmother, namely, the joys of family life.

Paging through Golda Meir's autobiography (*My Life*) also confirms one's impression that representing women was not the leaven of her political activity. In *My Life* Meir tells her readers about her work in the Women's Labor Council, but emphasizes that she was attracted to this organization not because it concerned women as such "but because I was very interested in the work they were doing, particularly in the agricultural training farms they set up for immigrant girls" (Meir 1975, 88). Furthermore, Meir could not have been a women's representative because she insists that for her there was no gender problem. In her own words: "The fact is that I have lived and worked with men all my life, but being a woman has never hindered me in any way at all. It has never caused me unease or given me an inferiority complex or made me think that men are better off than women—or that it is a disaster to give birth to children. Not at all. Nor have men ever given me preferential treatment" (Meir 1975, 89).

Golda Meir boasts of the fact that "she spoke like a man." She enjoyed her description (which she attributed to Ben-Gurion) as "the only man in the cabinet." She observes with pride that when invited to speak to the Pioneer Women in the United States, she did not talk only about the Women's Labor Council but about the Histadrut in general, about the problems of immigration and the political situation (Meir 1975, 112). Yet there is another angle to Meir's feminist identity. The woman who reached such prominence and fame in world politics did not repudiate her sex, but underlined only those attributes associated with traditional family life. Although Golda Meir divorced her husband and travelled around the world leaving the care of her two children to paid helpers, she took great care to emphasize her maternal devotion. Her book is replete with pictures of her strolling with her infant grandchild in a baby carriage. Her famous "kitchen" served as a meeting place for secret deliberations where the most critical state decisions were allegedly made (Hazleton 1977).

Association with family and children was not unique to Golda Meir. Nearly all women MKs have maintained the fact that their political career does not displace their family responsibilities. To give a few illustrations: When Nava Arad was first elected to the Knesset (in 1981), she was asked if her political activity hurt her husband. She took the opportunity to explain how happy she was in her marital life.[9] Shoshana Arbeli-Almozlino, another Labor MK, lamented the fact that she gave up having children due to her political activity.

Many other women MKs have ignored their sex interests, promulgating instead their general political beliefs. A volume containing speeches chosen by MKs as the most significant in their political careers sheds light on this phenomenon. Of the 137 speeches presented, ten were delivered by women. Of these only two (by Tamar Eshel, Labor, and Emma Talmi, Mapam), focused on women's issues. The former (made in February 1979) dealt with battered women; the latter (made in January 1963) proposed civil marriage in Israel. Talmi, an avowed socialist, reminded her audience that "the family is the most fundamental social nucleus, and the law's basic function is to sustain its stability and integrity" (Stiel 1992, 402). Other women raised a variety of issues, selected as being most important (or typical) in their political career. Shulamit Aloni criticized the government established in the aftermath of the October (1973) War, headed by Golda Meir, for ignoring the postwar protests; Haika Grossman (Mapam) berated the allied powers for their silence on German atrocities during the Second World War; Geula Cohen, a veteran of the anti-British underground and a renowned nationalist, submitted a bill declaring Jerusalem the eternal capital of the state; Hanna Lamdan, a member of socialist Mapam, was concerned with the problem of "who is a Jew" and demanded the adoption of a more flexible definition of Jewishness; Edna Solodar, a kibbutz member (Labor), was concerned about democracy and legality in Israeli society. Tova Sanhedrai (NRP) spoke about dismissal compensation. Why ancient Jewish law had been disregarded in the formulation of legislation, was her foremost care. Nuzhat Katzav (Labor), responsible for consumers' affairs in the Histadrut, spoke with some length about the alleged lack of concern for regulation in this area; and finally, Sara Shtern-Katan, a religious woman representing the NRP, lamented the failure of the Jews of the Diaspora to immigrate to Israel and their remaining in their countries of residence despite the horrors of the Holocaust. Not one word was uttered by these eight MKs on the plight of women in Israel. Not a single sentence was pronounced on the inequality between men and women in the Promised Land. This collection, as stated, presenting choices made by the MKs themselves, indicates that women elected to the Israeli legislature, have not, by and large, represented women.

A study of women in top party institutions (Yishai 1978b) found that a majority of them did not regard themselves as representing the female constituency but rather the public at large. The tendency to shy away from specific women's interests was positively correlated with political rank. The higher her position, the less inclined the woman politician to view herself as a protagonist of the women's cause. This is probably less true now than it was some sixteen years ago, as contemporary women representatives in Israel are increasingly emphasizing gender issues in their political campaigns. They also stress that their political advocacy is not confined to women's issues. It thus appears that gender alone is not yet a sound basis for a successful political career in contemporary Israel.

Women in Local Authorities

Women's representation at the local level was documented to be higher than in national legislative institutions. In Britain, for example, women constituted 14.4 percent of county councilors in England and Wales in 1983. Interestingly, following local election in 1983, women also constituted 14 percent of the membership of the French Conseils Municipaux. In West Germany, by 1983 women accounted for 13 percent of all local government councilors (Lovenduski 1986). In the United States there were likewise 14 percent women members in municipal and township governing boards in 1985 (Randall 1987, 105). As expected, the proportion of women serving on local government institutions is far higher in the Scandinavian countries, where their representation is around one-third of the total (Haavio-Mannila and Skard 1985).

The reasons for the relatively high number of women fulfilling political positions in local government are rather obvious: subject matter and family constraints. Local governments tend to focus on welfare, education, culture, community affairs, and other matters of traditional concern to women. Women are more familiar with these topics than men because they tend to deal with them more frequently. Furthermore, the fact that politics takes place near home is of great advantage to women, who are less mobile owing to their family responsibilities. A student of women in Israeli local politics asserted, "If we take the traditional division of labor as a given, local politics should be a good ticket for women to enter politics" (Herzog 1991, 234). In Israel the advantages of women in local politics are accentuated because this level of government is secondary to national politics. Being a unitary centralized state, local authorities are almost completely subservient to the Ministry of the Interior, operating from Jerusalem, the state capital. In 1975 the local government law was radically reformed allowing for the direct election of mayors. The reform was intended, among other things, to decrease the influence of political parties in the local arena. This goal, however, has been only partially achieved, as parties continue to wield power over many aspects of local government politics. What effect has these factors had on women's representation?

Data (presented in figure 2.2) show that contrary to expectations, women's representation in local authorities has been extremely limited. In the first local elections, held in 1959, women in the Jewish cities and local councils gained 4.2 percent of the seats. This low representation decreased even further, reaching its nadir in 1965 (3.2 percent). Since the late 1960s, however, it has increased steadily, reaching 10.9 in 1993. Although the proportion of women in local authorities has gradually risen, on the average there are no more than two women on each local authority. The picture is even darker when mayoralties are under consideration. During the state's existence only six women have served as heads of local councils, none of them in a city with a population over 10,000. In 1989 only one women was elected as a council head, in a small suburban local authority. This woman failed to be reelected in 1993. Currently there is also one, and only one, woman heading a (small) local council. Among women mayors was a Christian Arab (Violet Khoury), who made history by her victory in the local election. By and large, women's representation in the Arab sector is nil. For the country as a whole, including non-Jewish local authorities, the proportion of women representatives is only 7.3 percent.[10]

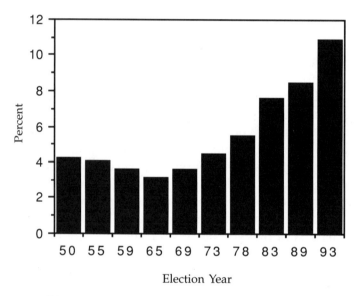

Figure 2.2 Women in Local Government Councils, 1950–1993 (percent)

Source: Information leaflet, Women's Network, February 1994.

In her study of women in local authorities, Herzog (1994) explored the path followed by women entering local politics. According to her findings, in the 1950s, some 75 percent of the women received their places on the list through the party machine or nomination committee, whereas in the 1980s, only 43 percent owed their places to the party. Among women candidates there were fewer party members than in the past. In 1989, twenty-nine women competed for mayoralties as heads of independent local lists, though only one succeeded in being elected. Herzog concludes that party membership is no longer a political resource for women interested in local politics. At the same time, women within political parties do not succeed in converting their investment in political activity into political bargaining power. Women thus try to by-pass obstacles within the party, by using their local reputation and personal resources. Their efforts, as proven by the data of recent elections, have been only modestly effective.

Women and Political Parties

In their relation to political parties women manifest two features: they act *within* political parties, and they act *as* parties, that is, they attempt to establish parties based on the gender theme.

Women's Parties

Israel provides a hospitable climate for the emergence of what has been termed "interest parties" (Yishai 1994). Interest parties are "interest groups in disguise." They are interest groups by virtue of the scope of interests they represent and by virtue of their organizational characteristics prior to elections: autonomous activity as voluntary associations. They are "parties" in that they submitted a list for popular vote in national elections. In all thirteen electoral contests that have so far taken place in Israel, interest parties appeared on the scene. These included lists of new immigrants, war veterans, ethnic groups, pensioners, and women. The appearance of these lists was encouraged by three basic attributes of the polity: First, electoral laws are extremely malleable in regard to party formation. New contenders are required to present a list of about 1,500 signatories and a modest cash deposit (not returnable in case of failure to enter the Knesset). Up to the 1990s the structural barriers for election were very low: only lists winning less than one percent of the vote were excluded from the Knesset. The threshold, also termed the "blocking percentage," was raised to 1.5 percent in 1991. The second inducement lies in state support for new contenders. Assistance is manifested in free media (radio and television) time and in financial support. Finally, the belief that political parties are the source of power in the country, and that party politics is a legitimate, perhaps preferred, way to influence policy issues has also encouraged the transfer from the group to the partisan arena. Women's groups were no exception. They, too, tried their luck in national elections, albeit not with much success.

Prior to the elections to the First Knesset, Rachel Kagan, activist in the movement called Women International Zionist Organization (WIZO), founded a women's party and won a Knesset mandate. Not much is known of the circumstances that led WIZO, known for its conservative positions regarding women's role in society (to be discussed in the next chapter), to endorse Kagan's candidacy. In any event, history was made when the first woman entered the first session of the fledgling Israeli parliament as a clear-cut and outspoken women's representative. Kagan was faithful to her mission. A review of her activity in the First Knesset reveals high concentration on women's issues. It was Kagan who submitted to the plenum the first proposal to legislate on women's equality. Following her initiative, the government proposed its own draft adopted as Women's Equal Rights Law perpetuating exclusive religious jurisdiction over personal status (Raday 1991b, 20). Kagan herself declined to support the law, which in her opinion constituted a "fraud regarding women's equality" (quoted by Sharfman 1988, 66). Her unwavering position regarding women's status in general and religious ruling over personal matters in particular made her unpopular in WIZO circles, particularly abroad. It was feared that extreme positions on gender equality would harm the recruitment of members in the United States. Furthermore, it was claimed that "a voluntary association that contributes to society and to women should not be involved in political activity" (Greenberg and Herzog 1978, 106). Hence it was decided not to resubmit her candidacy to the elections to the Second Knesset.[11] The first women's party was disbanded and faded from Zionist history.

A women's list reappeared on the electoral arena in 1977, in readiness for the election to the Ninth Knesset.[12] It was one of twenty-two lists running on the ballot in that election campaign. Upon its foundation in January 1977, the party issued a statement specifying its objectives, the gist being as follows: "Past experience proves that equality will be achieved only by our own activity, in one united women's front." The primary goal of the new party was to mobilize all women in Israel to promote women's issues. This goal was converted into organizational regulations, as the party declared it was open to all women, regardless of their previous party affiliation. Furthermore, in line with a familiar theme, the party undertook not to erect "a hierarchical organizational structure, based on power struggles." Declaring that the Women's Party "is not left-wing, not right-wing, and not center, we are above all," its activists aimed at attracting the widest possible support among women of all political shades. It promised its supporters a grassroots organization whose one and only purpose was to advance women in the economy, in politics, and in society. Likewise, the party introduced strong feminist strands into the political discourse. It promised "to dissolve prevailing myths and to change norms." Taking a programmatic stance, the party proclaimed that "Today's utopia is tomorrow's reality." Even this women's party, however, did not escape the gender dilemma in Israel, as revealed by a central sentence in its electoral platform advocating both women's equality and contribution to the national cause: "The equality we demand, in the areas specified, is essential to the creation of conditions that would enable every woman to live by her own values and to choose the type of work that fits her aspirations and competence. Only under these circumstances will the woman be able to greatly contribute to society at large."

The Women's Party secured only some 6,000 votes and failed to pass the blocking percentage. In retrospect, it was conceded that "Most of us did not believe in the possibility of winning" (Freedman 1990, 160). The party's first priority, so its founders claimed, was to raise consciousness, not to win votes. Still, the electoral defeat was striking. The party's failure was attributed to three factors: First, most adherents lacked political experience. The party explicitly chose a political path, departing from strategies of a grassroots feminist movement. Many women felt uncomfortable in the new, unfamiliar, environment. According to Freedman, there were never more than fifty activists for the Women's Party, and toward the end there were only about fifteen (1990, 165). Second, although the party declared its antagonism to internal hierarchy, the organizational imperative dictated division of labor. Candidates for the Knesset list had to be selected. "Sisterhood" remained a dead letter as internal tensions and personal rivalry mounted. "We hadn't foreseen the feelings of disappointment and distrust that slate selection entailed. The anger of some of those who lost insinuated itself into the collective" (Freedman 1990, 163). Consequently, the party splintered into cliques and was riven by factionalism. Third, Marcia Freedman, the founder and the acknowledged leader of the Women's Party, drew increasing resentment primarily because she radically deviated from mainstream Zionism. Breaking her previous affiliation with the Independent Socialists,[13] she was subjected to fierce criticism. "I felt like a bird with a broken wing," she recalled, "flying so high on the success of my political maneuvering to bring about the Women's Party and suddenly grounded, not by men I struggled against, but by the women who were my sisters" (Freedman 1990, 164).

The third, and to date the last, attempt to form a women's party occurred in the elections to the Thirteenth Knesset (1992). The direct cause of its foundation was the frustration of a feminist (heading a women's shelter for battered wives) at not being elected to the Civil Rights Movement's (CRM) slate. In cooperation with Shin, a voluntary association propagating women's representation in political institutions, veterans of the 1977 Women's Party were remobilized to take part in the electoral campaign. Once again feminist slogans were introduced into the political discourse. In 1992, however, the Women's Party did not confine itself strictly to gender issues but stated its views on general national concerns. The party proclaimed that "apprehensive of the fate of our society, we will act to promote the quality of life and the environment, and will protest against all forms of violence and discrimination in Israeli society. We aspire to eliminate hatred in the region by peaceful means" (excerpts from the party platform). The party further committed itself to negotiating the occupied territories and calling for a referendum before their return. The new Women's Party was less radical than its predecessor, focusing on increased opportunities for women rather than revolutionizing society.[14]

In contrast to the previous experience in women's partisanship, in 1993 the activists had political experience in political parties or in voluntary associations. According to their testimony, they were forced to run on their own because other organizations had failed to advance the women's cause. Despite this advantage, the Women's Party completely floundered in its electoral bid. Only 3,000 voters cast their ballot in favor of a separatist women's party, signifying a retreat from previous support. Once again it was proven that women (and obviously men) did not favor women's independent partisanship. A national survey carried in 1993 revealed that nearly half the female respondents did favor a separate women's party. This endorsement remained on paper only and was not manifested in the ballot. Rather, activity within existing political parties, leashed to the flag and directed by the symbol it carries, appeared a more appropriate channel for women's political behavior.

Women within Political Parties

In theory, liberal democracies offer women the means to claim equality of representation by utilizing the political opportunities offered by the party system (Lovenduski 1993, 3). In Israel, however, the parties have responded only partially to this claim, as women are underrepresented in the governing bodies of all political parties.

Women operate within political parties under two categories: in specific women's sections and as individual members. Where women's activity is organized in a specific subunit, this is expected to play a dual role: to recruit support for the party among women's constituencies, and to promote women's representation in the party. Consequently, some arrangements ensuring quotas for women are evident. In the absence of such a subunit, women engage in the power struggle as individuals.[15] There is also a third way, whereby a women's section does provide the party with its members' support, but the party does not reciprocate by allocating safe seats to women activists. The first pattern is typical of the left-wing parties; the second of "new" parties formed after 1967; the third of Herut and the NRP.

Most veteran parties include women's sections. Among them are the Labor Party (previously Mapai), whose women's section (established in 1955) served as a vote-securing agent. The section was concerned neither with policy-making and policy initiatives, nor with the coordination of the activities of Mapai's women representatives in the Knesset, Histadrut, or municipalities (Medding 1972, 73). In its platform the Labor Party included a paragraph devoted to women, ensuring representation, employment, and social security.[16] Women's sections have also operated in the NRP, Herut (the antecedent of the Likud), and in the Liberal Party (also currently a Likud component). Emuna, affiliated with the National Religious Party, is the most active among the three. It is widely engaged in charity and in providing child-care and educational services. The major purpose of Emuna is to instill religious values in women and youth and, obviously, to attract women to the NRP. Emuna, however, has political aspirations of its own. As noted above, only two NRP women were ever elected to the Knesset, but Emuna puts a heavy pressure on the party leadership during every electoral campaign to include at least one of its members on the list. These pressures are often accompanied by a so far unimplemented threat to run in a separate list.

Women's sections in the right-wing parties have receded since the formation of the Likud. Nevertheless, they still operate day-care facilities, old-age homes and educational activities, aimed at disseminating party values among women. A women's section operates also in the ultra-orthodox party Agudat Israel. Needless to say, the section is not involved in party politics but focuses only on educational and charity work.[17] In the newly established parties, most notably the CRM, and in left-wing parties (Mapam, the Communist Party), women act as individual members, unorganized in a special subunit. Regardless of the form of organization, however, women are underrepresented in all political parties, though to a varying degree.

Data compiled by the Women's Network in 1992 (table 2.2) reveal the paucity of women's representation in political parties. A distinction is made between large, popular forums, such as the party convention, and small, elite organs, such as the secretariat or bureau, where critical decisions are taken. As shown in table 2.2, left-wing parties have an edge over right-wing parties as regards women's representation. In the Labor Party there is a regulation (article 161a in the party's constitution) requiring that women be allocated at least 20 percent of all party positions. The Labor Party has rigorously stuck to this rule: in the last general conference (including 2,995 delegates) there were 613 women representatives—that is, approximately 20 percent. In the party center, operating as the dominant forum between conventions, some 20 percent of the delegates are women. Even in the bureau there was an impressive representation of 23 women out of a total of some 100 members. Note, however, that in the last census, taken in 1990, 48 percent of the total party membership was women. The fact that women constitute a fifth of the party's elite body may be commendable, but this proportion is far less than merited in view of the size of their party membership.

In the small left-wing parties women's representation is more impressive than in the Labor Party: in Mapam, women constituted 26 percent of the general convention in 1992, 26 percent of the party center, and 34 percent of the party secretariat. In this party, though, the quota for women is as high as 40 percent, so achievements do not match legal party requirements. No data are available on the proportion of women in the party membership. The Civil Rights Movement (Ratz) is expected to show the highest rate of women's representation. Not only was this party founded and led by a woman (Shulamit Aloni, the incumbent minister of science and communication), but also it has steadfastly upheld civil rights, including women's rights. Table 2.2 shows that women constitute over a third (35.5 percent) of the party executive, 26.2 percent of the national secretariat, and 32.5 percent of the party council. Yet it ought to be remembered that women comprise more than 60 percent of the party membership.

Likud fares worse in terms of women's representation with only 13.3 percent women in the party center, numbering a total of 3,300 individuals. In the party secretariat (including thirty members) the proportion of women is only 3.3 percent (one woman!). In Tzomet, a nationalist party headed by a former chief of staff (Rafael Eitan) there are seventy-two members on the governing board, of whom only two are women.

Table 2.2 Women in Party Institutions, 1992 (percent)

	Conference	Center	Secretariat
Labor	20.4	19.6	22.5[a]
Likud	–	13.3	3.3
Ratz	32.5[b]	26.2[c]	35.5
Mapam	25.6	25.2	33.8

Source: Information leaflets, Women's Network, 1992.

[a] *Bureau.*   [b] *Council.*   [c] *Executive.*

Comparing the data in table 2.2 with those collected fifteen years earlier (Yishai 1978) reveals dramatic changes. In 1977 the proportion of women represented in top party bodies was far lower.[18] Women have come a long way, although their representation still lags behind their contribution to the total party membership.

Women in the Bureaucracy

The Israeli "mandarins" (the term used by Dogan [1975] to describe senior civil servants) are no different from their counterparts in other Western democracies: they are predominantly male. Data on the civil service in Israel are staggering: at the top administrative level there are only two women compared with 155 men. Currently not one single woman serves as a director general of a government office, nor is there a woman heading an important government agency. The two top-level women are employed in the Ministry of Justice, where women constitute a majority. Male legal professionals prefer to make their living in the free market, where income is far higher than in government service. As the rank descends, the proportion of women increases. In the second rank from the top there are 40 women compared with 378 men, that is, 10.5 percent; in the three lowest levels of the civil service the proportion of women employees amounts to 68 percent (Annual Report 1993, 181). There is thus a clear-cut pyramid in the state bureaucracy, with men situated at the narrow apex and women at the wide base.

A study of women in senior civil service ranks was conducted by the author in the winter of 1993–94. These women were compared with their male counterparts at the top of the bureaucracy on the one hand, and with women in a junior rank on the other.[19] The study revealed far greater discrepancies between men and women (of the higher bureaucratic ranks) than among the women's groups. Women were found to have a higher standing on a scale describing their human capital. They were more educated, from a "better" ethnic origin, and had grown up in a more affluent environment. Women were found to be highly integrated into the administrative network, but they scored significantly lower than men on the scale of "political contacts." They, contrary to their male peers, had to work their way up by investing a tremendous amount of effort and ingenuity, unable to rely on political savvy. Women, furthermore, whether top or middle-rank civil servants, lacked a sense of equity. Men were positive that there was no gender discrimination and that both men and women shared the same opportunity to make strides in their administrative career. Women were emphatic that there was inequality, both in opportunities and in career advancements.

One striking finding relates to the importance of family in the officials' lives. First, a traditional division of labor was found to exist even at the highest echelons of the civil service, where women engaged in traditional house chores far more than men, who were generally responsible for the family's finances (and cars). Second, women, in a proportion far more significant than men, reported on compromising their own career in favor of their husband's. Data reveal that many women gave up family life altogether. In contrast, the proportion of single or childless men was negligible.[20] Finally, women were more liberal than men in some attitudes regarding women's place in society. The major difference among women concerned work centrality, which was far higher among senior women than among their junior colleagues. All in all, it appears that despite the absence of formal barriers to women's promotion to power positions in the state administration, the mere fact that they are subject to constraints unshared by men impedes their way to the top.

Women in Trade Unions and Interest Groups

Although women comprise nearly half of the Histadrut (Israel's Labor Federation) membership, they are conspicuously absent from the leadership of most trade unions, and are poorly represented on the federation's central bodies (Buber-Agassi 1991, 208). There has never been a woman secretary-general; only once did a woman run for this office. The fact that women in the Histadrut are organized in a specific subunit—Naamat—has prevented women from competing for power even within general Histadrut bodies. The highest Histadrut organ is the Central Committee. In 1992, six out of the forty-two members were women, that is, 14 percent. On the Executive Committee, the second highest body, only 15 out of 196 members were women— less than 8 percent. Out of forty-five individual trade unions only three are headed by women.[21] The powerlessness of women is reflected in the fact that even unions with a majority of female members, such as the Teachers' Federation and the Social Workers Union, are headed by men. Local workers' councils, representing the Histadrut in practically every locality in the country, are also governed by men. In 1993 there were only two women secretaries-general of these councils, both in remote peripheral towns.

Women play a limited role in other associations as well. The Israel Medical Association is currently chaired by a woman physician who was elected to office as a compromise candidate, despite her being a woman. Dr. Miriam Zangen is totally oblivious to gender interests and disengages herself from women's issues. A woman heads the Organization of Post-Elementary Teachers. She, too, concentrates on professional affairs and is constantly involved in wage disputes, having little to do with feminist affairs. No other woman is known to be active in Israeli associational life. On the Council of the Manufacturers Association, the all-encompassing business group in the country, there is a sole woman among the men. Likewise, the Chamber of Commerce, also an influential national association, has elected to its board one woman, and twenty-eight men. The Committee of the University Faculty Members, which gained national fame after a two-month strike, does not include one single woman. It may thus be concluded that women are active in civic society principally in specific women's associations; these are discussed in the next chapter.

Women's Underrepresentation: Some Explanations

That women in Israel are underrepresented in political elites runs counter to evidence showing that an electoral system with a wide district magnitude, including many voters' low threshold for winning a parliamentary seat and a strict list system is favorable to women's parliamentary representation (Brichta and Brichta 1994). Israel neatly fits this description: the whole country constitutes one electoral district, the threshold stood in the last elections at a low 1.5 percent, and the list system is extremely rigid as voters are not permitted to change the candidates' places, eliminate candidates, or add any to the list. Why, then, have women failed to secure their due representation in the Knesset? Explanations focus on three major factors: structural, behavioral, and environmental.[22]

Structural Constraints

The method of nomination is regarded as having impeded women's political progress. Until the mid-1960s the nomination of candidates to all elite positions in the country was practically monopolized by small and oligarchic nomination committees. Very few women belonged to them. It may be argued that men controlled the channels leading to elite positions, barring the way to aspiring women. The case of Golda Meir, moreover, proves that the rise of one woman to a position of power does not necessarily lead to the addition of women to the political elite. Since the early 1970s most political parties have changed the system of candidate selection by transferring the nomination function from small select committees to the central party organs, where the composition of the list is decided by personal and secret ballot. The number of party members in these organs ranged from a few hundred (Mapam) to several thousand (Labor). Prior to the elections to the Thirteenth Knesset, the Labor Party introduced another electoral reform: of the total of forty-four "safe" Knesset candidacies on the list, half would continue to be selected by the party's center, and half would be elected in the eleven party districts by closed and direct primaries. The introduction of this reform has not enlarged the number of women in the political elite. In the initial phase of the primaries 170 candidates presented their names, among whom only 10 percent were women. In the districts, only nine of the ninety-nine candidates competing for the twenty-two Knesset seats were women; only one woman won a safe seat. In the primaries for the election of the party's leader (and premier-designated), a women—Ora Namir—participated. She came out last among the contenders, winning only about 5 percent of the vote. Evidently, all these structural devices have not increased women's representation. Brichta and Brichta (1994) suggest that greater participation by women in the contest for nomination could significantly increase their number in the Knesset. The primary reason for the small number of women in the elite is thus to be sought in the women themselves—who are reluctant to leap into the cold water of politics—rather than in structural constraints.

Behavioral (Self-imposed) Constraints

Women activists in political parties have failed to organize an effective lobby to advance their interests for three main reasons. First, women's associations, particularly Naamat, have proved unsuccessful in converting their abundant resources into political assets. As is shown in Chapter 3, women's voluntary associations are extremely resourceful in terms of budgets and members; they are also in contact with diverse groups of service recipients. All of these assets are not turned to political use and are not traded for power (Azmon 1993). Women seem to have been satisfied with an informal, tacit agreement with Labor Party leaders to safeguard the quota arrangement which granted them, at best, only one-fifth of the total representation. Women often showed their dissatisfaction and threatened to withdraw from the party, but their warning was not taken seriously. Women were not perceived as political rebels.

Second, one of the reasons for the ineffectiveness of intraparty strategies to advance women to leadership positions lies in the fact that women barely support women. Women's associations have increasingly demanded that women be represented in decision-making institutions. A survey conducted by Naamat reveals how important this question was to the movement's activists. But even when women did compete for elite positions, there was still a problem of attracting female support. An editorial in Naamat's magazine pleaded for women to support women-candidates in the following words: "Even when we do not find ideal and competent [women] candidates, we must remember that not all male candidates are perfect either. We must unite around our candidates, even though their selection is not exactly what we wanted. We must stand by their candidacy and support them after elections, we must make them feel that they have a supportive and encouraging backing. We must increase our activities in all-women frameworks, as an intermediary measure, until women are fully integrated [into political life]."[23]

The fact that Ora Namir, running for the party leadership, secured barely 5 percent of the vote, shows that women party members do not necessarily support a candidate simply because she is a woman. The women's movement urged women to elect women candidates, but the call fell on deaf ears. The need to put vote-winning candidates on the party slate thus worked to the disadvantage of aspiring women.

Third, women in Israel, probably like women in other Western countries, are less likely than men to aspire to political or other high-powered careers (Epstein and Coser 1981). This explanation is supported by a study of Tel Aviv University students, which found that female students tended to be far less ambitious than their male counterparts and to opt more frequently for what were traditionally considered "female" (e.g., child-related), occupations which usually are relatively low on the power scale. (Shapira et al., quoted in Etzioni-Halevy and Illy 1993, 246). On the basis of these findings (and others, e.g., Tiger and Shepher 1975), it may be supposed that Israeli women shy away from the participation in the political power struggle.

Because of this unwillingness, they do not fill senior positions in proportion to their numbers.

Environmental Constraints

A major impediment to women's representation is the order of the national agenda, dominated by the security question. The gravity of national issues, over which the parties differ, has relegated gender equality to a secondary place. A "serious" politician is not expected to run on the subject of women's issues. The striking failure of women's lists in Knesset elections reflects the low priority of the gender problem in national politics.

Also among environmental constraints is the influence of religion on public affairs. The notion that "A woman's honor is in her house" is unfavorable for women's political careers. Orthodox Jews, comprising some 25 percent of the population and generally holding close to 15 percent of the seats in the Knesset, rebuff the very idea of women's participation in the political process. An Orthodox MK, chairman of the important Finance Committee, even suggested, in a notorious speech, denying women the right to vote.[24] The more moderate NRP has occasionally granted symbolic representation, but as noted by Brichta and Brichta (1994), "it is hard to expect that an orthodox Jew, who prays every morning 'Blessed be He that did not make me a woman,' would support the election of women to the Knesset."

Similar constraints are evident in other sectors of Israeli society, namely, the Arab sector and particularly the Sephardi constituency. The high percentage of people of African and Asian origin in the Jewish population has had an indirect influence on the low representation of women in politics, since families of this origin discourage active political participation of women altogether. Furthermore, most of the places allotted to the non-Ashkenazi sector in the different parties whose nominations were influenced by political institutions or "Landsmannschaft" organizations, were filled by men, thus decreasing the number of women representatives. As a sector entitled to compensation on account of deprivation, women had to compete with the Sephardim, who as a group were potentially more powerful and more active in political life.

Conclusions

Israel has been portrayed as a dynamic, rapidly developing society. It has absorbed literally millions of immigrants; it has sustained an expanding economy; and it has advanced cultural and scientific endeavors. Yet women's representation in the elite, decision-making institutions has remained consistently low, or at best has grown extremely slowly. In the Knesset, in the government, on the local level, in the top echelons of public administration, in voluntary associations—even those where women constitute a majority—power has been retained by men. The foregoing has provided ample data indicating that women are on the margins of politics and that they lack the resources to determine the course of events. Furthermore, it has been shown that even women who have entered the halls of power have not been committed to promoting the interests of their sex. Rather, they have become politicians by virtue of their opinions on issues of national interest having little to do with gender equality. In this respect, women politicians have largely integrated into the polity. The few attempts made to mobilize women outside the purview of male-dominated political parties proved abortive. Integration, however, was not fully achieved because women were perpetually underrepresented in all decision-making bodies.

The reasons for the paucity of women's representation are similar to those explaining women's position in general: alleged absence of political ambition, traditional mores, structural constraints, and last but not least vacillation between gender interests, relegated to inferior status in the order of priorities, and national imperatives, affecting the lives of each and every Israeli. All these have worked to the disadvantage of women's political careers. Full integration in structures of authority as manifested in women's representation in the political elite has thus been delayed. The incumbency of two women in the current government (June 1994), the creation of the women's subcommittee in the Knesset, and the increased proportion of women in party leadership forums may herald brighter prospects for women on their arduous road to equality at the top.

CHAPTER 3

Women's Associations
and Movements

Women's associations have been at the forefront of the struggle for women's equality in Israel, invariably confronting the well-known dilemma between national goals and gender objectives. Some women groups have ignored it, arguing that working toward the implementation of collective ends is not incompatible with liberating women; other groups, however, have made a clear-cut decision to favor one target over the other. Some associations have chosen to act from within. By selecting the so-called "internal path," they have allied themselves with political parties and other established groups and have been ardent proponents of collective values. Others have chosen to act from without, by mobilizing the women's constituency and forming grassroots organizations that have challenged the existing political and social order, treating it as the main culprit for women's inequality. This dual approach, while not unique to Israel, has been influenced by the particular historical, cultural, and political characteristics of the country. Women's associations have made their presence felt since the early days of the Jewish settlement in Palestine. They have mobilized broad constituencies, increased public awareness of women's plight, and influenced public policy on women (discussed in chapters 6–8). But their activity has been steadily overshadowed by their vacillation between the flag and the banner—affiliation and autonomy. This chapter will describe the development of the women's movements from the pre-state era to the present, focusing on their internal resources as well as their mutual relationships.

The Pre-State Era

Women's movements were interwoven into the effort of national revival pursued by the Zionist movement in mandatory Palestine. Disregarding women's groups operating within political parties, such as Emuna, two women's associations dominated the scene: the Women Workers' Movement (WWM) and Women's International Zionist Organization (WIZO).

More than any other organization in the country, Naamat (the Hebrew name of the WWM since 1976) has successfully coped with its two-pronged role: being a branch of the labor movement and being a leading women's movement in the country. The WWM developed within the Labor Zionist movement in reaction to the disappointment of a small group of women with the limited role they were assigned in the emerging society (Izraeli 1992). As members of socialist parties in their country of origin, pioneering women shared with their male co-workers ideas of social justice and human liberty; as Zionists they endorsed national redemption in the old-new homeland. Women assimilated the collective goals of the settlers in pre-state Israel; yet they were also aware of their unique needs. In her seminal book on women workers in the Yishuv (the pre-state Jewish settlement in Palestine), Bernstein (1987a, 24) describes the first-ever exclusive meeting of women in pre-state Israel which took place in Kinnereth in 1911. At the meeting, closed to men, the women complained about their confinement to kitchen and service work and about the general indifference to their predicament. They unanimously concluded that the only solution lay in autonomous political and economic activity. To this effect, the first agricultural training camp was opened, with the purpose of expanding the number of women engaged in "productive" occupations. Political organization followed, as women increasingly realized that their goals could not be won through the existing structures of the Labor Zionist movement. In 1914 the organizational arm of the women's movement was created.[1]

Following the establishment of the Histadrut in 1921, an affiliated Women's Workers Movement was organized. This body was not officially represented at the founding convention, because representation was based on political party membership, and the women viewed their association as nonpartisan (Swirski 1991a, 287). However, realizing their vulnerability in political parties women demanded, and were granted, official representation on the Histadrut council (Izraeli 1981, 103). Adhering to the socialist ideology, women suffered under the pressing circumstances of the time. Contending with immediate physical and economic needs in a poverty-stricken, barren land left little time for feminist activity. Yet these women were deeply concerned with problems that today may be termed "feminist": the perception of women as an oppressed group, the creation of all-female organizations, and the establishment of alternative institutions (Swirski 1991a, 285).

From the start, the WWM faced four vital issues, namely, the nature of the desired social change, the program of action, the appropriate form of organization, and primarily the nature of its relationship with the Labor movement (Bernstein 1987a; Ram 1993, 62). These questions were settled in a manner unfavorable to women's equality. This is remarkable, as the change sought was, indeed, revolutionary in nature. Women workers aspired to be equal to men, without reservation or qualification. The WWM aimed at eradicating the fundamental roots of inequality, not merely its symptoms. Yet reality proved that such an eradication was to remain an unfulfilled dream. Personal relations between men and women, division of labor, and political activity were forged on the basis of traditional mores. As much as women workers desired social change, the family remained outside its domain (Bernstein 1992a). The gap between the dream and its implementation was detrimental to the advancement of women.

Although serious and sincere attempts were made to promote social change, the program of action remained ambiguous. Women established self-help units to attend to their own needs. These networks not only provided social support and mutual aid, but inculcated ideas of autonomy and equality. Women were active in defining needs and supporting services funded by national authorities to other women. But the recipients remained mostly passive, uninvolved in the struggle for women's equality. They themselves did not aspire to the social change being promoted on their behalf by others. They did not supply the women's movement with the resources necessary for autonomous activity. Consequently, the WWM rapidly turned into a service organization rather than a political grassroots association.

The organization of the WWM was also highly problematic. On the one hand, desired social change necessitated a strong, centralized structure. On the other hand, without wide mobilization of women in the periphery, without the activation of wide strata of members, the achievement of the movement's goals would be hampered. The heterogeneity of the WWM aggravated the organizational dilemma. In the pre-state period, concludes Bernstein (1987), the Histadrut leadership, both in the central male-dominated institutions and in the women's Moetzet Hapoalot (the Hebrew name of WWM at the time), was oblivious to the needs of the common man/woman. The overall passivity of women, struggling to get by in the hardships of their new country, was a major impediment to organizational viability.

The vacillation between affiliation and autonomy was perhaps most detrimental to the promotion of women's status. Had it resolved this dilemma successfully, the WWM could have enjoyed the benefits of both worlds in the pre-state days: it could have ensured the Histadrut's support for women's advancement, and could have contributed to the consolidation and organizational expansion of the Histadrut. This was not the case, as relations between the two consisted of a combination of dependence and indifference. Women accepted as their major structural framework the Histadrut, where they had gained official recognition. But the male-led Labor Federation showed no interest in women's affairs; WWM enjoyed a marginal autonomy. The women's movement experienced growing tensions between the "radical" minority, favoring a strong, separate organization free of party control and in contact with grassroots members that would focus on women's affairs, and the "loyalist" majority, propagating strong alliance with male-dominated institutions.[2] The majority view was that women's role was to reeducate and train women for participation in national public life. Organizational segregation was also objectionable because it implied lack of faith in the men (Maimon-Fishman 1929; quoted in Izraeli 1992, 196).

The establishment of the state found the women's movement in an inferior status, with the four underlying problems unresolved. The victory of the "loyalists" proved to be abortive in terms of power resources. Furthermore, the WWM was able to exact only a small reward from the Histadrut for its active support. Thus, remarks Izraeli (1992, 190), "although the women's movement brought about important cultural change in the norms regarding the woman's role, it did not institutionalize a social structure to serve as a power center in relation to other organizations in the Yishuv."

The Women Workers' Movement was not alone on the scene of female activity. The domination of the political arena by Mapai, however, blurred the contribution of other organizations. Alternative efforts also attracted much less research and scientific interest. WIZO, the second largest women's association, was established in 1920, under the title "Federation of Hebrew Women." It aimed at "improving the standard of life for women and children in Eretz Israel," and to train women as mothers, wives, and economic partners of men. In 1933 it joined the Women's International Zionist Organization. WIZO declined to adopt a political stance. Being basically a charity association, attracting upper-middle-class women who wished to act on behalf of the needy, it had escaped the many political dilemmas faced by the WWM. Its prime goal, as stated in the movement's official publication, was "to provide an education and to give expression to the masses of women of diverse backgrounds who came from all countries of the world."[3] The national theme was unequivocally emphasized: "WIZO set itself the task of making these human wrecks into good useful citizens of the country." In the first years of its activity, WIZO established baby clinics, day-care institutions, training courses for sewing and homemaking, playgrounds for poor children, agricultural schools, and youth centers. This list demonstrates the traditional orientation of the women's association, keeping clear of the political scene.

Beside these two giant associations there were other, smaller, but no less effective women's groups. The most noted among them was the suffrage movement, whose members, unhappy about women's political status, aimed at political reforms. In 1917, a Women's Society was organized for the purpose of winning the right to vote in the Tel Aviv–Jaffa city council elections. The major opponents of this move were ultra-orthodox rabbis, who wished to remove women from the political arena. After winning the franchise in local elections, the women established a national nonpartisan association, the Union of Hebrew Women for Equal Rights in Eretz Israel, whose purpose was to elect and be elected to the Jewish self-governing bodies which were being organized. To this end, the union made an unprecedented move: it ran an independent women's list in the elections for delegates to the first Jewish Representative Assembly. Its success was stunning. Elections were held in 1920, with women participating, and fourteen women were elected as delegates. This success spurred organizational activity. In the first national convention of the union (held in 1922), WWM members also took part. The two associations united in their efforts to achieve legal suffrage, which was obtained in 1925.[4] By the end of the 1930s the struggles of the union had subsided. The association gradually shifted its focus to philantrophic activity until it amalgamated with WIZO.

What has been the course adopted by women's associations during the forty-six years of Israeli statehood? How have they coped with the political, economic, and social changes engulfing Israeli society? Answers to these questions will focus on the objectives, organizational resources, and membership mobilization of women's associations in Israel.

The State Era

Israel gained independence in 1948. The striking changes undergone by the country in its demographic composition, economic infrastructure, international status, and political makeup had only minor impact on the array of women's associations until the early 1970s. For more than two decades the veteran associations, namely, the Women Workers' Movement, which changed its title to Naamat in 1976,[5] and WIZO, continued to dominate the scene. They became, in fact, part of the ruling elite. The WWM enjoyed the fruits of political power controlled by its patron party—Mapai; WIZO membership reaped the economic benefits of the business community with which it was affiliated. As noted by Swirski (1991a, 293), "women slowly took on a 'social service' orientation, in keeping with their new class positions." These new orientations also fitted nicely with the needs of the state, overwhelmed by the massive tasks of absorbing immigrants. Women volunteers filled a vacuum left by the state's continued failure to cope with pressing social demands. During those twenty-odd years some changes took place in the objectives, strategies, and organizational structure of women's associations. Only in the past decade, however, have these changes been considerable. The Feminist Movement (FM) was the harbinger of change. Splinter associations focusing on specific feminist issues followed, complementing FM activity. Toward the mid-1980s another important association, the Women's Network (Shdula in Hebrew), entered the arena; it has both signaled and accelerated a change of course in Israeli women's politics.

The participatory revolution (also termed the "silent revolution") documented by social scientists (Inglehart 1977) was late to arrive in Israel. Israelis were preoccupied with demography, security, and the pursuit of the good life (Gottlieb and Yuchtman-Yaar 1983) rather than self-fulfillment and individual rights. Postmaterialist values have not dominated the agenda. No flower children rejecting the materialistic assets of the technological society were visible. Students did not challenge the institutions and convictions of higher education; consumers did not organize to protect their usurped rights, and women remained rather passive, accommodating themselves to their traditional roles and inferior social status. The change did not well up from within; Israeli women were entangled in their commonly sanctioned images and roles. Instead, it was first imported by women who immigrated to the country from the United States in the late 1960s. Israeli soil, however, was ripe for change.

The inception of the Feminist Movement was in Haifa in the early 1970s. The Israelis, exhilarated by their dramatic victory in the Six Day War, became more exposed to winds blowing from the Western world. The initiative for establishing the FM came from two professors at Haifa University, both newcomers from the United States. Seminars jointly conducted by them were continued later as consciousness-raising groups attended by students and teachers. In 1972 activists associated with these seminars formed the first radical women's group in Israel, Nilahem (Hebrew acronym for Nashim Lemaan Hevra Mehudeshet— Women for a Renewed Society; the word also means "We shall fight"). Separate sister organizations sprang up soon after in the two other big cities, Tel Aviv and Jerusalem, the former displaying a liberal stance and emphasizing the struggle against legal inequality, the latter a more leftist-socialist one, highlighting the link between the struggle of women and of other oppressed groups, particularly the Palestinians (Ram 1993, 52–53). It was a kind of women's auxiliary to Matzpen, a radical socialist, anti-Zionist, peace faction. The Tel Aviv group began by petitioning for enactment of the Law of Community Property,[6] and for abortion on demand. The Jerusalem group staged demonstrations against "Woman of Valor" and beauty contests (Swirski 1991, 295).

During the years that followed feminist activity spun off. Feminist centers, shelters for battered women, and rape crisis intervention centers were established in the big cities. Feminist movements were also involved in educational and consciousness-raising activities. Centers for women's studies were established in major universities. Feminist publications regularly appeared on the scene. In 1984 a new group joined the feminist arena with the formal establishment of the Women's Network (WN). The network was established by women academics in Jerusalem in August 1984. The setup of the group resulted from a meeting sponsored by the American-Jewish Congress dealing with Jewish women. Thirty-two women took part in the meeting; some of whom were willing to take part in the establishment of a nonpartisan body focusing on gender equality. In the mid-1980s women's status in the country reached one of its lowest nadirs: legislation regarding equality in the workplace was not carried through, there was no law regarding violence in the family, and women's Knesset representation was meager. Naamat was preoccupied with returning to power of its patron party, ousted from government in the 1977 political "upheaval," and the Feminist Movement did not gain ground in public opinion. The Women's Network was a self-declared lobbying association whose main (perhaps even sole) purpose was to influence gender legislation. Initially, WN served as a loose umbrella organization for women of all political parties, providing a coherent, coordinated framework for the female voice in Israeli politics. However, after gaining visibility on the national arena it has become, as will be described shortly, a highly institutionalized autonomous women's association.

Political Agenda

During the first thirty years of statehood, members of the Working Women's Movement were first and foremost workers and only then women. The task at hand was to absorb the influx of immigrants and to sustain the vulnerable Jewish homeland in its first steps. That national goals were predominant is evident from what the movement's leaders said and what its members did. "All these years," said Beba Idelson, the secretary-general, on retiring from the Knesset, "I carried in my heart the sense of specific responsibility which was conferred upon me. Every time I entered the Knesset I felt obligated. To whom? To the nation, to the citizens, to the Histadrut, to my party, to the whole women constituency, and to my colleagues in particular."[7]

This quotation vividly portrays the order of priorities that guided the women's movement in Israel. The WWM leader reiterated this point by adding: "I did not make do with acting within my movement. Nor have I seen this activity as distinct from the problems encountering the country and the Histadrut. My purpose has been to promote working women *within* society and *for the sake of* society. Hence I shunned activity aimed exclusively at women."[8]

As noted above, in 1965 Beba Idelson declined to present her candidacy for the Knesset following an unpublished party headquarters' decision to leave her off the list. In the movement publication there were increasing references to women's political vulnerability. Idelson went so far as to propose, in a revolutionary article written in 1966, the creation of women's parliament consisting of women representatives from all political parties.[9] The idea was ignited by her realization that "we have not yet achieved the social equality we deserve. We are aware of a situation which has no justification whatsoever, from the woman's point of view and from the perspective of society as a whole." The fact that the number of women in the Knesset fell in 1965, that not a single woman was nominated to a ministerial position, that no women were represented on the central committee of the Histadrut, in the trade unions, and in the bureaus of economic enterprises, dictated a change of course. Establishing a forum where women could advocate their gender interests seemed appropriate. This article was like a voice in the wilderness. There was no follow-up, either in the WWM or in other women's organizations. No action was taken to implement Idelson's ideas. The seed, however, was sown. Nearly twenty years later the Women's Network was established, approximating the dream of this frustrated women's leader.

The mood of integration gradually changed as Naamat shifted its focus from the national domain to the women's arena. The turning point in the Naamat's history occurred in the mid-1970s. The establishment in 1976 of a public Commission on the Status of Women by Prime Minister Rabin has been noted above. The commission was chaired by Ora Namir, a former WWM activist. Naamat worked closely with the commission and exerted a decisive influence on its deliberations. The political upheaval which brought the Likud to power in 1977 contributed, however, to the turning of the wheel as Naamat enhanced its integrative efforts. A month after the elections its incoming secretary-general, Nava Arad, has stated: "We suddenly realized what politics implies, and that Naamat is a *political* movement, and not only a women's association." Politicization of Naamat served two purposes, ostensibly mutually exclusive: it emphasized the association's allegiance to the party, tantamount, in the eyes of its leadership, to loyalty to overall national goals. But it also provided an opportunity to advance the status of women.

Since the late 1970s, Naamat has attempted to increase its function as a political lobby by establishing a Department for the Status of Women. The origins of this department, however, were grounded in national imperatives. Formerly known as the

Department for Legislation, Legal Counseling and Social Security, the department focusing on women's status evolved after the Six Day War, when the Labor-held Ministry of Defense asked Naamat to establish an agency to assist bereaved families and war widows. Currently, the department offers legal advice on job discrimination and violence in the family. One of its major undertakings is drafting legislation concerning women's rights particularly in these domains. In 1988 Naamat issued a formal declaration on the Rights of Women calling for equality in the workplace and equal representation in all public bodies.[10] The petition, signed by thousands of women across the country, was presented to the prime minister. Even this declaration, however, aimed at promoting the status of women, reflected adherence to national objectives. For example, one of the provisions recommended that women serve in the armed forces or do some other form of national service (Pope 1991, 232).[11] Each year, on the eve of Independence Day, Naamat's secretary-general took the opportunity to remind the movement's membership that Naamat would continue, assiduously and unabashedly, to be faithful to the nation: "Whither thou [the nation] goest, we [the women's movement] will follow you."

These orientations have influenced Naamat's agenda and shaped its objectives. Naamat adheres to its traditional role and image in providing welfare services. The movement takes pride in vocational courses offered to women. Every person trained, it was claimed, "adds power to the IDF, to the working people, to the quality of life in Israel."[12] Vocational training, however, is centered on traditional female interests. Courses are offered in fashion, beauty and cosmetics, child care, sewing, secretarial work, and home design. The justification for this range is that "these women need to support themselves and will not come to us if we offer them computer sciences," (personal interview with the author). But the message is nevertheless clear: women's place in society is defined by their traditional roles.

Naamat reiterated its traditional orientation when it adopted a controversial slogan as a central theme in a Status-of-Women Month in 1984: "Be a man! Give her a hand." This dictum was well meant: encouraging husbands to aid their wives in domestic chores, emphasizing that it is not "unmanly" to do housework. Naamat's secretary-general expressed this orientation through the question, "Can we ignore the division of labor, still pervasive in the Israeli society, assigning women roles different from those of men, a practice determining our mode of behavior?"[13] But the message that came through was antifeminist as it perpetuated the old-time division of labor, making house work the women's responsibility, the men being kindly requested merely to assist. Furthermore, it was said that "Women's progress in the two domains—workplace and political life—cannot be achieved without family support, or more accurately without cooperation of the husband when the woman is married or the boyfriend if she is single."[14] Naamat also reiterated its rejection of radical strategies, denouncing the application of "political pressure": "A solution to our civic problems will not be achieved by engaging in a pressure activity," stated an editorial in its monthly magazine.[15] Social-welfare activity has thus remained at the top of Naamat's agenda even though it has incorporated many feminist ideas.

Naamat's order of priorities is manifested in the annual budget during the last decade. Feminist orientations may be traced in the share of total expenditure allocated to the bureau for legal consultation, responsible for drafting legislation, and to the department on women's status (including a budgetary item entitled "public dealing with women's status"). The figures show that the amount of money devoted to women's status tripled from 1983 to 1993 and that the funds allocated to legal advice increased sevenfold. But this bright picture is somewhat dimmed when the sums, rather than the improvement of percentages, are presented. Even in 1993 Naamat appropriated less than one percent of its NIS 94.7 million annual budget to legal advise, only 2.7 percent to the status of women, and a trifling 0.008 percent (!) to "public dealing with women's status." By comparison, the proportion of the budget allocated to "political education," "Zionist education," and "family and community" amounted to 6.8 percent of the total budget in 1993, three times more than the sum designated to the specific promotion of women's status.

The largest women's movement in the country has thus distanced itself from the nationalist orientation that dominated it in the first three decades of statehood, but it has a long way to go in terms of feminist orientations and activities. In the midst of the Lebanon War (1982–83) Naamat praised its members, mobilized at the outbreak of the fighting, for contributing to the national effort, in the following words: "We found them [Naamat's members] in every corner: they distributed soft drinks to soldiers at the intersections, they packed gifts for soldiers in the Soldiers' Welfare Committee, they visited the wounded in the hospitals, and they supported the families of the casualties."[16] An emphasis on compassionate voluntarism was still evident in the 1980s.

To conclude, Naamat developed as part of the Zionist movement, which was inspired by the drive for building a national homeland in Palestine. After independence it remained part of the Labor-Zionist establishment and, as a result, its feminist objectives have been tempered by national and partisan concerns. Yet Naamat has increasingly subscribed to interests unique to women, adjusting its agenda to the growing awareness of feminism among Israeli women.

WIZO, notably a conservative women' association, has not escaped the winds of change, although to a lesser extent than other women's groups. In the early years of statehood WIZO adopted a feminist posture. As noted in chapter 2, it was WIZO that in cooperation with the Women's Union for Equal Rights, ran in the elections to the First Knesset and won a seat. However, feminist activity was short-lived, as a conservative leadership took over, reemphasizing WIZO's traditional objectives focused on the welfare of women and children. During the forty-seven years of statehood, WIZO has incorporated new issues into its agenda. As will be shown below, it played a major role in bringing the problem of battered women to the forefront of public attention.[17] In 1992 the department for the status of women and the legal advice bureau issued a Scroll of the Rights of Victims of Family Abuse, specifying the legal rights of those subject to violence. (No particular reference was made to battered wives.) This activity, however, was in line with the general welfare orientation advocated by the association. Only seldom was WIZO involved in political activity or in lobbying authorities on behalf of women. According to WIZO's advocacy, "good citizenship" is equivalent to charity. This term was defined in the association's publication as follows: "What is the meaning of 'Good Citizenship'? When a woman who has benefited from WIZO's aid comes to realize how much she has received, and that the time has come for her, in turn, to give of herself and to help those who are in greater need. When she is aware of that, we know that this woman has adjusted well to her environment. She no longer asks what WIZO can provide for her, but rather asks what can she give to WIZO, and consequently to her country."[18]

Despite its emphasis on women's traditional roles, some evidence of feminism can be traced in the WIZO agenda. In 1955 WIZO established the "Council for the Status of Women" whose purpose was to fight for women's rights. The fifteen branches of the department for legal advise further enhanced WIZO's role in promoting gender equality. The council's activity yielded four important laws: the Inheritance Law (1965), whereby a widow is entitled to half the family's property; the Common Property Law (1973), establishing an equal division of property upon divorce; an amendment to the National Insurance Law providing social security (1965), providing that mothers receive a direct financial child-allowance from the state; and the Alimony Law (1972), obliging the national insurance to pay the alimony (Greenberg and Herzog 1978, 115–16). Despite these achievements, WIZO's leaders insisted that the association is "not a lobbying group. We prefer to aid women, and they need us. Politics is somebody else's business, and not ours." Needless to say, the core of WIZO's activity has remained the family ("The Youth of Today Are the Parents of Tomorrow," stated a headline in one of WIZO's publications). In 1993 WIZO's slogan has remained "Right through Life." Recalling its accomplishments, the association has noted that its "comprehensive network of 680 institutions and services throughout Israel reaches out and enriches the lives of infants, children, adults and senior citizens." It has remained a charity association whose goals are closely associated with national objectives. In its annual address, WIZO's top leader (Israel branch) called upon the association's members to contribute more to immigrant absorption. Under the headline "Promotion of women's status," the chair exalted efforts made by the association and notified that "immigrants absorption has been raised to WIZO's top agenda."[19] This traditional mood has not prevented WIZO from joining forces with other women's associations in the struggle over specific issues of great concern to women in the country. In fact, "To advance the status of women in Israel" was noted as the second organizational objective, the first being: "To provide for the welfare of infants, children, youth and the elderly."

The emergence of the Women's Network revolutionized the arena of women's associations. Unlike Naamat and WIZO, from its inception WN confined itself to the political arena. Its first move was to pressure the prospective leaders of the National Unity Government to include women in the cabinet and to precipitate the implementation of the report issued by the Commission on the Status of Women. The founders of the network believed that women's status would not be advanced through charity and providing welfare, but by legal action and political pressure. The first and major objective of the WN was "to eradicate all trace of discrimination against women, and to obtain adequate and equal representation of women in all centers of power." The second aim was "to change attitudes and policy in areas such as the economy, employment, health, education, communication, and advertisement." Power has thus been a core theme in the WN's objectives. It was believed that "Only if women are equal partners enjoying equal status and rights in all forums of policy making, where critical decisions are taken and economic and human resources are allocated, only then will our dreams on an egalitarian, thriving, just, and efficient society be realized."[20] In 1993 a special coordinator for legislation was nominated to direct and regulate contacts with women Knesset members (of all political parties) to expedite lobbying efforts. Training courses were offered to women aspiring to political careers. Recently, the network has expanded its activity to domains of major importance to women's lives, such as health. It declines, however, to provide services and steadfastly adheres to its "political" commitment.

The goals of the Feminist Movement can be learnt from its publications and from the memoirs of one of its founders, Marcia Freedman. Unlike feminist movements in other Western countries, the Israeli FM did not cut itself off from the national mainstream; its letterhead read "The Feminist Movement of Israel," followed by "*Pro-Zionist*, not party-affiliated" (emphasis mine). During the October 1973 war the Haifa feminists went to local military authorities to volunteer for the war effort. "They, too, wanted to serve their country in its hour of need" (Swirski 1991, 296). FM, however, advocated objectives distinctly from those of the conventional women's groups. From its inception FM focused on body politics, on abortion, and on battering of women. As will be shown, it was FM that presented the Knesset with the pro-choice version of the abortion law. Unlike Naamat and WIZO, FM was not concerned with equal rights in the workplace, the family, or even in politics. Child-care and vocational training were outside its domain of interest. Acting on behalf of women suffering a clear and present constraint (violence, unwanted pregnancy) dominated the feminist agenda.

During the 1980s the Feminist Movement altered its agenda by including issues of war and peace among its top priorities. In its initial phases the Arab-Israel conflict was not perceived as a legitimate feminist concern. Following the war in Lebanon (1982–83), a group of feminists formed Women Against Occupation. Since the eruption of the Intifada (1987) feminists, many of whom were active in peace organizations, have organized all-women peace groups to demand an end to the occupation. Particular attention was given to Palestinian women detainees. Concomitantly, there has been increasing cooperation between Jewish feminists and Palestinian women in the occupied territories (Swirski 1991a, 298). Some splinters of FM, such as Women in Black, have targeted all their efforts at protesting the continued Israeli occupation of the territories, rather than at gender issues.[21] Despite these modifications FM has not veered from its original course: to influence public opinion, to raise consciousness and to generate awareness to women's needs (and subsequently to the needs of other deprived groups such as the Palestinians), rather than to directly lobby policy-makers.

Organizational Resources

The availability of resources is one of the fundamental criteria for assessing the propensity of an association to influence public policy (Walker 1991). The origin of resources may serve as an indicator for assesing the prospects for associational autonomy. Generally, women's associations in Israel have amassed impressive resources. Naamat is a highly structured mass-membership association, with a rigid institutional setup administered by a written formal constitution.[22] Elections to national and local positions within Naamat are held every four years at the same time as elections to the Histadrut. All candidates are presented according to party lists covering almost the whole gamut of Israeli politics. Likud is obviously a major contestor for power, but among the lists are also minor parties such as the Communists, the Civil Rights Movement (now in alliance with two other parties under the name Meretz) and others. Since its inception, however, Naamat has been controlled by the Labor Party, consistently securing a clear and decisive majority in the elections to the group's institutions.[23] Unlike the models of Western feminist movements, most of which are based on grassroots organization outside political parties and mainstream institutions (Randall 1987), Naamat is bound to a framework of political interests—forged by internal electoral processes and leadership nomination—determined by party institutions. Naamat operates its complex organizational network with some 5,000 employees.

Compared with other women's associations, Naamat is also replete with financial resources, amounting to NIS 94.7 million in 1993 (approximately $31 million). The annual budget reflects the range of activities undertaken by the association. Early child-care constitutes a major budgetary item , 90 percent of which is covered by parents' fees and 10 percent by the government. Likewise, vocational training is heavily subsidized by the state. The fees received for administering child-care facilities and vocational training account for about 65 percent of Naamat's budget. Approximately 30 percent of the budget is derived from Histadrut resources, depending on the size of membership and the share of dues. The remaining 5 percent is received through Naamat's sister organizations (formerly Pioneer Women) in the United States, and in twelve other Western countries. Evidently, Naamat does not derive its financial resources from grassroots fees but relies heavily on institutional resources. Although women pay for child-care they do not perceive this payment as part of their commitment to feminism but rather as a fee for a necessary service.

WIZO, too, does not derive its resources from rank-and-file women but from contributions solicited abroad. The budget (NIS 256 million in 1994), is allocated to the administration of day-care institutions and to charity activities. The largest item of expenditure—"family welfare"—accurately reflects the association's order of priorities. Consciousness-raising activities (termed "A Woman's Platform") receive only a scant share of the total budget. Specific projects, such as building day-care institutions, usually receive the support of a government ministry or a local authority, but voluntarism still plays a major role in the group's activity. In this respect both WIZO and Naamat perpetuate the use of women's cheap time and energy.

The Women's Network was initially set up as a nonstructural association. Soon, however, it faced the organizational dilemma confronting grassroots associations: how to gain influence without organization (Costain 1989). With the passage of time the WN has yielded to the organizational imperative by setting up an administrative staff. Organizational expansion is highly impressive. The group started out with one salaried person; a decade after its establishment the number of employees is fifteen. Concomitantly, the network expanded its institutional structure, which now comprises four branches and two standing committees, the legal committee and the political committee.[24] Additional forums deal with abusive advertising, education, and women's health. As membership dues constitute only a marginal portion of the total budget, WN, like WIZO, is heavily dependent on external resources. Its major patron is the New Israel Fund, a U.S.-based organization funding associations contributing to enhancing democracy in Israeli society. The network's budget is divided among salaries, daily maintenance, information centers, and membership recruitment.

Among women's associations in Israel the FM has the lowest financial resources. Starting out as a grassroots movement, it never enjoyed the affluence attached to affiliation with the political establishment. In fact, FM as such is without any resources—organizational, human, or financial. But, as will be shortly explained, it has succeeded, despite its vulnerability, in proliferating and disseminating feminist ideas and practices among the Israeli public.

Mobilization

Naamat does not conduct membership campaigns as its members are recruited by virtue of their affiliation with the Histadrut. There are no accurate numbers of Naamat's current membership, estimated to be around 750,000, including some 100,000 Arab women. Any woman who belongs to the Histadrut or whose husband does automatically becomes a member. For many Naamat women membership is merely a routine and passive. Many are not even aware of belonging to the organization. In an undergraduate course on women and politics for political science students, the women students (about half the total) were asked who belonged to Naamat: only one raised her hand. When asked who belonged to the General Sick Fund (Kupat Holim), membership of which derives from Histadrut membership, all but one raised their hands, indicating that in fact they all belonged to Naamat but did not know it. In the past decade, the Histadrut has been engulfed in a serious crisis, which made an impact on the membership rate. Bankruptcy of its industrial enterprises, ideological perplexity, and prospects of better health care in rival sick funds prompted many Histadrut members to withdraw from the organization. It has been reported that in 1992, 125,000 members ceased paying their dues to the Labor Federation. The increase in Histadrut membership in that year was only by 0.6 percent, compared with a 4.2 rise in the total population.[25] These figures imply a decline in Naamat membership as well. Yet Naamat can still claim that it represents 60 percent of Israeli women.

The Naamat's membership comprises heterogeneous social groups. People who join the Histadrut do so mainly because they wish to join the General Sick Fund, not because they identify with Israeli trade unionism. Workers, business people, farmers, and professionals belong to the all encompassing Labor Federation. Membership composition, however, makes little difference to the association's daily operation as Naamat is not a grassroots movement but a group in which a small minority of members are active. Far more women are subject to indoctrination ("education") and mobilization. The option of joining the General Sick Fund without joining the Histadrut, which was recently instituted by the National Health Insurance Law (adopted by the Knesset in July 1994), may limit Naamat's recruitment of new members.

In the early 1990s WIZO numbered some 100,000 members in Israel. Every year a membership drive is held (for one month), but the number of members has remained fairly stable. No dues are required from prospective members, simply enlistment for volunteer activity, presented as the substance of WIZO's life. In its membership drive WIZO appeals to women's enthusiasm for self-fulfillment and giving. Headlines such as "My Greatest Joy is to Give to Others" and "A Volunteer's Confession" are common in WIZO publications. The association highlights the satisfaction derived from volunteering to help the needy and the importance attributed to welfare work in the Jewish tradition and social heritage. No political strands are interwoven in the campaign to attract new members. No enduring commitment is required, just a notification. By virtue of its historical heritage, membership in WIZO is still associated with affluence and a right-wing political orientation. Joining WIZO is akin to class identification. It has been inconceivable for women associated with the labor movement or one of its social branches to become a WIZO activist.

The Women's Network expanded its membership impressively during the ten years of its existence. In 1993 membership, as judged by dues payment, was 1,500, the overwhelming majority of it being urban, educated, and professional women of European origin. The network has failed to mobilize membership in development towns and urban neighborhoods, not only because women in these localities shy away from feminist ideas, but also because its activities are incompatible with poor women's priorities. Yet members take an active part in the association's life. During 1986, two years after the network was established, general elections were held followed by the set up of democratically elected governing bodies.

At its inception, the Feminist Movement had only fifty active members in the entire country (Freedman 1990, 51). Although feminism in Israel has significantly expanded, it remained, until several years ago, an elite association, attracting mainly well-to-do, upper-class women. As noted by Swirski (1991a, 299), so far the movement has failed to become relevant to the majority of Israeli women, whether they live in urban centers, development towns, or agricultural settlements. This does not imply that FM has remained incognito. In fact it has widely proliferated into grassroots organizations running highly publicized activities on women's physical safety, health, and media status.[26]

The extent to which women's associations have been successful in raising awareness of their activities was examined in a national survey carried out in 1993 (for methodological details, see chapter 4). Respondents of a national sample (men and women) were asked if they ever took part in any activity initiated by a women's association. The answers indicated a low level of mobilization, as only 12.8 percent of all Israeli women gave a positive answer. Respondents were further asked if they had been helped by a women's association during the previous year. Findings show that although day-care services are nearly monopolized by women's associations, only a fraction of Israelis (3.6 percent) were assisted by them. It may be, however, that the clients dissociated the service from the provider and that they did not know who its owners were. Results were more encouraging when the respondents were asked about the influence of women's associations on public policy. If mobilization is tantamount to acknowledging this influence, then women's groups may take pride in their accomplishments. The scale of importance attributed by the women respondents generally reflects the seniority and magnitude of the association in question. Naamat took first place, with an overwhelming acknowledgment (89.4 percent) that it has greatly or to some extent contributed to legislation regarding women's equality. WIZO came second, with 81.9 percent acknowledging its contribution; the Women's Network followed with 44.7 percent; last on the list was the Feminist Movement, thought by 36.6 percent of the respondents to have influenced gender legislation. Needless to say, the answers reflect images more than reality, as the contribution of the WN to the formulation of public policy has been at least as substantial as that of

Naamat, whereas the Feminist Movement and WIZO did not perceive legislation as a major target. The upshot of these findings is that women's associations have not been very successful stimulating women to activity and instilling in them gratitude for their services. They have been more fortunate as regards general assessment of their activities, an assessment shaped by seniority and publicity more than by factual evidence.

Relations with Political Parties

Relations with political parties have been on the agenda of women's associations since their inception. As noted, the Women Workers' Movement vacillated between establishing a separate organization and joining forces with the party-controlled Histadrut. The latter opinion eventually prevailed. The WWM came increasingly under the control of the central Histadrut organs, which controlled financial resources. The party affiliation of Naamat, WWM's successor, is not only a historical memory but a contemporary reality, particularly in regard to nominations. From the start, the association's top leadership has been selected by party organs. Naamat's secretaries-general are well aware of their patrons. On taking office one of them stated: "In order to promote issues in our political reality we ought to emphasize the deepening of our linkage with our organization and the Labor party, and we ought to strengthen our party identity." She further added that "as long as Naamat is not an independent movement, and as long as it is integrated with the Labor Movement and acts in concert with its Knesset faction, it cannot afford to do what a marginal extremist minority group such as the Feminist Movement is doing: it cannot struggle for its goals as it sees fit itself."[27] Electoral reform, transferring the selection of candidates and the election of leaders to the general membership in national primaries, has loosened the party's grip on the internal electoral process, but candidates for major positions, such as the secretary-general, could not possibly seek support unless endorsed by the party. The linkage between Naamat and the Labor Party is, however, two-sided, as the association drafts the gender-related planks in the party platform.

Relationship between Naamat and the party are formally mediated by the Women's Department in the Labor Party, designed to fulfill a dual function: to represent Naamat in the party institutions and to represent the party in Naamat decision-making bodies. This distinction, however, has remained on paper only as the two bodies act in concert, with overlapping membership. Many of Naamat's activists serve as members of the department's governing bodies; the department activists are supported by Naamat in their bid for leadership positions. Naamat activists utilize their movement's potent role as a springboard into mainstream political institutions. It has become a tradition that after one or two terms in office Naamat's secretary-general is elected to the Knesset on the Labor Party's list.

The close link between Naamat and the Labor Party has often tarnished women's politics. This was the case particularly under the Likud government, when adherence to the women's cause could have been detrimental to Labor's interests. Naamat activists praised Sarah Doron (Likud), a minister without portfolio, for shaping a feminist agenda. At the same time a question arose: "We are contributing to Doron's prestige. How will the party accept this? . . . The public appreciates a minister more than it does a movement like Naamat, and a minister always represents a party."[28] Partisanship in Naamat has, nonetheless, somewhat abated. Debates in the association's secretariat reflect the inclination toward the party on the one hand and the wish to tear away from institutional politics on the other. One of the activists said: "We are party members and party delegates, but it is inconceivable that we, as Naamat activists, would present ourselves as a women's cell at the service of the party. All in all, our campaign is founded in the party, but the Naamat movement is also essential. I reject the notion that Naamat is akin to the Labor Party. Naamat sustains the party rather than the reverse. . . . That we serve the party is obvious, but we have to safeguard Naamat."[29]

This equivocation, however, dwindled as elections approached. Naamat activists readily campaigned on behalf of the party. Women were requested to hold home-meetings and to solicit support for the party. "The task of a Naamat activist is to involve other women in the electoral process and mobilize them in order to make them follow the movement, rain or shine."[30] Women's campaign activity was considered more effective because "women were familiar with the people. They could enter houses and be greeted by the people."[31]

The Women's Network started out as a professed apolitical association. Within a short time, however, it was penetrated by political parties as candidates to elected institutions were identified as party activists. WN responded to party infiltration by setting up a political committee, comprising representatives of all political parties. The committee's diverse membership is united around two goals: to place women's issues on the agenda of all political parties, and, primarily, to enhance women's representation in state and local governing institutions. Assertiveness seminars have been held and (modest) funding is provided to women running as candidates. WN prides itself on the fact that activists associated with both coalition and opposition parties smooth over their differences when women's issues are at stake. This is true not only for grassroots activists but also for women Knesset members who are at each other's throat on problems of Israel's peace policy. A Likud delegate in the network's political committee was warmly commended by a member of Mapam, a left-wing party, after deciding to run for a senior position in her party. The fact that the committee is co-chaired by a Labor and a Likud activist both reflects and fosters the all-party nature of the Women's Network.

The Feminist Movement is currently detached from party politics. In its short history, however, FM did undergo an episode of partisanship. When the Citizens' Rights Movement decided at the last moment to run for the 1973 elections, its leader, Shulamit Aloni, requested FM to help her obtain the number of signatures required to enter the race; in return, a feminist activist (Marcia Freedman) was allotted a third place on the party's list, which seemed unlikely to win a Knesset seat at the time. The October War, and the ensuing protest movements, gave CRM an unexpected victory, resulting in Freedman's election to the Knesset. Immediately after the elections tensions arose over Freedman's allegiance to the party versus the feminist movement. From the very start, wrote Freedman, "we disliked and distrusted one another" (1990, 140). Aloni tried to persuade her to relinquish her Knesset seat; when she refused, Aloni cold-shouldered her for five years as punishment. FM did not appreciate Freedman's Knesset membership either, and failed to provide support in her perpetual conflicts (Swirski 1991a, 295). One of the chief reasons for the unfavorable environment was Freedman's position on the Arab-Israeli dispute. In her own words: "I was already infamous as a militant feminist in a country where the liberation of women was seen as a threat to national security. I was an upstart immigrant who went too far too fast. By coming out, in 1975, in favor of a two-state solution, I became more notorious and more isolated, even within the feminist community" (Freedman 1990, 108).

Freedman was wanted on the list because CRM needed FM's membership resources, meager as they were. When the feminist MK broke away from her party and joined Yaad, a small radical leftist party, the Feminist Movement was once again deprived of partisan assets.

"Sisterhood" among Women?

Having no common parents, women's associations in Israel hardly ever act as "sisters." A Labor activist has noted that "the impediment to the advancement of the women's cause emanates from controversies among women themselves."[32] Rivalry was at its worst among women who did climb up the ladder of success. Shulamit Aloni was forced out of the Knesset and later of the Labor Party owing to the animosity shown to her by Golda Meir. Aloni and Freedmann were on no better terms. In her memoirs Marcia Freedman describes how, from their first encounter, "Aloni and I brought out the worst in each another." Perhaps the hostility between women had to do with self-hate, she remarked (1990, 169). Furthermore, women who have climbed the political ladder are not always loyal to their association of origin. For example, Naamat complained that the chairperson of the Knesset Labor and Welfare Committee, a former secretary-general of the association, did not grant its representative the right to speak during a meeting dealing with battered women.[33] Bad blood between this particular MK and Naamat was seen to prevail in other gender issues.

The political committee of the Women's Network has provided an umbrella to members of opposing political parties.
Activity in the committee has attracted such strange bedfellows
as members of the arch-nationalist Tzomet and left-wing Hadash
(the Israel Communist Party). But WN has antagonized feminist
groups, alleging it monopolizes fundraising for the women's
cause. For example, Shin, the group focusing on women's political representation, claimed it ceased to receive financial aid
because WN held there was no need for splinter groups on the
feminist front. Feminists also challenge the network on account
of its strong "national adherence."[34]

Among the feminists there have been clashes between the
Jerusalem women, who centered on the oppression of the Arabs
and the poor, and the Haifa women, who centered on feminist
issues (Freedman 1990, 51). There has been little collaboration
among FM's numerous chapters. From 1975 to 1977 attempts
were made to coordinate activities of FM branches. Committees
were set up for this purpose, but conflicts and dissension could
not be overcome (Swirski 1991a, 296). In the following years
national conferences were organized annually in an effort to
increase cohesion among feminists in Israel. These endeavors,
however, have been abortive. A recent conference attended by
some 700 women, displayed a serious rift between Sephardi
feminists who recently joined the movement, and the veteran
FM membership, mostly of European origin. The former charged
the latter with ignoring the problem of underprivileged women
in Israel. "Their [the veteran feminists'] problems are not mine,"
one was quoted as saying.[35]

Impediments on sisterhood may, however, belong to the past,
as during the past decade two attempts at coordinating women's
efforts have proved highly successful: the first—Bat Adam—is a
coalition combating violence perpetrated against women; the
second—Ikar—focuses on eliminating laws discriminating
against women in matters of personal status. The improvement
in relations among major women's associations may partly be
because allegiance to the banner has taken precedence over
adherence to the flag. The issues around which Bat Adam coalition formed were both the least controversial and the most
propitious for action. Furthermore, with the passage of time

there has been a turnover in leaders, all of whom now are of the same age group, and with similar life experiences. Smooth personal communication has thus replaced historical and political rivalries and animosities.

Grassroots Women's Associations

Women's movements were not confined to the institutional arena but emerged at the grassroots level, particularly in the late 1980s. The grassroots associations were significantly not organizations with broad constituencies and many interests, but specialized groups representing particular constituencies and focused interests. Growing awareness of women's special needs and, more importantly, changes in Israel's security situation, were important factors in the formation and operation of several of these new women's groups. Most notable among them were: Claf (Community of Lesbian Feminists), created in 1986 for the promotion of its members' interests; Women in Black, established in 1989 and advocating the end of the occupation over the territories captured in the Six Day War; sister-association, Women's Network for the Promotion of Peace (formed in 1989), which set about disseminating the idea of peace among Israeli women. Another group, Women and Peace (also established in 1989), in addition to its advocacy of peace also aimed at raising women's political consciousness and increasing cooperation between Israeli and Palestinian women. These three associations were joined by a fourth: Coalition of Women and Peace, aiming (in the language of one of its activists) to "pressure the government to cease violence, end the occupation, curb militarism, and to advance women's participation in processes of decision-making on issues of peace (and war)." More important than pressuring the government was the goal of instigating women to act on behalf of peace.

All these women's associations manifested similar organizational characteristics.[36] First, there was the lack of organizational resources in terms of membership[37] and budget. Except for one (Women and Peace), these grassroots associations operated without a fixed budget and without professional staff. Second, despite the conspicuous paucity of resources all associations reported successful recruitment. Women in Black, for example, initiated its activity with only a hundred women. Four years later the number of its activists had tripled. Claf increased its size tenfold (from 25 in 1986 to 250 in 1994). Although in terms of absolute numbers the gains were not impressive, the idea of women's grassroots activity has nevertheless gained ground. Third, true to their nature women's grassroots associations were not governed by structured leadership of elected representatives but practiced direct democracy, with all activists taking part in the decision-making process. As one of them has put it: "Our association is not hierarchical. Any woman can join us, participate and turn into a 'leader'." In some associations (for example, Women in Black) a self-appointed committee, comprising women activists volunteering for minor organizational work, steered the group. Fourth, all associations (except Claf)[38] enjoyed access to decision-makers. Activists reported that requests for meetings with politicians or government officials were accommodated. Yet none of the associations reported being invited to testify before a Knesset committee. Access was thus granted on a personal basis but not ensconced in structured legitimacy.[39] From the information provided by women activists it emerges that grassroots associations employed a variety of strategies to further their goals. Most prominent were street demonstrations, but they were supplemented by media campaigns, contacts with political parties and in one case (Women's Network for the Promotion of Peace) court appeal.

As this brief overview indicates, there has been a proliferation of women's movements focusing on peace. Attempts to combine the activities of these associations under one umbrella organization largely failed. Women's groups acted separately, each soliciting its own modest funds and managing its own activity. Given this fragmented scene, it is no wonder that women's grassroots associations found it difficult to cope with organizational vulnerability. External circumstances were more compelling. The precipitation of the peace process with the Palestinians removed women's peace groups from the public eye. Protests are no longer held, the voice of the women pacifists was finally heard and listened to. Sociopolitical developments had a different effect on Claf. Since 1986 Israeli society has dramatically changed its attitude toward people with different sexual preferences. Male and female homosexuals have gained legal rights and recognition. Notwithstanding this change in the political arena, social norms are still inimical to lesbians, many of whom are not yet ready to openly admit their sexual preferences. Consequently, Claf is not content with raising the feminist banner, but seeks a space on this banner for women whose way of life is still viewed as aberrant by the Israeli public.

Arab Women's Movements

A discussion of women's associations in Israel cannot be concluded without reference to the non-Jewish sector of the population. As faithful members of a traditional society, Arab women have not been active in public life, and if they have been involved in politics it has usually been in the context of establishment parties and voluntary associations, such as the Communist Party or Naamat. Some local women's associations in the Arab community, such as the Organization of Acre Women, are involved in welfare activity and promotion of education for young children.[40] In 1990 the first seed of Arab feminism was sown with the establishment of Al-Fanar (The Lighthouse), an organization dedicated to fighting "honor killing" and the perceived systematic oppression of women in Arab society. The message of the Arab feminists was revolutionary, challenging fundamental traditions and mores of the Israeli Arab community. Al-Fanar has targeted a series of practices which it says are symptomatic of a society dominated by a patriarchal regime: forced marriage of women to their relatives; sexual and other physical assaults on women by their husbands and male relatives; denial of education and job opportunities to women who are taken out of school as teenagers and kept at home to carry out domestic chores; and the spread of defamatory rumors and gossip about women as a means of controlling their behavior. Al-Fanar started informally as a study group on the status and treatment of women in Arab society. It began publishing an internal newsletter in which members put forward their own views on feminism. A demonstration in Nazareth held in protest of a "family honor" slaying turned Al-Fanar into a public phenomenon. Shortly after its establishment the organization attracted wide criticism. Arab political parties challenged Al-Fanar for taking independent initiative. MK Miari (Hadash) suggested more restraint should be employed. "We live in a traditional society. I do not advise shattering its foundations." But the most virulent denunciations of Al-Fanar have come from the growing Islamic fundamentalist movement.[41] Despite the hostile reaction in Arab circles, Al-Fanar has successfully broken the social taboo on discussion of domestic violence and maltreatment of women. Articles on the subject began appearing in the Arab press, including anonymous personal accounts by women who had been victimized by men. A growing number of women responded to Al-Fanar's advertisements, appealing to the organization for help. The group has also received assistance from a Jewish-run shelter for battered women. Currently Al-Fanar runs on a modest budget and is supported almost entirely by its members, though it has registered as a nonprofit organization and is seeking contributions from supporters. It publishes a quarterly newsletter which is distributed door-to-door, and it has published articles in the Israeli Arab newspaper.[42] No accurate information is available on membership size. It is known, however, that its activists are university graduates, mostly single, residing in Haifa.

Conclusion

Recapitulating the story of women's associations brings about an ambivalent picture portraying both integration and mobilization. The more veteran, and so to speak, more conservative women's associations have largely retained their traditional themes. Both Naamat and WIZO (the first to a lesser extent, the latter to a greater extent), have avoided a struggle against male organizations. Both have defined themselves in terms of women's traditional interests. Both Naamat and WIZO still emphasize the importance of family values; both urge women to volunteer their time and energy to aid the needy; and above all, both invest the major part of their resources in welfare activities, providing services to women constituents. Taking care of young children and supplying vocational education to poor women, mainly in traditional female jobs, have remained typical organizational endeavors, encouraged by the political authorities. The provision of these services has granted the veteran women's associations legitimacy, recognition, and some state funding. It is unlikely that either Naamat or WIZO will eschew their traditional roles in favor of a more radical course as concentrating on family needs has been their way of integrating into the polity. One may conclude, therefore, in line with the well-known French dictum, that the more things change the more they remain the same. Despite this perpetuation, discernible changes have occurred.

First, the entrance of new actors to the women's movement arena has made a lot of difference. The Feminist Movement, while poor in resources, has sown a seed that almost unnoticed produced impressive fruits. In its advocacy it has emphasized women's feminist identity placing the focus on what women *are* rather than on what women *do* for others. Depicting women as having their own interests was a novelty in Israeli political discourse. It was FM that first detached women's associations in Israel from mainstream collective aims. Even the Feminist Movement, however, has eschewed a serious confrontation with society's principal values and institutions. It has abstained from comprehensive and penetrating criticism of the political structure. Rather, as noted by a feminist commentator, Israeli feminism "has been deeply submerged in the prevailing order without challenging it; and it exploits the prevailing conceptual framework without disputing it."[43] Despite these drawbacks, FM has spurred the spread of feminist activity. Extensive organizational proliferation has brought to the scene many small self-help movements attempting to raise women's identification with feminism by focusing on specific women's issues.

The inception of the Women's Network further enhanced the role of feminism, and moreover gave it a political tilt. Whereas FM concentrated on mobilizing women and inculcating them with feminist ideas, WN directed its efforts precisely at the center of power. For the network, women's equality was defined in terms of public policy rather than ideas, identities or services. Participation of women in decision-making bodies, and the output of these bodies regarding gender roles and rights, became chief organizational targets. Not one single association has remained indifferent to these changes. Even WIZO, which basically remains loyal to its charity posture, has spelled out slogans compatible with feminist aspirations. Naamat took organizational measures to prove its allegiance to the women's cause, such as invigorating the activity of the legal department and the department for the status of women. The newly elected secretary-general stated at a press conference, that "the movement [Naamat] is shifting from the phase of protest to the phase of determination."[44] Giving priority to women's representation in decision-making bodies, Naamat has actually joined the network's political campaign.

Notwithstanding these changes, however, the dilemma of the flag versus the banner has not been totally resolved. In 1993 Naamat still regarded family life as a major value, not only to be reckoned with, but in fact to be embraced and encouraged. For WIZO, family life has remained not only at the center of the scene, but the only scene. Naamat has probably attenuated its ties with its patron party and has distanced itself from national collective goals ("We are not the 'taken for granted' of the state!")[45] but party activity is still flourishing. Senior positions in Naamat still constitute a springboard for party office. The network has worked wonders by bringing together representatives of various parties to form a coalition promoting women's interests, but it too is harnessed to tradition, though much less than the veteran women's associations. The direction women's associations are taking is thus ambiguous. There has been a noticeable, undeniable movement toward feminism, but it is feminism Israeli style, imbued with values and norms that are alien to the very essence of feminism.

PART II
Ordinary Women in Political Life

CHAPTER 4

Political Participation:
Women in the Party-State

Israel has been described as a highly politicized society, a party-democracy in which political parties wield influence on social and political life (Arian 1989). Although the impact of the parties on society has somewhat eroded now compared with the state's formative era, considerations based on party politics still loom large in public life. "Political" issues linked with the Arab-Israeli conflict still dominate the public agenda. Politics, in this regard, is not an abstract term concerning a small active group of "gladiators" or even "spectators" (Milbrath 1968), but an everyday matter involving each and every individual. In contrast to Americans described as shunning politics, the Israelis accept it as daily routine. Consequently, people are interested in politics: they seek information by being avowed consumers of media news; they discuss politics at social gatherings; they are emotionally involved in political affairs, and many of them hold firm views on political issues. Whether one adheres to the notion of Greater Israel or is willing to make territorial concessions for the sake of peace is not only a political stance but may determine a way of life—choice of residence, friends, and media consumption. Furthermore, Israelis tend to participate in political life at least once every four years, when they are called to cast their ballot. Israeli elections have drawn a turnout which is among the highest in the democratic world (on the average over 80 percent of those eligible to vote), especially as the participation in the elections is voluntary, rather than enforced by law. In short, for Israelis, politics is not a marginal activity, but a central domain incorporated into daily life.

How do women fare in this domain? Scholarly attention has centered mostly on the role of women in the elite (e.g., Bubber-Agassi 1991; Azmon 1993; Etzioni-Halevi and Illy 1993). This chapter focuses on the role of the ordinary Israeli woman in political life. Who is the Israeli political woman? Does she tend to participate? Is her participation different from that of men? Does she manifest in her political participation the underlying dilemma facing women in Israel? Is her participation conducive to political mobilization?

Women's Political Participation: A Comparative Perspective

Before delving into the Israeli case, a short summary of findings regarding women in other Western countries is in order. In recent years the problem of gender differences in political participation has proved controversial. Within the literature three major perspectives can be identified: The first maintains that women's participation in political life is *inferior* to that of men. Maurice Duverger (1955) was the first to point out that women fare better at home than in political life. Many other scholars followed suit: Almond and Verba, in their seminal study of civic culture, asserted that in each of the countries they studied, "men showed higher frequencies and higher intensities than women in practically all the indices of political orientation and activity" (1989, 325). Lipset (1963, 187) asserted that "men vote more than women"; Dalton (1988, 49) reiterated that "gender is an important social determinant of political activism." Milbrath (1968, 16) went even further by suggesting that women's lower levels of participation in politics was one of the most thoroughly substantiated findings in social science.

The second approach maintains that women are not inferior to men regarding political participation, nor are they superior to them. Women, in fact, are *equal* to men when socioeconomic variables are controlled. This conclusion, reached mainly by women scholars (Bourque and Grossholtz 1974; Welsh 1980; Sapiro 1983, 59–60; Skard and Havvio-Mannila 1985; Norris 1991) is based on a variety of empirical studies looking at the patterns of women's political participation.

The third perspective presents a different argument by stating that women are neither inferior nor equal to men; they simply behave *differently*. Women are more likely to participate in protest activities and to hold distinct views, tending to either the conservative or the liberal pole of the political spectrum (Barnes, Kaase, et al. 1979; Eduards 1981; Goot and Reid 1984). How do Israeli women fit into these three perspectives? The discussion will center on the three major characteristics of political participation: conventional participation, unconventional participation, and political orientations.

Conventional Political Participation

The definition of political activity, in this context, follows that offered by Milbrath and Goel (1972, 2) focusing not only on active roles that people pursue in order to influence political outcomes but also on passive support activities. Political participation was thus described in terms of a spectrum ranging from inner feelings of confidence in one's ability to influence policy decisions, through the commitment to acquire political information, to the performance of actual participatory activities. The survey conducted for this study[1] presented a scale including the following items:

1. Political efficacy, measuring confidence in one's ability to influence public policy;

2. Regular viewing of a leading political program on national television (*Moked*, meaning focus), indicating the quest for political information;

3. Political discussions held with friends and family;

4. Partisanship (ranging over a scale from unsalaried party member, through unsalaried party member with a formal position, to salaried party member with a formal position), indicating actual political activity;

5. Voting behavior.

Political Efficacy

Political efficacy is one of the most widely discussed concepts in political science. It constitutes the feeling that one is capable of influencing the public decision-making process. Studies of political culture have confirmed that in democratic societies, such as the United States and the United Kingdom, the individual sense of civic competence is widespread, even among women. Israel too belongs to the community of democratic nations, but one particular attribute distinguishes Israeli democracy from its counterparts in the industrial world: a strong emphasis on statehood. From the very start of the Zionist endeavor in Israel the Jewish settlers perceived themselves as soldiers on the front, committed to the fulfillment of national goals. This is not to suggest that Israelis are forced to act on behalf of their country, but that they are effectively mobilized to do so. Israel has been described as a "nonliberal democracy" (Ben Eliezer 1993), where political participation is the result of manipulative tactics employed by political elites. Government "paternalism" (Lehman-Wilzig 1992) is a result of both historical legacy and contemporary circumstances. The development of the "collective democracy" has been attributed to the heritage of Eastern European ideologies, imported by the early settlers who immigrated from Russia, and to the imperatives of nation-building in a hostile environment. The encounter with the Arab intransigence, as well as the hardships of daily life, necessitated wide mobilization that left its imprint on the citizens' sense of their political efficacy.

Studies of the Israeli political culture in the 1960s and 1970s revealed astonishingly low rates of political efficacy. A positive response to the question, "Do people like yourself have an influence on the government?" was given by only a quarter of a national sample in 1960 (Arian 1973, 27–33; Etzioni-Halevi 1977, 68–79; Galnoor 1982, 32). This proportion has increased through the years. In 1993 almost a third of Israelis had a sense of effectiveness; they believed in their ability "to influence the government policy." Furthermore, data (presented in table 4.1) reveal a very small gender-based difference, and what there is favors women over men. That women have gained a sense of political efficacy is evident also from the pronouncements of women's leaders. In the early 1960s Beba Idelson, WWM's secretary-general, lamented the lack of appreciation of what women are doing. Women's striving against human suffering and negligence was underestimated. In her own words: "Unfortunately, I cannot say that our revolutionary work is adequately appreciated by our leadership."[2] The women's leader urged her followers to slough off their inferiority complex and to know how powerful they could be. Apparently, her call fell on deaf ears. Thirty-odd years later, however, the spirit of abnegation had completely faded. In 1994, Naamat's incoming secretary-general stated that "The battle has ended but the war starts. No more protests. We start determining."[3]

The increasing political efficacy of Israelis compared with the past is evident also among its non-Jewish population. A study of political participation conducted in the small Arab town of Shefar'Am,[4] revealed a high rate of political efficacy, even higher than among Jewish respondents. Among the non-Jews, however, a gender gap was clearly visible, as the percentage of Arab women giving a positive answer to the question on their belief in their ability to influence a policy decision was far lower than among the men. The discrepancy between the two ethnic communities—the Jewish and the non-Jewish—may be explained by the intense interest Israeli Arabs show in politics. Arab residents of a small community may have perceived "government decisions" in terms of local affairs rather than in terms of national policy.

Political Interest

Israelis yearn for political information: they read newspapers at very high frequency;[5] they are glued to the television screen when the news is broadcast. As in other Western societies, radio news is presented every half-hour. A remarkable silence reigns over public places such as intercity or urban buses during transmission, as people are eager to learn of recent events. The high interest is generated, first and foremost, because many Israelis have close relatives (sons, fathers, boyfriends) serving in the armed forces, daily exposed to hostile confrontations in the administered territories or on Israel's northern borders. The second and not less weighty reason is overall identification with the national cause. The high political temperature prevailing in the country is a major instigator of political interest.

Political interest, in this context, was tapped by a question probing the television-viewing of Israelis. Frequency of viewing a newscast was not considered a useful indicator, owing to the published high percentage of such watching. Instead, people were asked how often they viewed a political broadcast in which a central political figure was interviewed (a program which may be likened to *Face the Nation* in the United States). Results were not surprising as a high proportion of the respondents did report watching this program (regularly, or at least once a month), but a gender gap was visible: based on these results, 72.6 percent of the men and only 66.4 percent of the women may be labelled as having a high interest in politics. A previous study of political participation in Israel reached the same conclusion: Israeli women exhibited significantly less interest in politics than Israeli men (Wolfsfeld 1988, 67). In this respect, too, Arab women lead their Jewish counterparts in showing a great interest in politics. No gender gap between non-Jewish men and women was traced.

Discussion of Political Affairs

Engaging in a political discussion is one factor in the so-called "communication" dimension. It is different from having subjective feelings about politics in that it is an active form of participation. Living in a free society that allows freedom of speech is a precondition for reporting discussion of political affairs. The frequency of people talking politics was found to be significantly higher in the Western democracies whose political culture had been studied than in other states.

Israeli respondents were asked if, and to what extent, they discuss politics with their friends or family members. Their answers reveal a similarity to findings for the United States and the United Kingdom (thirty years ago). Women, however, tended to score lower on this indicator of political participation. The conjecture, based on universal findings, that women have less interest in politics than men is valid for Israel too, as the gender gap is quite visible.

Party Affiliation

The predominance of parties in Israeli politics is not only a historical legacy but also a contemporary reality. Political parties are still heavily involved in the provision of social services, the foremost of which is health care. Although measures have been taken to disengage medical services from politics,[6] partisan footprints will be probably endure in the near future. Political parties still control the political arena by mobilizing wide constituencies, imposing discipline on legislators, penetrating the state bureaucracy, and exerting decisive influence on the formulation of public policies (Yishai 1991, 31–43). How has all this affected individual affiliation of citizens with political parties?

The relevance of party affiliation to political behavior has been highlighted by the literature. Nearly three decades of research have confirmed the association of party identification with political participation (Milbrath and Goel 1977, 54). The impact of partisan attachment on political activity seems to be independent of socioeconomic variables: at all levels of education or income strong partisans tend to participate more than weak or even moderate partisans (Verba et al. 1980, 308). Membership of a party is not an incentive for participation but participation itself. This type of political activity, however, is reportedly declining dramatically. Data published in 1993 show that practically in all Western democracies (except Belgium) there has been a striking decline in the proportion of people reporting party membership (Katz and Mair et al. 1992). A survey conducted in Denmark revealed a significant gender gap with women scoring lower on party membership (9 percent) than men (12 percent) (Togeby 1992). Higher rates of party affiliation were expected in Israel owing to the high politicization of society. This expectation, however, has been invalidated.

A surprisingly substantial proportion of the respondents in the survey conducted for this study reported no contact with political parties. Among the women nearly half (44.3) percent stated that they did not support nor were they active in any political party. Among men the proportion was lower (39.1 percent) but also higher than expected. This does not mean that Israelis distance themselves altogether from party life, as a considerable part of them (43.9 percent of the men and 44.6 percent of the women) stated that they did continuously support a political party, although they had not registered as members. Only a small minority of the respondents reported actual membership in political parties: 17.0 percent of men and a mere 10.9 percent of the women. Among the men some 3 percent (of the total) constituted the "gladiators," that is, the _active_ members performing an organizational function; among women the party activists constituted a fraction of the total—less than one percent. The gender gap, perhaps not prominent in some aspects of passive political participation, is starkly evident when the partisan arena comes under review. Having a higher stake in politics (to be discussed in the next chapter), Arabs were more inclined to partisanship. This inclination was reflected in the higher proportion of men registered as party members. Non-Jewish women, however, did not differ from their Jewish counterparts in regard to partisan activity.

Voting Behavior

As noted, Jewish women were franchised in the mid-1920s. Since those early days they have firmly established their voting rights. Israelis, regardless of their sex, age or degree of orthodoxy, flock to voting booths on election day. Why they do so, with a rather low sense of efficacy, remains a mystery. They regard it as a national duty, a way of identifying with a social class (Ashkenazim tend to vote for Labor and its affiliated parties, while Sephardim cast their ballot for the right-wing or religious parties); they also express their views regarding the future fate of the occupied territories, but primarily they respond to a successful mobilization campaign. By voting they express their allegiance to the Israeli polity—to the regime, if not to the party of their liking. Casting a vote is the Israelis' avowal of legitimacy, of the system, its laws and its fundamental beliefs. There is no noticeable difference between men and women regarding the act of voting. Among the respondents some 85 percent of both sexes reported on having voted in the last elections (held in 1992). Among the Arab respondents the picture is similar, although women demonstrated a higher rate of voting (89.1 percent) than men (80.5).

Having confirmed the comprehensive scope of electoral participation in Israel, the question still remains how far is gender relevant to casting a ballot. Respondents of the national sample were presented with a series of questions looking into the salience of gender equality in regard to choosing a party to vote for. The first question concerned information regarding party positions: "Has the party you voted for in the last elections expressed any positions on gender equality?" The answer was striking: over half of the women (52.6 percent) and about half (49.5 percent) of the men stated that either they were not aware of such a position or that to the best of their knowledge the party had not expressed an explicit stand. The respondents were further queried to find out if the issue of gender equality had affected their electoral choice. In view of their slight knowledge of party positions on the issue, their answer is hardly surprising. An overwhelming majority of both men and women (81.1 percent and 79.2 percent, respectively) replied that the issue did not have any impact whatsoever on their voting behavior.

To further test the relationship between electoral behavior and gender politics, a question exploring the issue in the local arena was presented to the respondents. One may presume that national politics is dominated by critical questions relating to war and peace and to the state's economic fortunes. Local politics is characterized not by "high" affairs but by problems relevant to daily life. Women have been singled out as the best candidates for dealing with these problems. The respondents were asked to express their views on the importance of the gender issue in the local elections. More specifically, they were asked if the problem of gender equality would have any effect on their vote in the (then) approaching local elections. The answers reaffirmed the small relevance of the gender issue to the electoral arena. Only 23.4 percent of the men and 28.7 percent of the women said that the issue would have any influence on their electoral preferences. All this tells us that women are active participators when it comes to conventional political participation, but that their participation is not gender-oriented. Rather, political participation, in its conventional forms, serves as a means of identifying with the nation, not with the problems of women in general and the issues propagated by feminism in particular. When acting within the confines of conventional political participation, Israeli women tend toward the national flag more than toward the feminist banner.

Unconventional Political Participation

Parameters of participation not defined by elections, party membership, and the like, are considered "unconventional," although they need not be confined to what is usually described as protest politics. In the Israeli case these include voluntary activity, membership of public associations, and participation in protest demonstrations. Unconventional participation in politics differs from conventional participation in several ways. Primarily, it accentuates the role played by the individual in social life. This is especially true in regard to voluntary action. In a country where "entitlement" is the order of the day (Eisenstadt 1985), and where the state is expected to take care of people's daily needs, any person volunteering to perform a social function operates outside the conventional circles of civic participation (unless voluntarism is performed through a party-dominated association, such as Naamat). Second, in the Israeli jargon a "public organization," is associated with challenging authority. Israelis do not regard membership of the Labor Federation, for example, as falling within the confines of "public organization," but they do tend to associate unconventional political participation with affiliation to political movements. Finally, taking part in a protest demonstration differs significantly from conventional participation, because it implies direct *confrontation* with political authorities.

The picture regarding unconventional political participation, as reflected in the data collected for this study, is quite gloomy.

There are several obstacles to voluntary action in Israel. The first is the belief that the government is responsible for taking care of virtually every problem and is expected to intervene in every aspect of life (Kramer 1982, 88). Second, the centralization and bureaucratization of the country also militates against grassroots voluntarism. Finally, the overwhelming influence of political parties leaves little leeway for nonpartisan activity, which is practically dominated by party-affiliated groups. In view of these obstacles the answers given by the respondents to the question probing their voluntary activity are hardly surprising: more than 80 percent of both women and men stated that they never or only rarely engaged in voluntary activity. Contrary to the common image of women as being more involved in aiding others, no gender gap in this regard was found in Israel.

Membership of voluntary associations did not fare better. Practically all Israelis are members of "voluntary" associations such as trade unions (with the highest membership rate in the democratic world) and professional organizations. The reason for the high density of organizational membership stems, in part, from a series of laws obliging workers to belong to the group representing their branch of employment. Israelis join the Histadrut not only because they are overwhelmingly salaried employees (82.1 percent of the labor force in 1992; Statistical Abstracts 1993, 373), but because until the National Health Insurance law was approved, this was the only way of acquiring the services of the major health insurance fund in the country (Kupat Holim). As for affiliation with a genuine citizens' group, the proportion of Israelis engaging in such activity is dismal. Among the respondents, an overwhelming majority stated they are not affiliated with, nor are they members of any "public association." The gap between men and women, however, was statistically significant, confirming, in this case, the greater inclination of women to non-conventional political activity. Worthwhile noting is the significantly higher proportion of Arab women stating they were members of "public associations." Living in a small town in the Galilee mountains, community life seems to assume greater prominence than in the big urban centers, where the Jewish respondents in the study reside.

The paucity of unconventional forms of political participation was confirmed in the question probing the frequency of demonstrations. Lehman-Wilzig (1990, 124) noticed that during the last two decades the protest phenomenon has been growing fairly steadily to the point where it now is accepted as a "normal" part of the general political process. The increasing difficulties of establishing effective political communication with the central government has been one of the chief reasons for the growing scope of protest demonstrations. This description is accurate as long as the *number* of protests are counted. But when asked who had taken part in a protest demonstration during the three years preceding the study, only 11.9 percent of the women and 13.5 percent of the men gave an affirmative answer. Among the non-Jewish population, constantly challenging the political authorities, the rate of participation in protest demonstrations was somewhat higher than among the Jews (14.2 percent of the women and 13.4 percent of the men), but it nevertheless remains rather low. Wolfsfeld (1988, 67) reported that Israeli women scored significantly higher than Israeli men on the "blocked opportunity" scale. Consequently, they were more likely to justify direct action owing to cynicism about institutional means of influence. As the data collected in this study show, this attitude does not manifest itself in behavior and is not translated into political activity. A summary of data on both conventional and unconventional political behavior is presented in Table 4.1

Table 4.1 Political Participation, by Sex and Nationality, 1993 (percent)

	JW	JM	AW	AM
Efficacy	32.2	30.0	36.5	48.7*
Seek information	66.4	72.6*	77.0	79.4
Discuss politics	66.9	73.7*	52.0	55.9**
Party member	10.9	17.1**	11.1	21.2*
Voted in last election	84.7	85.1	89.1	80.5**
Member of association	17.6	11.6**	37.5	21.7*
Demonstration	11.0	13.5	14.2	13.4
N	641	523	339	117

JW—Jewish women; JM—Jewish men; AW—Arab women; AM—non-Arab men.

Source: Survey conducted for this study.

*p < 0.05   **p < 0.001.

Opinions on War and Peace

Politics is the arena of the major power game, replete with competition, aggressiveness, and pugnacity. Judged by their stereotype image, women are unsuitable for politics. They are, supposedly, gentle, caring, and they shy away from aggressive behavior and loathe power. It was hoped that "a polity that included women as active participants would . . . abolish poverty, protect family life, and raise educational and cultural standards; an international society made up of nations in which women had the suffrage would not tolerate war" (Almond and Verba 1989, 325). Feminine compassion was considered not only a personal asset but as a key to eliminating belligerence from political life.

At the turn of the century a woman appalled by the horrors of the Boer War (1899) wrote: "it is our [women's] intention to enter into the domain of war and to labor there till in the course of generations we have extinguished it" (Shreiner 1914, 59). This mood was corroborated by findings revealing that women tend to oppose military measures at a higher frequency than men (Goot and Reid 1975, 20). Females were more likely to support withdrawal from wars already started (Pomper 1975, 79) and to be less receptive to the idea of peacetime conscription. Surveys consistently showed that more women than men classify themselves as being doves (Baxter and Lansing 1983, 59). The moderation of women was attributed to two major factors: biological and sociocultural. Being those who give birth, women are presumably more reluctant to destroy life. As women in most societies are socialized into nonviolent and passive behavior patterns, the pursuit of power is commonly conceived as incompatible with femininity (Kirkpatrick 1974, 15). Have Israeli women adopted the apparently universal inclination toward political moderation on issues of war and peace?

The significance of security in Israel has been already discussed. Both the human and the economic costs of war have been excessive as a large proportion of the national budget is devoted to security; some 20,000 young men, furthermore, have lost their lives in the bloody conflict with the Arabs. At the top of the political agenda is the question of the territories occupied in the Six Day War (1967) and their inhabitants, the Palestinian Arabs. The territorial issue has been a source of deep friction within Israeli society (Yishai 1987). Political parties and public movements are pitted against each other, advocating opposite solutions to the problems of the lands and people living on them. The right-wing parties, sustained by the militant movement Gush Emunim, have promulgated the idea of Greater Israel, justified by religious and/or security arguments. The Israeli hawks have been unwilling, under any circumstances, to return the territories captured in 1967. The center and left-wing parties, supported by Peace Now, advocate territorial concessions in return for peace. Although there are many shades of opinions between these two extreme views (How much territory should be returned? On what conditions? To whom? In exchange for what? When?), the demarcation between these two camps is quite clear. The division is between those wishing to retain the territories, and those willing (or even pressing) to relinquish them. Have Israeli women, as predicted by findings in other Western societies, joined the peace camp?

Data collected since 1968 by the Israel Institute for Applied Social Research present a different picture from that of other Western societies. They reveal that more women than men are unwilling to return lands (an average of 65.8 percent and 60.4 percent respectively between 1968 and 1981). Surveys taken during the first phases of the Lebanon war attest to similarities between the attitudes of men and women rather than to women's moderation (Yishai 1985, 199). Women were not, as depicted by the literature, compassionate doves seeking peace and reconciliation. A 1992 survey confirmed this finding. Respondents (among the Jewish urban population) in a pre-election survey[7] were requested to state their opinions regarding four crucial aspects of the Arab-Israel conflict. The first question was straightforward: Should Israel be required to choose between two alternatives—to return most lands captured in 1967 or to annex them—what would be the respondents' individual preference? Second, should Israel accept the autonomy proposals put on the agenda of the Madrid Conference held a short time earlier attended by Israeli and Arab leaders? Third, should Israel be prepared to negotiate with the PLO, anathema for right-wing militant Israelis? Fourth, should Israel agree to the establishment of a Palestinian state, equally abhorred by the proponents of Greater Israel?

First and foremost, the answers reveal the mood of the country: at the time the survey was conducted (1992), before the Oslo agreements that cleared the way to direct negotiations with the PLO, Israelis were reluctant to withdraw from the territories. Less than half the respondents preferred the return of lands to annexation, an option not openly discussed by the Israeli political leadership. Once again, the proportion of those holding dovish attitudes was slightly lower among women than among men, although the difference was marginal (38.2 percent and 40.8 percent, respectively). Both men and women adamantly opposed the establishment of a Palestininan state. That women were, in fact, more militant than men was evident also from the answers to another question: significantly fewer women than men supported the idea of granting the Palestinians in the territories autonomy (see table 4.2). Asked if the issue of the territories would affect their vote, the answers of both women and men revealed how important the subject was in their electoral considerations. One only has to compare the slight importance of gender equality in the electoral calculus with the importance of the territorial issue to appreciate the weight of the security question in the lives of Israelis. An overwhelming majority (about 82 percent) of the respondents stated that the issue of lands would influence their vote to a large or to some extent. No significant difference between women and men was discernible.

Table 4.2 Attitudes toward Security Policy,
by Sex, 1992 (percent)

	Women	Men	Difference
Willingness to return territories	38.2	40.8	−2.6
Approving the autonomy	53.5	63.5	−10*
Negotiating with the PLO	43.9	42.3	+1.6
Palestinian state	29.1	29.0	−0.1
Influence of territorial issue on vote	82.9	81.1	+1.8
n	624	556	

Source: Pre-election survey

*$p < 0.001$.

Even if women and men are no different in their attitudes toward the territories, they might still be distinguished on the basis of the electoral choice, which in Israel is closely associated with positions on the Arab-Israel conflict (Shamir and Arian 1993). Earlier findings in several countries on women's electoral choices present a paradox when applied to the Israeli reality. In the first phases of gender research it was widely assumed that women tend to lean more toward the right-wing of the political spectrum and that their political orientations are more conservative than those of men (Duverger 1955; Inglehart 1977). Regardless of regime, continent, political culture, or political history, women were found to penalize left-wing parties in terms of votes and membership. In West Germany women cast significantly more votes for the Christian Democrats than for the Socialists; in Italy, men account for about two-thirds of the vote for parties on the left, while women provide two-thirds of the support for the country's Christian Democrats (LaPalombara 1973, 444–45). All in all, as Randall commented, "female conservatism has also been, and in many cases continues to be, a feature of voting behavior in other West European nations" (1987, 71). In Israel, however, voting for right-wing parties does not necessarily imply social conservatism, but mainly identification with the cause of Greater Israel. Here, the two major findings elsewhere in the world on women's political preferences—moderation and inclination toward right-wing (and/or religious) parties—would be mutually exclusive.

The Israeli case neither confirms nor refutes women's inclination toward the right. It simply shows that no gender gap is visible. When asked to state their electoral choices in the last elections, respondents reflected the balance between parties affiliated with Labor and those affiliated with the right-wing Likud (including religious parties). That the voter happened to be a man or a women made no difference in casting the ballot.

The final test for women's opinions on the issue of peace and security was in revealing their attitudes to government spending. Respondents (in the pre-election survey) were presented with a series of questions relating to government expenditure. They were requested to indicate if they thought the state should allocate more, less, or equal amounts of money among nine different policy areas: education, the environment, religious institutions, health, security, immigration absorption, aid to the unemployed, settlement of the territories, and producing jobs. According to the usual findings, women might be expected to show greater concern for social welfare issues, supposedly owing to their maternal instincts, their humanitarian compassion, extension of their concern for the family to public life, and their adult experience being confined to the domestic role (Sapiro 1983). In terms of the above question, therefore, they might be expected to recommend increased spending on education, the ecology, health and immigration absorption. By virtue of their alleged dovish nature, they might be expected to reject the option of increasing budgetary allocations to security; on account of their domestic role, they would presumably show less interest in "pure" economic affairs, such as creating jobs for the unemployed.

The data (presented in table 4.3) show that none of these propositions was confirmed when applied to Israeli women. From the range of issues presented to the respondents, it appeared that an overwhelming majority of Israelis would like to see more spending on the creation of jobs, on education, and on health. In this regard women and men were very similar. Only in one policy issue was there a striking gender discrepancy.

Table 4.3 Public Preferences Regarding Government Spending, by Sex, 1992 (percent)

	Women	Men	Difference
Education	86.1	84.2	+1.9
Environment	40.0	41.7	−1.7
Religious institutions	12.1	11.7	+0.4
Health	81.7	76.4	+5.3
Security	70.9	64.2	+6.7*
Immigrant absorption	51.5	48.5	+3.0
Welfare to the unemployed	57.1	52.6	+4.5
Settlement of the territories	24.0	22.2	+1.8
Job creation	91.5	91.8	+0.3
$\bar{X} =$	57.2	54.8	+2.4
n	624	556	

Source: Pre-election survey

*$p < 0.001$.

Contrary to expectations, women wanted more money to be spent on security. This preference casts further doubt on the widely hypothesized dovish inclination of women. Note, however, that generally, women tend to be greater spenders than men. More women than men believed that government should spend more than it actually does on all items (except the environment!). That women, more than men, long for a strong, active state is, perhaps, one of the symptoms of their vulnerability and their equivocation regarding their status in the collectivist society.

If Jewish women in Israel tend to display hawkish tendencies, their Arab counterparts may be expected to follow suit. Being subject to a double disadvantage (Moncrief et al. 1991) on both gender and ethnic bases, Arab women are likely to be more militant than Arab men. The positions of Arab women were examined by a series of questions focusing on the Arab-Israel conflict. The Arab respondents (both men and women) were presented with various proposed solutions to this enduring conflict, extending from a secular democratic state, an option favored by the extremists in the PLO, to the annexation of the occupied territories by Israel, an option preferred by the extreme pro-land proponents in Israel. The two major findings based on the answers by the Arab respondents show a clear difference between Arab and Jewish women. First, Arab women do not follow the lead of men, but hold opinions distinctly different from them. This is surprising in view of the traditional characteristics of Arab society in Israel. Second, Arab women tend to the two extreme poles of the policy spectrum. Put differently, they tend to be both more moderate and more militant than Arab men. Only a fraction of the latter endorsed a "secular democratic state" within the boundaries of the state of Israel; twice as many Arab women (8 percent) favored this option. Women's extremism was evident at the other end of the policy spectrum as well: only a negligible minority (3.2 percent) of the men endorsed annexation of the territories (while granting the Palestinians full citizenship rights), while three times more women thought that this move would end the belligerency between Arabs and Jews.

It thus appears that both Jewish and Arab women in Israel have broken the rule of female moderation. This aberration calls for explanations. The major source of the Jewish women's relative hawkishness is probably their desire to be more Israeli than the Israelis, and to super-conform to national-oriented norms. Israeli women are denied the opportunity (valued by many citizens) to contribute to the nation's defense. As noted, their military service is noncombatant and shorter than that of men. They do not serve in reserve units and do not climb the career ladder in the armed forces. Their contribution to the welfare of the nation may be displayed in nationalistic advocacy. Arab women face a different dilemma. They, more than the Israeli women, are caught between the hammer and the anvil. Being exposed to the syndrome of the "double disadvantage" of being females in a traditional society and members of a minority group in a nationalistic society, Arab women tend to exhibit more extreme attitudes than their men. The discussion of their identity (considered in the next chapter) will further illustrate their quest for acceptance in Israeli society.

Who Enters the Political Arena?

The political participation of both women and men in Western societies has been examined under the microscope. The problem of who enters the political arena has intrigued many scholars in the Western world. Their findings have become an inalienable asset of modern political science. That social class affects participation has become a truism. This holds more for women, traditionally associated with a lower position on the socioeconomic scale. Sex differences in political participation have been analyzed according to three distinct models: the development (Almond and Verba 1963), the generational (Christy 1987, 2–6), and the autonomy (Carroll 1988) models.

The development model holds that economic progress, namely, affluence, economic resources, and education, induce women to enter the political arena and reduce sex differences (Di Palma 1970, 133–37; Rokkan 1970, 378; Baxter and Lansing 1983, 23–27). This model has been very popular among the proponents of political culture, suggesting a correlation between socioeconomic status and political participation. Studies in the

United States confirmed that the gap between men and women is widest among lower-status and narrowest among upper-status people (Milbrath and Goel 1977, 117). It was thus assumed that economic and social development is slowly eroding the gender gap.

Is this model, based on findings visible in an affluent, peaceful country, pertinent also to Israel, with its huge population of immigrants? The answer appears to be equivocal. The relevance of the development model has been explored by looking into the rates of participation of women across socioeconomic strata. The variables considered were education and ethnic origin, the two hallmarks of social class in the country. Educational attainments are highly correlated with the fundamental stratifying factor in the Israeli society, ethnic origin. Forty-six years of independence have not eradicated the social differentiation between former immigrants from Asia-Africa and their descendants (by now third-generation Israelis) and the Jews of Euro-American descent. National efforts at turning Israel into an egalitarian society have been either insufficient or ineffective. The ingredients tossed into the "melting pot" have simply failed to blend. The educational disparity is most conspicuous among second-generation Sephardi women (Bernstein 1991, 193), who lag far behind women of European descent in their attainments.

If the development model holds true for Israel, then women from an Asian-African background, with their low educational accomplishments, would exhibit less propensity for political participation than their more affluent counterparts. The data, however, show us that only in political discussions do Ashkenazi women have the edge over women of Sephardi origin. In other measures of participation the picture is reversed, as women of less privileged ethnic groups appear to be more involved in politics than their affluent counterparts. These findings are confirmed when the educational criterion is applied. Once again, college-educated women engage more frequently in political discussions; their sense of efficacy, and their partisan affiliation, however, are lower than those of women of lower socioeconomic status. To sum up, the development model, as presented in the literature, is not very useful in explaining the Israeli scene.

The generational model proposes that the gender differences diminish as younger, more egalitarian generations of women replace older, more traditional generations (Duverger 1955, 191). Age in itself, however, may not be as important for crystallizing attitudes and behavioral patterns as the life circumstances that are linked to it. Inglehart's famous thesis on postmaterialism postulated that younger age-cohorts are more inclined to support egalitarian values (including feminism) because their socialization was different from that of their parents (Inglehart 1990). The generational model may be expected to explain some aspects of women's political participation in Israel. Younger women have been more exposed than their mothers to egalitarian ideas. They have grown up in a world where mass communication has transcended political boundaries and they have been susceptible to the feminist winds blowing from the Western world. The general change in women's role may have affected their political behavior.

But the findings of this study provide only minor support for the generational explanation. If anything, age affects women's political participation in a direction contrary to that expected. Women under forty have probably been exposed to the feminist advocacy more than their older counterparts, yet the effect of this on their participation has been disappointing. Data show that younger women tend to score higher on the participation scale only in the quest for political information. Older women tend to discuss politics more and to have a higher sense of efficacy. They are also more inclined to take an active part in party life. This finding may be attributed to the fact that the younger women are preoccupied with raising their young children and perhaps advancing their careers. It may also lend support to Inglehart's theory about the decline of institutionalized parties (Inglehart 1990, 363–68). All in all, younger Israeli women tend to shy away from conventional patterns of political participation.

The autonomy model argues that the independence of individual women from individual men induces women to join the political arena and diminishes the gender gap. Recent studies have emphasized "independence" as a crucial variable explaining political participation among women. The gist of the autonomy argument is that women's political behavior can best be understood if they are perceived as a disadvantaged or a vulnerable minority, disaffected because of their psychological and economic dependency on men (Carroll 1988, 238). As a result of their dependency, they are expected to be less politically active and to demonstrate the characteristics identified in the early days of research on women and politics, namely, apathy and withdrawal from politics. Working, single women are, presumably, the most autonomous. At the other end of the spectrum, one may find the married woman who is not employed outside her home. She is the most dependent.

During the last two decades the proportion of working women in Israel increased from 31.2 percent to 41.6 percent (Statistical Abstract 1994:365). It has to be noted, though, that joining the labor force does not imply immediate or automatic "independence," as women tend to cluster in a small number of large, female-dominated occupations, especially in the service sector, where wages are extremely low (see chapter 6). One major reason for this job segregation is precisely the lack of autonomy— the need to balance work and family obligations. Data on family life in Israel published in the yearly statistical abstracts further reduce the validity of the autonomy factor in political participation. As will be elaborated below in some detail, Israel is a family-oriented society, in which family stability is a ground rule. How has the combination of a growing female labor-force participation and a strong family orientation affected the political participation of Israeli women?

A comparison between married and single women in this study has shown remarkable differences, to the disadvantage of the latter in terms of political participation. Married women are enthusiastic watchers of political television programs. They also tend to join political parties at a high frequency, double that of single women. Surprisingly, married women's sense of efficacy is higher than that of single women, and they are more inclined to discuss political affairs with friends and family. Judging by the rate of political participation among married women, it may be concluded that family and politics are closely intertwined. The politicization of family life is also evident from answers to another question put to the respondents. They were asked to state whether their voting decision was influenced by their spouse or reached independently. About three-quarters of the respondents, among both men and women, stated that "we did not influence each other." Among those admitting they were influenced by their spouse, the proportion of women was double that of men (10.5 percent and 4.7 percent, respectively). The proportion was reversed when the respondents confirmed that they had influenced their spouse. Although the findings are not conclusive, it appears that men not only have more voice in politics, but a louder voice as well, especially in regard to ballot preferences.

Working outside the home has a limited effect on women's propensity for political participation: the proportion of women discussing politics and having a sense of efficacy is far higher among working women. Outside employment, however, does not influence political activity. On the contrary, the homemakers are the ones who seek information and join political parties.

In conclusion, the portrait of the Israeli woman political participant deviates from findings in other Western societies. Generally speaking, political participation appears to correlate well with women's traditional characteristics: lower-status origin, mature age, being married, and to some extent homemaking. This holds more for partisanship than for discussion of political affairs. But the general picture is consistent (see table 4.4).

Table 4.4 Women's Political Participation, by Demographic Indicators, 1993 (percent)

	A	S	−40	41+	M	S	W	H
Sense of effectiveness	32.4	28.5	32.7	34.6	33.4	30.1	34.9	27.1
Discuss politics	62.5	70.7*	57.9	72.1**	68.6	62.4	67.3	65.3
Seek information	68.5	59.5*	82.1	53.7*	73.8	49.8**	64.4	71.1
Party membership	12.1	9.1	9.6	13.7	13.6	7.0*	11.7	13.3
Leftist parties	40.2	69.4*	49.5	61.4*	55.5	51.1	58.3	40.9*

A = Ashkenazi; S = Sephardi; M = married; S = single; W = working outside home; H = homemaker.

Source: Survey conducted for this study.

*$p < 0.05$.   **$p < 0.01$.*

What Has Changed?

That feminist politics of the 1990s is unlike that of the 1960s is evident even from a cursory glance. In those early days of statehood, women were portrayed as distant from all public or political involvement. They were expected to act, to contribute, to devote time, energy, and money for aiding the underprivileged, particularly for absorbing new immigrants, but not to raise their political voice. At a meeting of the WWM, its leader urged the members "not to demand but to *give*" (emphasis in the original). The reporter noted that for "the participants of the meeting, most of whom are 'veteran' volunteers in this country, Beba Idelson's call reflected their own mood."[8] Women were described as being uninterested in, and incapable of, pursuing a political career. In the commentator's own words: "A woman's contribution to social life is reflected in her utmost loyalty to her duty and her commitment to fulfilling it; in the supremacy of the goal over her personal career, in her ability to maintain a warm and personal contact with those seeking her aid, and in her ability to identify unspoken misery. A woman is characterized by her unique attitude toward the vulnerable and the insecure, in her ingenuousness and purity of heart."

This quote (from the minutes of a symposium held in Mapai's headquarters in Jerusalem in September 1959, cited by Sharfman 1988, 75) vividly describes the mood that filled the air. Israeli women of the 1990s hardly resemble their mothers in this respect. They are more assertive, less submissive, and more vocal in stating their case.

Changes in the environment prompting women's political participation are compatible with the diffusion theory. This postulates that time alone is sufficient to induce changes regarding the gender gap. As society advances toward more openness and awareness of injustice, values and symbols regarding the role of women in society are bound to change (Ruschiano 1992). The test of the diffusion model lies in the comparison of women's behavior and attitudes across time. Admittedly, this model can interact with other factors, since as time passes women are gaining more resources, younger generations are reaching political maturity, participation in the labor force is tending to rise, and family patterns are becoming altered. Yet tracing changes across time, albeit not in their net form, is instructive in terms of understanding women's political behavior.

The examination of changes was made possible by the use of data from a pre-1973 election survey, comparing them with those of a pre-election survey conducted in 1992.[9] The comparison centers on both women's political activity and the gender gap: how women have changed their behavior compared with men. The overall picture of women's political participation exhibits a dramatic increase in some measures, while at the same time showing a decline in others. For example, there has been a marked increase in political effectiveness among women, which grew from 27 percent in 1973 to 38 percent in 1992 (see table 4.5).[10] Contemporary Israeli women are no longer the passive citizens of a manipulative state, but believe they are capable of bringing about changes. Second, discussing political matters has also become much more widespread—the proportion of those reporting that they engage in such activity has nearly doubled. Women's greater involvement in politics is also evident from the decrease, by more than half, of those stating they did not intend to vote. In one indicator of political activity, though, there has been a decline during the past two decades: the incidence of those women (and men) reporting party membership significantly declined (from 14.9 percent to 6.3 percent among women, and from 19.4 percent to 11.9 percent among men). As noted earlier, these findings correspond with the evolution of political behavior in other Western democracies.

To isolate the effect of time on women's political behavior, the parameters relating to men were also scrutinized. Evidently, men too have changed the practices of their political participation. But the effect of time is far greater on women than on men. In all parameters, without exception, the change was more noticeable among women than men. Political efficacy, for instance, rose among men by only 6.8 percent between 1973 and 1992; the equivalent figure for women is 11 percent. The practice of discussing politics with friends has expanded for both men and women, but more so for women. These findings portend a greater measure of political equality between men and women in the country. When the gender gap is under review, however, the reliance on time alone does not fully justify this expectation. Data (table 4.5) reveal that this gap has narrowed with respect to the sense of political efficacy, as women have gained more confidence in the political system. A (marginal) decline is evident also in regard to the gap in electoral participation, which was high at the time of the first survey and has remained so to the present. In the two remaining indicators, discussion of political affairs and party membership, the gap has actually widened rather than narrowed. It may thus be concluded that with the passage of time women increase their participation in politics but this increase is not sufficiently high to bridge the gender gap, which is still considerable.

Table 4.5 Political Behavior, by Sex
and Year, 1973, 1992 (percent)

	Women		Men		Gender Gap	
	73	92	73	92	73	92
Sense of political effectiveness	27.0	38.0	47.6	39.5	−20.6	−1.5
Discuss politics	33.6	61.6	32.7	70.0	−0.9	−8.4
Party membership	14.9	6.3	19.4	11.9	−4.5	−5.6
Non-voters	7.0	3.3	3.8	2.1	+3.2	+1.2

Source: Compiled from Yishai 1995, 117.

Conclusion

The examination of Israeli women's political participation confirms their political inferiority when compared with their male counterparts. Data on political participation, both conventional and unconventional, reveal that women are less active than men in politics and that there is a clear gender gap. The discrepancy between women and men is even more evident among the non-Jewish constituency, which still widely adheres to traditional mores (to be discussed in the next chapter). Consequently, women's associations can hardly count on the female constituency as a human resource readily available for political mobilization.

The answer to the question, "Who is the woman taking part in politics?" reveals a pattern somewhat different from other Western societies. Socioeconomic variables have a limited effect on political participation, and even then, it is not in the expected direction. This is particularly true when party politics are at issue. It appears that the more affluent and educated the woman is, the more likely she is to shy away from affiliation with political parties. The data also show that the passage of time works wonders on women's political participation. Comparison of younger women with more mature women yields some results. Yet the gender gap has not disappeared with the passing years, although it has shrunk in some respects. This finding may be interpreted equivocally: the bad news is that women have made progress in politics, but the pace of men's advancement in terms of political behavior has been far more rapid; the good news is that women may be developing unique patterns of political participation. Their distinctiveness, however, is not necessarily congruous with feminist aims. To recapitulate the findings presented in the foregoing discussion (p. 108), Israeli women tend to cling to militant views on questions of war and peace more than men.

The hawkish stands women display on issues regarding the country's defense may be linked to their intrinsic dilemma. By being holier than the Pope (the Chief Rabbi in the case of Israel), women have demonstrated that they are loyal to the flag, that their fidelity to the national cause cannot be questioned. On the basis of the Israeli experience, it may be concluded that increased political participation in itself may not necessarily lead to feminism. Unless women identify with the feminist cause, there is no reason to assume that their political activity will be channeled toward the "banner." The poor showing of gender issues in electoral politics offers another reason to suspect that distinct political participation does not necessarily emerge from adherence to anti-establishment feminism. Under these circumstances, the option of the political mobilization is hardly open to the women's movement in Israel.

CHAPTER 5

Women's Gender Identity: "Who am I?"

A headline in Naamat's monthly captured the essence of womanhood in Israel: "I Am Not a Feminist, but . . . " The article recalled that Israeli women, even the "progressive" ones, often state that although they are not "feminists" they support women's quest for equality. Rejection of feminism is deepened by the extremist image of feminists. It is therefore not surprising, asserted the writer, that "the majority of women, used to being indulgent, yielding and pleasant, and lacking the courage to go their own way and express their own desire, join the chorus denouncing feminists and denying feminism."[1] This short quote encapsulates the problems encountered by Israeli women in their feminist identity.

"Identity" in modern society is a multifaceted phenomenon. To the question "Who am I?" there is always more than one answer. But an order of priorities, not always clear-cut, does create self-boundaries and does shape self-images. Embracing an identity is particularly difficult in societies where values and norms are mutually exclusive. This is the case in Israel, where women are faced with a dilemma: to be faithful members of their national community or to be proponents of their gender rights. As elaborated above, the choice between the two entails a determination of priorities. The underlying question, therefore, is, how, and to what extent, have Israeli women incorporated these two identities to form a coherent frame of reference?

The clash between gender identity and other forms of refer- ence is not unique to Israel but is common to women world- wide. Several difficulties have been enumerated as obstructing the formation of gender identity and women's group- consciousness. First, widespread beliefs in meritocracy and intergenerational mobility in industrialized societies have incul- cated in women the feeling that they can make it without taking the feminist course. The economic success of women in the United States has on the one hand encouraged feminism, but it has also worked against gender separatism. Second, across the globe women share with men economic gains and losses and are emotionally bound up with males as husbands, brothers, or fathers. These bonds put heavy constraints on gender identifi- cation, implying, at least partially, confrontation with men. Third, recent experience has revealed that "sisterhood" is less viable in social life than expected. Women often compete with other women of more privileged status (Gurin 1985), a circumstance that works against group cohesion. Finally, the entrenched con- struction of women as a dependent target group, and their treat- ment as such by policy-makers (Schneider and Ingram 1993), often militate against gender identity. In Israel the problem is aggravated by the overarching "national vision," presumed to dominate all spheres of life. The manner in which Israeli women have coped with these difficulties is the subject of this chapter.

The Meaning of Gender Identity

Gender identity has been described as an "elusive concept" difficult to grasp. Any group identity implies a sense of a com- mon bond and of shared status. As women do not constitute a "group" in the classical sense of the term, the problem is aggra- vated. One way of probing women's identity centers on the affinity women feel for each other. Rinehart, for example, sug- gested that gender identity is "one's recognition that one's rela- tionship to the political world is at least partly but nonetheless particularly shaped by being female or male. This recognition is followed by identification with others in the 'group' of one's sex, positive affect toward the group, and a feeling of interde- pendence with the group's fortunes" (1993, 32).

The major indicator for evaluating gender identity on the basis of interdependence is the "group closeness" question, included in the U.S. National Election Study (see Gurin et al. 1980; Rinehart 1993, 51–55). The second approach regarding the examination of gender identity focuses on attitudes toward gendered issues, often covered by the title of feminism. Notwithstanding the vagueness of the concept and its controversial meaning, it is widely agreed that "feminism *at least* means insistence on equality of treatment, particularly equal access to all elements of public life, along with the equal rewards for activities" (Black 1980, 92). This approach attempts to capture collective orientations of women, assuming that they are discontent with their power in society and that they desire a change in the status quo, which favors men over women. In line with this approach, respondents in the study of Israeli women were asked to state their opinions on a number of items on gender-role issues relating to the polity, the economy and their status in society at large. Awareness of gender inequalities is thus treated as beliefs displaying gender identity. Respondents were also asked to state their hierarchy of identities regarding the choice between nation and gender. What is more important in their lives? Being a man/woman or being an Israeli?

Gender Identity: Scope and Intensity

The scale of gender identity in Israel constituted of ten questions relating to different aspects of gender equality. Not less important than the specific position toward each issue was the overall attitude. A resemblance among respondents, regardless of their sex, would have indicated that women's identity was in abeyance and that national consciousness had taken clear precedence (unless the men were avowed feminists, which was hardly likely). Adversely, a distinction between men and women (supposing women to be more equality-minded than men) would have implied that women had assumed a gender identity. Data collected in the survey for this study furnish evidence for the second conjecture. Women are, indeed, *different* from men. Their answers show that even if they do not constitute a group in the political meaning of the term, their opinions about their position in politics, family, and society are shaped by their particular female experience. As seen in the results presented in table 5.1, marked differences between men and women were found, in seven of the total ten statements presented. This is true even though both men and women in Israel accept gender equality as the order of the day. They do, however, attribute different weights to different items on the roster of equality.

Equality in Politics

The first question pertaining to women's equality in politics looked into women's independent partisan activity, discussed in chapter 2. As recalled, women's parties have not garnered electoral support and have failed to obtain parliamentary representation. Despite their defeat in the ballot, women's parties have become a focal symbol for feminism, a token of women's independence in the male-dominated political world. Support in principle for a women's list is associated with a high measure of gender identity. The results show that this type of feminist activity is not widely endorsed as both men and women tended to disapprove of separate female party activity. Shunning separate party activity may also be linked to the association of the past women's parties with radical feminism, abhorred by many Israelis. Though generally disapproved, a gender gap regarding women's parties was discernible, with significantly more women than men favoring this option. The negative attitudes toward a separatist women's political organization were revealed in the answer to another question. Respondents were asked to select the most effective strategies to promote women's status in the country, including "the establishment of a women's party." Only a fraction of the respondents of both sexes (6 percent) chose this as the most effective means for ameliorating women's position. Here no gender-based variation was noticeable. Yet despite these negative attitudes, it is worth noting that nearly half the women respondents did endorse the option of women's political parties. Obviously, they did not convert their opinion into deeds as they did not actually support the women's party running in the 1992 elections. Still, their gender identity appears to have been sufficiently comprehensive to encompass an activity unpopular in behavioral terms.

Second, attitudes regarding the adequacy of women in political life were examined by the common question, "Is politics too dirty for women to be involved with?," often used in questionnaires looking into feminist attitudes. In the United States, where feminism has taken major strides, this question may seem irrelevant. But in Israel, where nearly half the population originated in developing societies, where women are confined to home and children, the question of women's qualification for the public world still looms large. In fact, some quarter of the respondents (29.1 percent of the men) agreed with the postulate that "politics is too dirty for women to be involved with." Nearly four out of five women, however, dismissed this opinion.

The last issue regarding women's equality in politics centered on managerial skills. As shown in chapter 2, women in Israel encounter an invisible glass ceiling that prevents them from climbing to the administrative summit. An underlying question is if the obstacles to their promotion are (at least partially) linked to perceptions regarding their managerial competence. The respondents were asked if they agreed with the statement that "women's managerial skills are equal to those of men." An overwhelming proportion of both men and women rejected the notion than men are more competent in management than women. Even though women do not tend to occupy top administrative positions, either in public service or in the private sector, very few people seem to attribute their scarcity at the summit to their lack of managerial competence. A distinct gender gap is nevertheless noticeable, as more women than men tend to believe in women's penchant for management.

To sum up, both men and women were willing to condone the association of women and politics. They were less tolerant regarding women's political activity independent of mainstream politics. Despite the wide endorsement of women's equality in politics, a gender gap is clearly discernible. Women evidently share distinct views on their status in public life.

Equality in the Family

As will be elaborated below, family values are deeply embedded in traditional Jewish culture and evoke strong, group commitments to the protection of the weak and vulnerable, including women (Izraeli and Tabory 1988). The question is how do these powerful family sentiments impinge on gender equality? Have women acquiesed in notions confining them to the private world of home and family? Respondents were asked to reveal their attitudes regarding the sharing of domestic chores, parental responsibility, and careers by judging three relevant statements: "When both spouses are working outside their home, men and women should have an equal share in housekeeping and child-rearing"; "Women should pursue their own career even at the cost of some family discomfort"; and, "Working outside is not less important than taking care of young children."

The findings reveal that a gender gap manifested itself persistently as regards opinions on equality in the family. An overwhelming majority of both men and women endorsed, at least verbally, egalitarian families. Women, however, were more keen than men on sharing domestic chores. Agreement in principle to share home responsibilities does not imply that this is practiced in reality. A poll conducted in the early 1980s revealed that 70 percent of the women respondents stated that they were the ones who performed most of the domestic chores. A substantial proportion of the men interviewed in that study (59 percent) shared this view (Tzemach and Peled 1983, N11). Katz (1993) substantiated the universal finding that women are far more engaged in domestic chores than men. The study of top women civil servants showed that seniority and responsibility for crucial state affairs do not alleviate the burden of the "double shift."[2] The mass media confirm the women-home association, as appeals to buy domestic products are invariably addressed to women and phrased in the feminine (Hebrew grammar differentiates between the genders).

Wide endorsement of equality in the home seems to further dissipate somewhat when the woman's career is the question. Acceptance of a woman's right to pursue a career despite inconvenience to family members was far lower among both sexes than in the previous item, winning the endorsement of 67.4 percent of the women and 61.6 percent of the men. Similar proportions were evident when work outside the home was posited as more important for a woman than taking care of home and children. Here, too, a gender gap was visible—women showed less concern over the possible clash, but both sexes were reluctant to endorse the primacy of work over home responsibilities. The fact that most Israeli women do not tailor their occupational careers to suit these norms will be dealt with in the next chapter. Despite some deviations from mainstream feminism, the gender gap in attitudes toward equality in the family does reveal that Israeli women are aware of their particular interests and that they do shape their opinions accordingly.

Equality in Society

The respondents of the national survey were requested to state their opinions regarding general norms of gender equality in society. Reproductive choice has been considered as the linchpin of this equality. Approval of a women's right for abortion (to be discussed below) was deemed as an indicator of gender identity. Respondents were further asked for their views on gender equality by evaluating two concluding statements: "There is no justification for full equality between men and women in various domains of public life"; and "Women already enjoy equal rights. There is no need to act specifically on their behalf."

The exploration of general attitudes toward gender equality in society yielded surprising results. The good news, from the feminist perspective, is that an overwhelming majority among both men and women (75.9 percent and 80.2 percent respectively) sanctioned reproductive freedom. If this endorsement is not mere lip service to gender equality, then a serious gap is evident between existing legislation and public opinion, as abortion policy in Israel does not grant women free choice regarding reproduction. The bad news is that nearly a third of both men and women are of the opinion that either "there is no justification for equality between men and women," or that "women already enjoy equal rights. There is no need to act on their behalf." Nevertheless, the distribution of answers to these two questions reflects at least some inconsistency between women's and men's attitudes toward gender equality. A gender gap, placing women at the more liberal end of feminism, is clearly evident.

Finally, the quandary between gender and national identity was explored by means of a straightforward statement for respondents to evaluate: "My interests as an Israeli citizen are more important to me than my interests as a woman/man." The responses present additional bad news for the proponents of feminism in Israel. An impressive majority of all the respondents emphasized their national affiliation rather than their gender connection. In terms of numbers alone, this was truer for women than for men (74.0 percent and 71.5 percent respectively). These findings attest to the hegemony of the collective vision and the importance national identity plays in the lives of the Israelis.

Gender Identity: Determinants and Sources

Socioeconomic and demographic variables have been of little utility in explaining determinants of female political participa-

Table 5.1 Indicators of Gender Identity, by Sex (percent)

	Women	Men	Gender Gap
Separate women's party	48.5	36.6**	+11.9
Politics too dirty for women	24.5	29.1	−4.6
Women have managerial competence	89.7	82.1**	+7.6
Home chores to be shared equally	93.5	87.3**	+6.2
The right to pursue a career	67.4	61.6*	+5.8
Work is more important	66.4	61.0*	−5.4
Freedom of abortion	80.2	75.9	+4.3
No justification for gender equality	28.6	33.1*	−4.5
Women already enjoy equal rights	29.0	32.1**	−3.1
National interests more important	74.0	71.5	+2.

Source: Survey conducted for this study. The responses "Certainly agree" and "Agree" are combined in these figures.

*$p < 0.05$.   **$p = 0.00$.

tion. Yet these variables presumably enhance a woman's gender identity. In other words, young, socially privileged women, enjoying relative economic and psychological autonomy, are expected to portray a higher female identity than older, under-privileged women, who are homemakers. To these variables two other were added in this study: religiosity and personal experience of deprivation.[3] Observant women are expected to internalize norms unfavorable to gender equality. They have been raised to think that a woman's home is her sphere. Conversely, women who have been subjected to discrimination on account of their sex are expected to concur with statements indicating gender identity. The questionnaire did not specify specific types of deprivation women are believed to encounter (sexual harassment, discrimination in the workplace, etc.) but couched the question in general terms.

In general, the findings of this study (table 5.2) do support the conventional explanations regarding women's gender identity, as a gap among women was clearly identified. To begin with, the findings give full credence to the development model presented in chapter 4, associating a woman's identity with her socioeconomic standing. Indeed, high-status women tend to be characterized by a higher level of gender identity, being more supportive of issues associated with women's equality. For example, the gap between women with income higher than the average, and those with income lower than the average on the precedence of home and family over career, is stunning, as 78.5 percent of the more privileged, compared with only 53.7 percent of the less affluent, deemed career more important than home. Even the choice between national and gender identities is affected by socioeconomic status, as Ashkenazi women, with a college degree and a higher income, demonstrate a greater awareness of their gender interests than low-status women. In fact, income made a difference in eight of the ten items on the gender-identity questionnare (table 5.1). Education and ethnic origin were also pertinent to a woman's identity. The gap between the more and the less privileged women is often striking.

The development model, however, fails to explain the attitude toward one important variable studied in the survey. As noted, lower-status women tended to join political parties more than affluent women. Findings on the structure of gender identity corroborate this inclination, as these same women show greater support for a women's party. The ratio of less-educated to more-educated women who endorsed a women's party is approximately 3.2 (47.6 percent and 29.1 percent, respectively). Almost the same proportions divide Sephardi women, 57.9 percent of whom favor a women's party, and Ashkenazi women, only 33.6 percent of whom endorse it. Contrary to expectations, the association between organized feminism (in the form of women's party) and social privilege does not hold true in Israel, where the less-privileged women appear to show more feminist orientations, Israeli-style, than their affluent sisters.

The effect of age on gender identity was far less noticeable. Findings reveal the small significance of biological age on the formation of the gender identity with one exception. Women under forty did tend to identify themselves as "women" more than as "Israelis" compared with older women (at a ratio of 29.6 percent to 19.3 percent, respectively). But age had an impact when income was controlled, as younger, affluent women (in the highest economic bracket) showed a higher inclination toward feminism than other groups. This finding may signal changes in gender identity in the foreseeable future. Another factor linked to socialization had a significant impact on a woman's gender identity: the educational level and employment status of her mother. Daughters of educated mothers, employed outside their home, tended to adopt a higher gender identity, with one prominent exception: they, too, were likely to reject a separatist female party, which was mostly favored by women who grew up in more traditional homes. Yet the role model provided by the mother-achiever did stimulate the adoption of a feminist perspective, as the gap between the two groups of women—the daughters of educated/working mothers and of noneducated/homemaking mothers—was striking.

The difference between married homemakers and "autonomous" women was equivocal. Generally, married women did conform to more traditional values regarding women's role in society than their single counterparts (including widows and divorcees). They were less in favor of free abortions, and they were quite content with women's general social status. Nearly twice as many married women (33.9 percent) as unmarried ones

(18.8 percent) were of the opinion that "women already enjoy equal rights." More married women than single ones thought that their Israeli national identity took precedence over their gender identity. No difference was traced in opinions on other items in the gender-identity questionnaire. Taking a job outside the home, however, had a striking effect on women's perceptions, as the difference between homemakers and working women extended to all the ten components of the feminist identity. Once again, however, support for a women's party was more evident among the traditional women, as homemakers favored such an enterprise more than those gainfully employed.

That religion played a role in constraining gender identity came as no surprise. As already noted, according to the Jewish faith a woman is unequal to a man; her status is determined by her domestic achievements. She is judged by how far she meets with the ideal of *eshet hail* (the biblical term for the perfect wife and mother). Orthodox women were not expected to embrace the principles of modern, secular feminism. This prediction was largely verified. A difference between observant and secular women was visible particularly in regard to general views on the status of women in society, the suitability of women for political life, and the hierarchy of interests. Nearly 90 percent of the secular women advocated, for example, free abortions; among the observant the proportion was less than 60 percent; nearly 40 percent of the observant were content with women's status in Israel ("women already enjoy equal rights") compared with less than a quarter among the secular. A dramatic gap is visible in attitudes toward women's involvement in politics. This was branded "too dirty" for women by 36.7 percent of the orthodox women compared with only 18.7 percent of the secular. As national sentiments in Israel highly correspond with religious observance, it is not surprising that among the observant women the sense of national identity (supremacy of the national interest) was significantly higher than among the secular.

Finally, the effect of personal experience of discrimination was not decisive. That such an experience is common is evident from anecdotal information. Women soldiers complain of sexual harassment by superior officers; female students often complain they have been subjected to "sexual" interrogation upon applying for jobs ("Are you going to marry soon?"; "When do you intend to have your first child?") . Data collected in this study reveal the scope of discrimination, as over a quarter of the female respondents reported on having had to submit to such experiences. The data also reveal the impact of discrimination on the formation of gender identity, as "deprived" women were far more vehement in their insistence on the inferior status of women in contemporary Israeli society. At a ratio of 2:1 com-

Table 5.2 Gender Identity and Demographic Variables (percent)

	a	b	c	d	e	f	g	h	i	j
Ethnic origin										
Ashkenazi	33.6	14.8	91.6	98.7	66.5	73.7	89.8	17.9	22.7	69.0
Sephardi	57.9*	30.4*	88.7	89.6*	69.7	62.3*	72.5*	34.6*	33.2*	78.0*
Education										
College	29.1	10.1	93.1	94.3	69.6	80.4	81.0	14.0	18.3	68.7
High school	47.6**	25.4*	55.6**	91.4	65.9	71.9**	82.4	30.1**	27.3*	77.2*
Income										
Above ave.	42.0	17.9	88.6	95.7	69.4	78.5	81.2	20.9	24.2	70.9
Under ave.	52.4**	29.3*	87.9	89.4*	64.0	53.7**	71.6	34.1**	34.1*	76.5*
Age										
Under 40	49.4	23.3	88.0	93.1	65.3	68.5	81.7	28.6	25.8	70.4
Above 40	45.9	25.5	90.8	100	67.3	62.7	78.3	28.1	34.1	80.7*
Mother's education										
College	32.9	15.4	90.8	100	65.0	81.3	88.2	11.5	21.8	60.8
Highschool	54.1**	30.0**	88.0	90.2**	64.8	59.2**	75.0**	33.7	34.3**	80.7**
Mother's employment										
Working	43.1	17.2	91.6	97.2	68.8	69.8	83.0	23.9	27.8	54.3
Homemaker	56.3**	33.8**	87.1	88.6**	61.8	61.8**	77.5**	34.2	31.3	77.1**
Marital status										
Single	53.2	22.6	85.5	88.7	70.0	75.6	89.0	22.3	18.8	68.6
Married	43.2	26.6	88.9	94.7	70.1	63.2*	76.3**	30.8**	33.9	77.7*
Employment										
Working	42.3	22.8	90.9	95.4	71.3	73.5	80.7	28.3	17.9	73.5
Homemaker	45.6**	35.8*	85.5*	88.9*	61.1**	50.2*	68.1*	34.1*	32.8*	83.3*
Religiosity										
Orthodox	53.6	36.7	87.8	90.1	63.3	55.3	58.8	37.2	39.2	81.1
Secular	46.3	18.7**	90.3	95.0*	68.7	71.0**	88.72**	4.5**	24.4**	70.8*
Discrimination										
Yes	58.9	25.0	95.8	94.4	80.0	70.0	81.7	14.1	15.5	74.0
No	45.0**	24.5	88.8	93.3	65.5*	66.0	79.8	30.4**	30.8*	74.0

Legend: a = separate women's party; b = politics too dirty; c = women have managerial competence; d = equal share of home chores; e = the right to pursue a career; f = work more important; g = freedom of abortion; h = no justification for gender equality; i = women already enjoy equality; j = national interests more important.

*p < 0.05.   **p = 0.000.

pared with those who had not encountered discrimination on account of their sex, they rejected the statements describing the status of women in society as generally satisfactory. They also showed more support for a feminist political party.

In conclusion, women's identity, in terms of support of women's equality in public life, the family, and society, appears to be affected by a host of demographic variables as well as by life experience. Two unexpected findings merit special attention. First, age appears to make little difference, as the views of younger women on gender equality resemble those of their more mature counterparts. To this rule there is one glaring exception: for females under forty the fact that they are "women" is very meaningful. But support for organized feminism (in the form of a women's party) is confined to the less privileged among all age groups. This second finding reveals the obstacles facing the women's movement in Israel locked between those who embrace a feminist identity but do not support feminist activity and those who endorse feminist activity but do not advocate feminist norms.

Gender Identity: Outcomes and Effects

Whether or not a woman adopts a gender identity may have crucial implications for her orientation and political behavior. A distinction has been made between gender (in fact, any group) identity and an awareness of gender consciousness. The former lies in the realm of ideas. How one regards oneself is a personal affair, not necessarily bearing social or political implications. The latter extends to the behavioral domain. Gender identity may thus be perceived as a necessary, but not a sufficient, condition for political participation. Only a group consciousness, defined as "a commitment to collective action aimed at realizing the group's interests" (Miller et al. 1978, 18, quoted by Conover 1984, 761), provides the missing link, as it mediates between cognition and activity. The underlying question is if and how women holding high feminist identity differ from those who do not identify with the feminist cause. The answer to this question will be based on the comparison of political participation and political orientations between the two groups of women: those with a high gender identity and those with a low gender identity.[4]

The answers of the women respondents (table 5.3) reveal the startling impact of gender identity on political participation, but the difference between the two groups of women is not always as expected. Women who are aware of gender interests and identify with feminist advocacy indeed evince a greater sense of efficacy and are more inclined to discuss political matters with friends and family than women with a low gender identity. So one would expect that women with a high gender identity would tend to turn their cognitive orientation into behavior and that they would be likely to participate in activities bearing on political decisions. But data of the survey show that this is not so. The high-gender-identity women do precisely the opposite: they tend to *shy away from conventional political participation;* they are less inclined to watch political programs on television that generally reflect old-style politics; they join conventional political parties less than their low-gender-identity counterparts, and they are even less prone to vote (no significant difference between the two groups of women was found in regard to membership of a public association).[5] The shunning of conventional politics by high-gender-identity women starkly reveals the dilemma of women who are aware of gender interests but are still subject to the constraints of national "visionary" imperatives. Instead of making hard choices, these women have retreated from the political arena.

Table 5.3 Political Participation, by Sex and Gender Identity (percent)

	Women	Men	Gender Identity (women)	
			High	Low
Sense of efficacy	32.2	30.0	32.4	28.2*
Discuss politics	66.4	73.7**	75.0	54.7**
Watch political program on television	64.4	72.6*	59.5	70.5*
Party member	10.9	17.1**	8.4	13.2*
Voted in recent elections	84.7	85.1	77.8	83.0*
Member of public organization	17.6	11.6**	10.8	7.4

Source: Survey conducted for this study.

*$p < 0.05$.   **$p = 0.00$

Finally, the impact of gender identity on political orienta- tions was subject to examination. Women's political preferences are presumably shaped by their maternal roles and by their daily experience. As noted in chapter 4, women's attitudes to- ward the Arab-Israeli conflict are not compatible with this im- age, as women have not adopted caring attitudes toward Israel's adversaries. The question remains open, whether gender iden- tity makes a difference regarding the security issue, as well as other political matters. Do women who may be labelled femi- nists deviate from the traditional stereotype limiting their inter- ests to family and domestic affairs? The answer was sought in a question to the respondents regarding their interest in differ- ent policy areas.[6]

The answers (table 5.4) are instructive in two respects. First, the data show a clear gender gap. Women were distinct from men in showing a strong preference for issues associated with traditional feminine domains, namely, family planning, wel- fare, and education. Women were far less interested in issues dealing with "masculine" subjects such as energy and the economy. This finding touches upon one of the thorniest prob- lems addressed by feminist practitioners and scholars: *Should women concentrate on issues pertinent to their daily lives?* The struggle to turn the personal into the political does estab- lish a link between domestic and public affairs. But the con-

Table 5.4 Preferences on Political Issues, by Sex and Gender Identity (percent)

	Women	Men	Gender Identity (women)	
			High	Low
Family planning	61.9	47.0**	55.4	70.1*
Welfare	71.4	64.9**	69.0	73.1
Education	87.1	77.1**	91.7	89.6
Security	89.0	92.0	91.7	88.1
Energy	35.1	51.6**	32.7	35.1
The economy	62.5	71.9**	60.1	64.9

Source: Survey conducted for this study.

*$p < 0.05$.   **$p = 0.00$.

finement of women to traditional domains makes feminists at least uncomfortable, as these domains are marginal, in the public view, compared with important state matters. In Israel this dilemma has not been resolved, as women tend to focus on "private" issues, with one noticeable exception: the security of the state. The findings presented in chapter 4 are corroborated by the responses to this particular question. The defense issue not only attracted the widest response (some 90 percent of the respondents) but closed the gender gap. Both men and women showed interest in and concern over matters relating to the perpetuating Arab-Israel conflict.

The marked gender gap in regard to issues traditionally dividing men from women, and the unanimity on the importance and relevance of security, indicate that gender identity has had a minor effect on preferences for political issues. Comparison between women with a high and a low gender identity verifies this impression. The difference between the two groups of women was revealed only in one instance: women characterized by a high gender-identity were less interested than their low-gender-identity counterparts in family planning. In other respects, even women who have embraced attitudes congruent with feminism did not dissociate themselves from what has traditionally been perceived as women's *domain*. Rinehart (1993) has suggested that negative feelings toward feminists as a group need not co-vary with disapproval of feminist goals. The Israeli case demonstrates that wide endorsement of egalitarian measures need not generate the rejection of traditional female roles. It appears that contrary to the argument presented by Conover (1988) gender identity need not structure progressive political beliefs.

Arab Women in Israel: Between Gender and Nationalism

Caught between their national identity and their gender identity, Arab women face a dilemma even more serious than that of Jewish women. In theory, Arab women may choose one of the four paths:

First, they may forego their own gender interests in favor of a national effort. Arabs in Israel constitute a minority character-ized by strong nationalist orientations. Their growing sympathy with the plight of the Palestinians residing in the occupied ter-ritories has intensified their nationalist sentiments. A survey conducted by Smooha (1989, 87) in the Arab community in Israel revealed that nationality ranks first, reported by over 40 percent of the respondents as the most important identity. Throughout history women have fomented and engaged in national liberation movements (Davis 1983). Arab women could join their men folk in their quest for national emancipation, evincing strong nationalistic feelings.

The second option for Arab women in Israel is feminism. It has been suggested that nationalism, meaningful as it may be, is largely irrelevant to women's adversity. Regardless of histori-cal context, type of regime or economic circumstances, women have consistently been burdened by a structural inequality (Peterson and Runyan 1993). Realization of women's enduring deprivation could spur feminist sentiments among Arab women. Furthermore, attitudes favoring women's equality, so prevalent among the Jewish population, could be diffused among Arab women as well.

The third option is for Arab women to remain in what the literature describes as the "double disadvantage." It has been posited that the two variables—gender and nationality—co-vary, but in the negative sense. Consequently, they produce the double disadvantage phenomenon, which is suffered by minority women: one handicap is due to their sex, the other is due to their national (or ethnic) minority status. Arab women in Israel are perfect candidates for a double disadvantage: they are situ-ated at the bottom of the socioeconomic scale in Israeli society, with low educational and occupational attainments.[7] Many of them have maintained a traditional way of life with one of the highest fertility rates in the world, which confines them to do-mestic roles.[8] As members of a patriarchal society, Arab women have also been subject to deprivation in their own community. It was noted that even higher education does not bar sexual discrimination. Academic husbands may be progressive in the workplace but still suppress their wives at home.[9] At the same time, Arab women, like other Arab citizens in Israel, are subject to disadvantages affecting the entire minority community.

The final option is one combining nationalism and feminism. The significance of feminist orientations in the shaping of national demands has been widely discussed. It has been suggested that the organization of women around their own interests was closely interrelated with the nationalist movements in Third World countries. Accordingly, feminism is not a foreign, Western notion, separate from the struggle for national liberation, but a fundamental requisite for gaining human dignity. It has been further asserted that "struggles for women's emancipation were an essential and integral part of national resistance movements" (Jayawardena 1986, 8). Arab women in Israel could thus combine their gender identity with their national identity to produce a frame of reference unique to them. The frames of reference adopted by Arab women in Israel were explored in the Shefar'Am study. The findings (though preliminary, from a study conducted in one single Arab town) are illuminating.

The first question probed Arab nationalism among women. Respondents were asked a series of questions regarding possible solutions to the Arab-Israel conflict (see chapter 4). A comparison between Arab men and Arab women as to national sentiments revealed that in many respects the women differ from the men. The difference, however, is less significant than it appears statistically, as the bulk of both men and women (nearly half the respondents) favored one particular solution out of the six presented to them: the establishment of a Palestinian state alongside Israel. But women scored higher than men on the scale of national identity, as measured by their views on the conflict. Nationalism among women manifested itself in response to another question. A substantial majority of both men and women (71.2 percent and 72.3 percent respectively) agreed with the assertion that "Arabs in Israel are generally discriminated against, compared with the Jews in the country." In the words of one interviewee: "We cannot have the luxury of putting politics aside. First we will achieve our national liberation, and next we will start thinking about women's liberation."

Feminist orientations were also identified among Arab women, who were asked to respond to some of the same statements presented to the Jewish women. Opportunities available for Arab women to embark on a public career are extremely sparse. As earlier noted, there has never been an Arab woman in the legislature, and their share in local government is nearly nil. These facts are reflected in their attitudes toward gender equality in public life, as a higher proportion among them viewed politics as unsuitable for women, compared with their Jewish counterparts. The association between low economic standing and social deprivation on the one hand and a yearning for a "women's party" on the other was reestablished, as Arab women supported autonomous female partisan activity more than the Jewish women.

When other questions on gender equality were at stake, Arab women showed attitudes generally more conservative than Jewish women and more liberal than Arab men. The striking difference between the Arab and the Jewish respondents is evident in positions on reproductive choice. Apparently, breaking away from long-established tradition was unacceptable to many Arab women. The reader will recall that an overwhelming majority of Jewish women (about 80 percent) subscribed to a pro-choice stance. Granting freedom to a woman to decide on possible termination of her pregnancy was far less popular among Arabs. Less than half (44.5 percent) of the women and less than a third (30.1 percent) of the men were willing to vest women with the right to make such a choice. Arab women were also less eager than Jewish women to share domestic chores with their husband. They nevertheless insisted (in a higher proportion than Jewish women) that a woman need not be confined to home and children and she has an inalienable right to work (see table 5.5).

In conclusion, despite some aberrations, the data reveal that Arab women raise the gender banner higher than might be expected under the circumstances. There is a considerable gender gap between them and their men. Their similarity to Jewish women (confirmed by Duncan's Multiple Range Test) attests to their inclination toward feminist identity. The women interviewed in the course of this study spoke of the patriarchal attributes of Arab society. Stories were told about a political activists, including a member of the Communist Party, who

Table 5.5 Feminist Attitudes, by Sex
and Nationality (percent)

	JW	AW	AM
Separate women's party	48.5*	67.2	48.6*
Politics too dirty for women	24.5	29.1	37.6*
Women have managerial competence	89.7	90.5	76.8*
Home chores to be shared equally	93.5	85.8	76.6*
Work is more important	66.4	74.1	59.8*
Freedom of abortion	79.4	44.5	30.1*
N	576	339	117

JW = Jewish women; AW = Arab women; AM = Arab men.

Source: Surveys conducted for this study.

*$p < 0.05$.   **$p = 0.000$.

trumpet gender equality in public and treat women as second-class servants at home. Patriarchy, they maintained, was supported by the Jewish authorities, wishing to keep modernization of the Arab community at bay. Traditional norms were consolidated too, by the belief, prevalent among Arab women themselves, that they play an important role in preserving society (1991). Yet Arab women are increasingly contending with their inferiority. Most important for these women is "the liberation of women from [the] social tyranny" manifested in traditional customs. For example, "forcing young women in our Palestinian society to marry against their will is, in our opinion, moral dissolution. Stifling women in the prison cell of the kitchen and cleaning, and denying them equal participation in social and political life, has no connection whatsoever to morality."[10] This language, only recently proclaimed in public, is indicative of the flow of feminist ideas across national boundaries.

    If Arab women score high on both nationalism and feminism, the option of remaining in the double-disadvantage condition is ostensibly ruled out. Yet these women do feel deprived. As one of them put it, "I float. I just don't belong. I want to bang on the table and tell the whole world, Hey, listen—I'm here. Don't ignore me." Data reveal that four out of every five Arab women (74.3 percent) have experienced personal discrimination on account of their being *Arabs*, as compared to 66.6 percent of the Arab men. The proportion of women who have admitted to being subject to sex discrimination was somewhat lower (60.5 percent), though still high by all measures. That Arab women are often subject to discrimination is even more striking when the proportion of those admitting to having had such an experience is compared with that of Jewish women. Among the latter, some quarter of the respondents (25.8 percent) reported on ever having experienced some form of gender-based discrimination. It thus appears that in terms of both objective criteria and personal experience, Arab women have been subject to the double-disadvantage syndrome. This, however, has not had an impact on their opinions regarding gender interests.

The final option facing Arab women—combining nationalism with feminism—was found to be the mostly acceptable. The fact that Arab women were similar to, or more extreme than, Arab men on national issues means that they subscribe to a national identity. The fact that they demonstrated greater likeness to Jewish women than to Arab men on issues of women's equality means that they have internalized a gender identity. The division of the total Arab women interviewed in this study into four groups on the basis of their gender/national identity revealed that the largest group (34.5 percent) was characterized by both a high national and a high gender identity. These findings lends support to the presupposition that gender and nationality need not be mutually exclusive.

The double-identity—both national and feminist—of Israeli Arab women is clearly marked in statements made by Arab activists. Al-Fanar, the group discussed above, calls itself a "Palestinian Feminist Organization." One of its leaders stated explicitly: "Our identity is Palestinian. We are Palestinians living in the State of Israel, and we recognize the state. However, we maintain that we are oppressed both nationally and socially, and there can be no national liberation without the liberation of women first." An article in Al-Fanar's newsletter asserted that "it is impossible to separate the national struggle from the social-feminist struggle, and the liberation of the Palestinian woman is an integral part of the liberation of our Palestinian people."[11] This placing of women's liberation as the primary goal has set Al-Fanar apart from Palestinian activists in the territories. Though women are subject to the same oppression as men, the national struggle in the territories has been given priority over the fight for women's rights.

Determinants of the Gender-National Nexus

The search for socioeconomic and demographic explanations for the Arab women's identity produced some interesting findings. First, in contrast to the Jewish women, age among the Arab women did appear to have a considerable effect on identity, as those under forty scored high on both the national and gender identity scales. Among those plagued by the double disadvantage, the proportion of older women was predominant. Both feminists and nationalists were considerably more prevalent in younger age-cohorts.

The impact of education on Arab women's identity is even more striking: the higher the educational attainments, the more the woman is inclined to endorse both gender and national identities. A converse tendency is visible regarding the double disadvantage, which considerably weakens with education. In line with findings among Jewish women, feminism was more attractive to housewives than to those employed outside their home, but the combination of marital status (being married) and outside employment was most conducive to the emergence of gender identity (feminism). Nationalism, on the other hand, was highly associated with traditionalism, as 92.3 percent of the nationalist-inclined women were homemakers.

The importance of religion in shaping the attitudes of Israelis was evinced in the Arab town of Shefar'Am. Three-quarters of the nationalists stated that they observe religious tenets; some 90 percent of religious women stated that they had experienced the double disadvantage. The internal ethnic division within the Arab community has also affected identity. Muslim women identified most with the nation (75 percent); among the feminists the Christians were predominant (77.5 percent); among the double disadvantaged the Druze women constituted the majority (66.7 percent). Christians were also the leading group among the national feminists.

The final question concerned the impact of identity on patterns of political participation. The combination of nationalism and feminism appears to have a decisive impact on political participation, as those women belonging to this category are far more active on all its indicators. The influence of national-feminism is striking in unconventional participation. More than 60 percent of the nationalist-inclined feminists demonstrated for a political cause, compared with only 10 percent among the feminists and none among the nationalists.

Conclusions

To the question posed in the heading of this chapter, "Who am I?," two separate answers were given: one for Jewish women and the other for Arab women in Israel. Both groups of women face a dilemma, but of a different nature. Jewish women cope with the constraints of the national vision urging them to abandon their particular feminist ideas in favor of the collective endeavor. Arab women face a more difficult choice, not only between nationalism and feminism, but also between a mix—or a rejection—of these two options.

The choice before Jewish women is not easy. Any defection from mainstream politics could be costly in terms of both political influence and personal integrity. Many women, particularly among those who have climbed the social ladder, deny that there is any problem at all. A famous woman journalist once stated in a popular talk show that "feminists are struggling over nonsense." Another participant, a specialist in preventive medicine, publicly asserted that "I have no problem with discrimination."[12] Yet they are well aware of their unequal share in society's resources and do wish their voice be heard. As the study conducted with Jewish women shows, a quarter of the women made their gender identity a core issue, even when juxtaposed with national sentiments. This is a relatively small proportion, but under the pressure of a visionary democracy it is perhaps higher than might be expected. When the two foci of identity were not in opposition, women's interests garnered wide support. Those who scored high on the scale of gender identity were younger, more educated, more affluent, and more secular than women characterized by a low gender identity. The Israeli-style feminists also benefited from a role model: a working, educated mother.

Holding a feminist identity in Israel increases political interest and involvement, but in a unique form. Paradoxically, organized feminism has fallen prey to feminist views. Contrary to findings in other Western countries, those characterized as possessing a high gender identity shunned separate female political activity. They endorsed women's equality and liberation, but spurned segregated organizational structures. Radical political channels were not chosen as suitable means of eradicating the visible gender disparities. The extent to which women (including feminists) show interest in typical female preoccupations attests to their difficulty in adjusting to extreme feminist stances. It may be concluded that adherence to feminist attitudes, widespread among Jewish women, does not, in the Israeli case, lead to political mobilization. This finding deviates from the hypothesis offered by Katzenstein and Mueller (1987, 386) suggesting that the degree of overall feminist consciousness serves as a factor explaining women's mobilization. The disjunction between views on the one hand and patterns of political participation on the other may be partly responsible for women's vulnerability in the political arena. In the case of Israel, identity has hardly been turned into awareness of gender interests.

As regards Arab women, the findings of this study suggest that they have made a choice—to minimize inconsistencies by adhering to both nationalism and feminism. To some extent, much higher than expected, Arab women have internalized the principles of feminism; at the same time they have incorporated strong national sentiments. Arab women have thus renounced neither national nor gender identity, but rather have combined these two identities to form an aggregate of nationalist-inclined feminism. The study of Arab women in Israel reveals that feminism alone, while possibly gaining ground among Arab women, has not been sufficiently pervasive as a main focus of identity. Only when combined with nationalist orientations did Arab women entertain ideas commensurate with gender equality. The statistical association between feminism and nationalist-inclined feminism shows no causal relationship but it does suggest a coincidence between the two identities. The prevalence of nationalist-leaning feminism among Arab women in Israel is an empirical fact that inspires the hopes of the proponents of both national liberation and women' equality. By incorporating both identities, Arab women may serve as an effective link between the Jewish and the Arab communities.

PART III
Women and Public Policy

CHAPTER 6

Labor Policy: The Problem of Economic Equity

Women in Israel enjoy economic equality before the law. The most important paragraph in the Women's Equal Rights Law (1951) provides that "There shall be one law for men and women in all judicial cases, any regulation discriminating against a woman as such will be invalid." Still, economic resources are not equally distributed between the sexes. In Israel, as in other countries across the globe, women have joined the labor force; they are, furthermore, increasingly likely to be the family breadwinner, or at least to contribute to essential family income. Equality, however, has not been attained. That women are unequal to men in regard to employment is evident from many documented stories. "I Will Not Get Pregnant in My First Year on the Job. I Promise!"[1] was the headline of a feature focusing on the difficulties confronting women in the labor market. Neither education nor personal competence appear to mitigate these difficulties.[2] States respond to women's economic distress in three distinct ways, which need not be mutually exclusive: denial, protection, and encouragement. In the first case, authorities comply with unjust distribution of economic resources, justifying it by women's domestic roles. In the second case, the state acknowledges women's economic vulnerability and takes measures to protect them while perpetuating their presumed weakness. In the third case, the state takes active measures to rectify inequality by endorsing affirmative action. Israeli authorities have largely rejected the third option, concentrating on the other two. This chapter describes women's share in the country's economic resources. It further focuses on measures that have been taken to eliminate injustice. Finally, women's contributions to policies aimed at the eradication of economic injustice are discussed.

Women in the Economy

Data on women's economic position in Israel mirror two basic processes which are universally valid. First, the massive entrance of women into the labor force; second, an unequal distribution of economic resources. Many women are employed in a highly segregated labor market and in part-time jobs, where income differentials are clearly evident.

Participation in the Labor Force

One fundamental fact regarding women's economic status stands out prominently: that so many women are employed outside their home. The proportion of women in the civilian labor force has dramatically risen from 26.5 percent in 1955 to 41.6 percent in 1992 (see figure 6.1). On average, women's share in the labor market rose almost by half a percentage point every year, with the pace of change fairly steady except for a decline in 1966–70. The massive entry of women into paid work, evident worldwide, has been signified as the most fundamental change of recent decades (Fuchs 1988, 31). Women have joined the labor force because of personal needs and external, environmental inducements. As noted by Simone de Beauvoir, "it is through gainful employment that woman has traversed most of the distance that separated her from the male; and nothing else can guarantee her liberty in practice" (1961, 639). Women seek work because it provides them with income, social interaction, a sense of accomplishment and because it frees them from being "just housewives." This is incompatible with the notion that women work only because of economic constraints. As suggested by Fuchs, "many women view employment as the passport to full

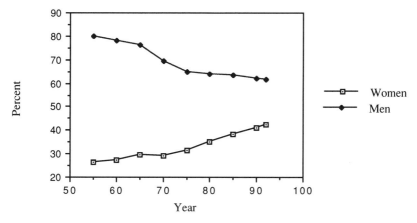

Figure 6.1 Participation in the Labor Force,
by Sex, 1955–1992 (percent)

Source: *Statistical Abstracts* 1985, 315–17; 1993, 356.

Note: Civilian labor force out of the total population, 14 years old and over.

participation in our society, just as the right to own land in Hellenistic Egypt marked a major advance for women in that society" (1988, 11).

Four factors account for the upward trend in women's employment in Israel: the falling employment rate for men, the entrance of young and married women into the labor force, the rise in female education, and economic growth. As shown in figure 6.1, the proportion of men employed in the labor market declined from a high of 80.1 percent in 1955 to a mere 61.8 percent in 1992. This considerable decline enabled women to fill vacancies unavailable earlier. Worth noting, though, is the fact that women as a whole are perceived as a relevant reserve of labor only after men are provided with employment (Bernstein 1993; Wolkinson et al. 1982). Women have also been the first to be fired in times of economic recession. Consequently, unemployment figures for women have constantly been higher than those for men.

During the past two decades there have been considerable changes in the age structure of working women. The share of women between the ages 25 and 54 increased from 50 percent of the total in 1970 to 73 percent in 1990. Simultaneously, the proportion of women younger than twenty-four declined by more than half, from about 36 percent in 1970 to 17 percent in 1990. Most significant is the rise in labor force participation of young women between the ages of 25 and 34. More than 70 percent of them have not been deterred by their being mothers of young children.[3] The availability of child-care facilities throughout the country has made this choice sustainable. In 1992, 68.3 percent of Jewish women whose youngest children were between two and four years old joined the labor force (Statistical Abstracts 1993, 127).

The educational level of women in Israel was found to be the best single predictor of their labor force participation (Bernstein 1991, 192; Hartman 1993). In 1970 the proportion of women with thirteen or more years of schooling was only 11.8 percent; by 1992 it had grown to 27.1 percent. Among educated women it is not customary to be a housewife. The ratio of employed women rises linearly with education. Among those with 1–4 years of schooling, only 11.2 percent joined the labor force; among those with 16 or more years of schooling the figure is a startling 75.7 percent. Figure 6.2 shows the impact of education on women's employment between 1970 and 1990, displaying the drop in the proportion of women with up to four years of schooling who seek work outside the home. The modernization of the economy has almost ruled out the option of employment for uneducated women. Women with secondary education (8–12 years of schooling) constitute the bulk of the female labor force, as they are those employed as secretaries and in the service industries. At the same time, the figure demonstrates the dramatic rise in the proportion of educated women in the female labor force, which grew from 21.1 percent in 1970 to 40.4 percent in 1990.

As noted earlier, educational attainments of women in Israel highly correlate with ethnic origin. This association is also reflected in employment statistics. Labor force participation is higher among women of Ashkenazi origin (47.9 percent) than among Sephardi women (41.2 percent). Arab women are less inclined to be employed outside their home: only a meager 8 percent were included in the labor force in 1992.

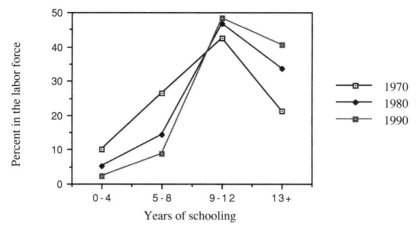

Figure 6.2 Women in the Labor Force,
by Years of Schooling, 1979–1990 (percent)

Source: *Statistical Abstracts* 1971, 543; 1981, 608; 1991, 603.

Finally, structural factors and processes, not dependent on individual choice were also found to influence female labor-force participation. Economic growth was noted to be the chief among these structural factors. The combination of security consider-ations and social absorption of immigrants induced Israeli gov-ernments to develop an approach of rapid economic expansion (Sanbar 1990), which in the first decade of the state's existence averaged nearly 10 percent annually. This extended period of growth was broken by a short period of recession starting in the mid-1960s. Expansion resumed, however, after the Six Day War (1967) and persisted up to 1973. Growth was made possible pri-marily by the mass influx of immigrants, by the attraction of private capital, and by the transfer of national resources to pri-vate hands via newly established financial institutions (Bernstein 1993, 70). These processes led to the expansion of labor-intensive, privately owned industries in which women played a major role. Female labor was also an essential component in the growth of the widening bureaucratic state apparatus.

The higher incidence of employment among women was not only a product of economic processes, but also of premeditated campaigns. Public figures repeatedly appealed to women to join the labor force and contribute their due share to the country's economic development. Two committees were appointed to suggest ways to encourage women to "go out to work," and the importance of women's work both for the nation and for themselves was emphasized (Bernstein 1993, 73). The Working Women's Movement added its voice to these exhortations. Women's employment outside the home contributed, indeed, to a rise in their status and income, but the positive trends were counterbalanced by a segregated labor market and by discernible income differentials.

Segregated Labor Market

Occupational segregation has been defined as "the disproportionate representation of one social category in a [particular] occupation, relative to the proportion of that category in the labor force" (Izraeli 1979). Being a major cause of women's lower wages, job segregation, pervasive in all Western societies, has been monitored closely by social scientists. The distinction between "men's jobs" and "women's jobs" is not unique to Israel but is a key factor in women's poor position on the labor market in many other Western societies (Bergmann 1986). Women tend to concentrate in a small number of large-scale, female-dominated occupations. A study based on data from the 1972 Israel Population Census reveals astonishing evidence of occupational segregation. It showed that 75.1 percent of the female labor force were employed in female occupations while 78.9 percent of the males were employed in male occupations. Relative to their proportion in the labor force, women concentrated disproportionately in clerical work, service work, and other typical feminine occupations such as nursing, teaching, and social work (Wolkinson et al. 1982, 467). In all, 64.9 percent of the women were concentrated in three of the ten aggregated occupational categories used in the study—semi-professional and technical workers, clerical workers, and service workers—compared with only 27 percent of the men. A leading authority on women's employment in Israel has concluded that every second woman in the country was employed in one of the following eight occupations (out of a list of 90): school teaching and headship, social and probation workers, nursing and paramedical work, bookkeeping, secretarial work, typing and keypunch operating, general office work, and sales (Izraeli 1991, 169).

By 1992 job segregation had abated somewhat, but was still marked (see figure 6.3). Data reveal that women are still heavily clustered (72 percent) in the three typical female occupations: teaching and nursing, clerical work, and service work. The respective proportion of men in these three occupations was only 28.5 percent in 1992. A study published in 1987 reveals that occupational sex segregation, measured by the Index of Dissimilarity across 354 detailed occupations, hardly declined between 1972 and 1983.[4] Notwithstanding the small decline in overall segregation, there were major changes in the sex mix of sixty-seven occupations involving about one-fifth of the workforce in 1983. On the one hand, women entered some pre-

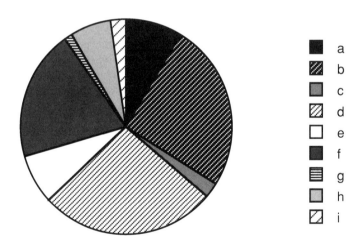

Figure 6.3 Employed Women, by Occupation, 1992 (percent)

Legend: a = Scientific and academic workers; b = Professional, technical and related workers; c = Administrators and managers; d = Clerical and related workers; e = Sales workers; f = Service workers; g = Agricultural workers; h = Skilled workers in industry, building, transport and other skilled workers; i = Unskilled workers in industry, building, and transport.

Source: *Statistical Abstracts* 1993, 374.

viously male-dominated lucrative occupations—mostly professional and managerial. On the other hand, however, women
increased their representation in a few very widespread occupations (mostly clerical) that were already female-dominated or
desegregated in the early 1970s (Cohen et al. 1987).

Horizontal work segregation—between male and female occupations—is accompanied by a vertical segregation within occupations. Although a significant proportion of the female labor
force is employed in the academic, semi-professional, and white-
collar occupations, in all of them the higher the position the smaller
the proportion of women. For example, Toren (1993) has noted
the paucity of women in the senior faculty positions in Israeli
universities. Three-quarters of the female faculty hold the lower
positions of lecturer and senior lecturer and only a quarter hold
professorial positions. Only 5 percent of full professors are women.
Women are rarely members of the boards of directors of big economic enterprises.[5] Reportedly, women constitute only 9 percent
of the total number of managers in industry.[6]

The highly segregated labor market may be attributed to the
sexually discriminatory employment practices that permeate the
Israeli economic fabric. As a result, women have more limited
career choices, fewer promotional opportunities, and inferior
wages and fringe benefits (Wolkinson et al. 1982, 486). There are
two additional factors inhibiting an egalitarian labor market:
first, the absence of affirmative action legislation and, unlike
the practice in other Western societies, the reluctance of career-
oriented women to delay childbearing (Izraeli 1991, 169).

The intrusion of family obligations into employment patterns has motivated many women to work only part-time. Comparative data on female labor indicate that women, in large
(and undiminishing) numbers, tend to work part-time. In the
United States, for example, even among employed women of
prime working age, one in three works substantially less than a
full week for less than a full year. If "full-time" is defined by a
more stringent standard, such as a minimum of thirty-five hours
per week and at least forty-eight weeks per year, one-half of all
employed women would be considered "part-timers" (Fuchs
1988, 44). In Israel, part-time work for women is no less prevalent. The proportion of women working part-time increased from

30 percent in 1970 to 42 percent in 1992. Seventy percent of part-time workers are women. The average working week is 29 hours for women and 40 hours for men. Note that part-time work is not penalized in Israel. In contrast to many other countries, part-time workers enjoy the same rights as full-time workers in terms of security of tenure, social security, and worker benefits. When asked to give reasons why they work part-time, women often cite their being "housewives" (21.7 percent) as the chief cause. None of the men mentioned domestic chores as a reason for part-time job. To this may be added the answer "not interested in a full-time job" given by 12 percent of the women, compared with only 2.7 percent of the men (Statistical Abstracts 1993, 381). Part-time work is thus a matter of choice. It results from the need to balance family and work. Women select to forego job opportunities or to avoid demanding occupations because they have to juggle their multiple roles (Izraeli 1988).

Income Differentials

Israeli law prescribes equal pay for equal work for men and women. Women, nevertheless, continue to earn less than men. Income differentials have, in fact, increased across time. Unpublished data reveal that only 30 percent of married working women earn a salary liable for income tax.[7] This is hardly surprising, as studies have confirmed that women, like racial minorities, are concentrated in the poorly paid occupations and in marginal industries. Moreover, it has been revealed that the economic returns on educational and occupational investments are considerably lower for females than for males. The income gap between the sexes was found to be larger than among ethnic groups in Israel. The combination of female sex and ethnicity yields, however, the lowest income. The income of males originating from Europe-America is the highest, while that of females originating from Asia-Africa is the lowest (Semyonov and Kraus 1993).

Efroni (1980) conducted a comprehensive study on gender income differentials in the civil service. She found that in the 1970s women earned 78 percent of what men with similar characteristics earned. She suggested, moreover, that if women were compensated for their education, training, and experience at the same rate as men, their income would be two percent higher than that of men. Income differentials were even more significant in the labor market as a whole, as official statistics indicated that women's income was 71.3 percent that of men in 1980. More recent data show that the gap between what women and men earn has narrowed only slightly. In 1991, women's income, calculated on the basis of an hour's work, was 76.5 percent that of men. In industry women still earned some 60 percent of their equivalent men's income, but the gap had closed somewhat. But regarding professional and academic occupations, the picture is reversed. One would expect professional women, having invested huge resources in education and training, to be equal to their male colleagues. This was not the case, as those employed as professionals earned only 77.4 percent of their male peers' income, compared with 82 percent ten years earlier. Even those working in "scientific and academic" jobs did not match men, as their pay was 79.2 percent that of men, also showing a decline of income over time. When income is calculated on the basis of monthly employment the gap is staggering, as women earned some half (56.4 percent) of men's income (see table 6.1).

The income differentials are attributed primarily to discrimination. According to Efroni (1980), employers discriminate between men and women in essentially similar jobs by means of differential allocation of fringe benefits such as overtime payments and car allowances, which account for 40 percent of the take-home pay.[8] In addition, different job titles are assigned to what is really the same work. As in other countries, women are denied promotion to more lucrative posts (Shenhav and Haberfeld 1988). Differences in human resources, such as a lower starting point, were also found to account for gender income differentials (Semyonov and Kraus 1993, 106). That women hold lower-paying jobs is also attributed to their own choice. Social norms regarding women's responsibilities for care of the home and children, as well as for many of the tasks which link the individual to society,

Table 6.1 Females' Income as a Percentage
of Males' Income, by Occupation

	1980(a)	1991(b)
Scientific and academic	82	79.2
Professional, workers	82	77.4
Administrators	72	79.6
Clerical workers	74	76.3
Sales workers	67	71.5
Service workers	75	80.3
Skilled workers	60	60.7
Unskilled workers	59	69.6
Total	**71.3**	**74.3**

Sources:
(a) Ministry of Labor and Welfare, *Major Trends in Women's Employment,* 1991, 33.
Derived from Central Bureau of Statistics, *Surveys of Income 1980,* Special Publication
Series No. 681 (Jerusalem: Central Bureau of Statistics, 1982).
(b) *Employees' Income (Individuals),* 1989, 1990, 1991. Special Publications Series No. 963
(Jerusalem: Central Bureau of Statistics, 1994).

Note: Based on one hour's income from wages or salaries of urban employees.

operate to discourage women from pursuing demanding full-time careers (Izraeli 1991, 171). The search for more convenient hours and job locations close to home militate against gender income equality.

The picture that emerges from this analysis is therefore not encouraging. The segregated labor market, the hurdles before women's promotion to high positions, and the persistent income differentials, all indicate that gender equality has not been secured in the economic sphere. Torn between her duty to the nation, substantiated as familial responsibilities and the rearing of children, and her desire to carve herself a place in the professional "masculine" world, the Israeli woman has sought employment outside her home, but equivocally: she has remained content with part-time jobs, often low-paid. Although she has been discriminated against, she herself has not pushed hard enough for advancement. This duality, based on the need to integrate work with family commitments, is corroborated and sustained by the law.

Women's Employment and the Law

State authorities have not been oblivious to women's economic plight. From the early days of statehood public policy has been formulated to equalize women to men. A review of legal arrangements regarding women's equality in the workplace reveals impressive attainments as regards policy intentions. Legislative efforts promoting female employment evolved in two phases: the protective phase and the egalitarian phase (Raday 1983; 1989; 1991).

The first step toward equalizing women's rights in the workplace to men's rights was taken in 1951, with the passing of the Women's Equal Rights Law, asserting that all kinds of discriminatory regulations against women are invalid. Unfortunately, the law did not have constitutional force as it could be used only to invalidate laws existing prior to its enactment. As far as subsequent legislation was concerned, it was considered merely a directive to assist in the interpretation of ambivalent primary legislation and a norm allowing invalidation of secondary legislation (Raday 1991a, 20).

A further step at promoting women's economic equality was taken in 1959, with the incorporation in the Employment Service Law of a provision forbidding discrimination on the basis of sex in regard to assigning a potential worker to a job. Likewise, an employer was forbidden to reject a worker on account of his or her sex. In 1964, the Knesset enacted the first version of the Equal Pay Law, providing that an employer had to pay female employees a wage equal to that of male employees in the same workplace for essentially equal work. The question whether "generally similar work" may be taken to include "work of equal value" has been posed before the Labor Court, but has not been resolved. Furthermore, the law contained no criminal sanction, but it authorized recovery of underpayments in the Labor Court.

In addition to these legal provisions, the state of Israel produced a series of laws (particularly the Women's Work Law, 1954) protecting women and granting them benefits on account of their maternity functions. In affording rights to women who become mothers while employed, Israel has followed traditions of other democracies. As early as 1919 the International Labor Organization (ILO) stipulated that women would not be permitted to work during the six weeks following childbirth and would be entitled to pregnancy leave. The European Social Charter of 1961 affords women employees even greater protection (Wolkinson et al. 1982, 480). Israel enthusiastically followed this path, as it perceived women first and foremost as mothers; work came second. Working women were given the right to three months maternity leave. During that period the employer was prohibited from employing the woman or from dismissing her, and she was given the right to payment in lieu of salary from the National Insurance Institute. After her maternity leave, the mother was given the right to take up to a year's leave without pay or to resign with entitlement to severance pay (Raday 1991a, 179). That these benefits were not granted on a biological basis but rather on social grounds is evident from the fact that a woman adopting a child (up to the age of 10) enjoyed the same benefits as a birth-giving mother.[9]

These rights were not the only ones granted by the state to mothers. A pregnant woman could charge her medical examinations to her employer. Her absence from work on account of her pregnancy could be counted as a sickness leave regardless of its duration. Women were encouraged to integrate work and family by other legal means: collective agreements provided that women could use part of their own sick leave to care for children and could work one hour less a day if they had at least two children under the age of 12. Young women of reproductive age (under 45), were banned from working in a job exposing them to radiation or lead. All these protective measures, notes Raday (1983), were of great practical value in facilitating the integration of motherhood with participation in the labor market. However, they were also responsible for the perpetuation of stereotypes, for they were based on a female role image as primarily caretaker of home and children.

Equality between men and women in the workplace was treated in another set of laws regarding working a night shift. As a rule women were prohibited from working at night,[10] save for those specific occupations such as nurses and customs inspectors. Even in these few cases there were certain conditions to be fulfilled as a prerequisite for women's work, which reflected women's unique difficulties. The employer had to provide a suitable place for a woman to rest, a hot drink, a recess of at least twelve hours between one workday and the next, and transportation to and from her home. All these provisions, positive as they may have appeared in the past, seriously curtailed women's equality in the workplace. Women themselves were not allowed to obtain permission to work at night at their own initiative. Employers, for their part, were reluctant to go through the bureaucratic maze necessary to obtain a permission for a women's night shift. Forced to grant female workers favorable conditions, employers were disinclined to hire their services unless they worked for low pay.

In the last decade, in both Europe and the United States, the belief has been growing that bans on night work are unfairly restrictive to women and they serve as vehicles of discrimination rather than instruments of protection.[11] Israel has also been affected by this mood. In a 1986 amendment to the Women's Work Law (1954), changes were inserted regarding women working night shift. Employers may not dismiss a woman who refuses to work at night for family reasons, but women are allowed to work at night, provided the conditions previously set are fulfilled: transportation to and from the place of work, a place to rest during work, a hot drink. None of these facilitating conditions were relevant to men.

Only in the second phase of legislation, taking place in the 1980s, has the Knesset made a serious attempt to deal with the problem of gender economic equality. This attempt has led to the adoption of a series of laws, the most important of which are the Retirement Law (1987) and the Equal Employment Opportunity Law (1988). The concept of equal opportunity between the sexes in employment was initiated by the labor courts in a landmark 1973 decision: *Edna Hazin et al. v. El Al Israel Airlines Inc.*[12] The decision was made in the context of a suit brought by air stewardesses against the airline to contest their exclusion from the rank of chief steward, the highest rank for cabin crew (Raday 1991a, 180). As noted by Raday (1983), although there was no existing legislative framework prohibiting discrimination in employment conditions, the Regional Court and the National Labor Court both held that the promotion provision in El Al's collective agreement was discriminatory and that the court had the power to declare such discrimination void as contrary to public policy. The Hazin case opened the way for extensive litigation against discrimination in employment. However, the potential of this case was not realized as in the ten years following the judgment only once did a court (the Haifa Regional Labor Court) invalidate a labor decision—in this case by the civil service not to employ a plaintiff. The dearth of litigation, according to Raday (1983), is explained, among other things, by the inadequacies of the legal remedies available from the Hazin case. In the circumstances of this legal void, the second phase of employment legislation was initiated.

Equal Opportunity in Employment (1981)

In 1981 the first bill on equal opportunity in employment was introduced to the Knesset. The enforcement of equal opportunity by law was adopted as a major recommendation by the Prime Minister's Committee on the Status of Women. But the change of government and the inception of the peace process with Egypt, culminating in Sadat's dramatic visit in Jerusalem (19 November 1977), shelved this recommendation and pushed aside the problem of gender equality. Once again national objectives were given priority over gender issues. The entrance of new actors into the political arena, however, gave rise to private initiatives. Sarah Doron, a woman MK belonging to the governing Likud faction, introduced a private member's bill regarding equal employment opportunity. Doron was not the sole actor, and in fact the Department for Women's Employees in the Histadrut, the female branch in the trade union department, took the credit for initiating the legislation. Doron, however, was more visible. As a member of the governing coalition, she could muster the majority necessary to approve the bill.

The Knesset debate on the motion (15 March 1978) vividly displayed the force of the national principle. Sarah Doron, introducing the bill, said:

> I hope ... that this House, or those responsible for the membership of the House, will grant an adequate ex-

pression to half the population [the Hebrew word is Yishuv, a term associated with the bond among the Jewish settlers in pre-state Israel] and enable them to make their contribution, which I regard as perhaps no less important than the contribution of others, to the development and prosperity of the state. I think it is a shame that half the population [Yishuv], with an intellectual, technical potential, with a warm and sensitive heart, with clear-headedness and sense not inferior to others, is not utilized for the advancement and development of the national economy.[13]

The minister of labor and welfare reiterated this theme by emphasizing "the national importance of offering women equal employment opportunities."[14] In short, there was a wide consensus on the need to incorporate women into the labor market. Equal opportunities were conceivably a widely endorsed means toward this end. The bill, however, encountered foot-dragging and even opposition. Among those confronting the law were other women MKs, unhappy with the party affiliation of the original sponsor. The fact that Naamat was left outside the legislative process was a thorn in the flesh of the women Labor MKs, who attempted to hinder the smooth passage of the bill. In 1981 the bill was finally approved by the Knesset, but it was extremely limited. The new Equal Opportunities in Employment Law did not effectively add to the remedies available from the Hazin case. It did introduce criminal prohibition of discrimination in hiring job applicants, since under the ruling in *Hazin v. El-Al* the right not to be discriminated against was limited to the work conditions of persons already employed. But the law did nothing to improve the potential for implementation of this right through civil litigation, and the criminal liability which it introduced remained a dead letter. Not a single conviction has ever been made to date under the law forbidding discrimination in acceptance of job applicants.

Equal Retirement Law (1987)

The 1981 law, however, did have a psychological effect on women. In the early 1980s a series of suits were filed to challenge discrimination against women of retirement age. Although Israeli females, as their counterparts elsewhere, live longer than males, they were due to retire at 60, five years earlier than men. The story, told by Raday (1991a, 181) is as follows: In 1983, two women professors of medicine sought an injunction against the Hadassah Medical Organization to prevent it from forcibly retiring them five years earlier than their male colleagues. The early retirement was in accordance with the provisions of a collective agreement between Hadassah and the doctors' unions. The case terminated in an out-of-court settlement in which the plaintiffs achieved full equality regarding retirement age. In 1985, Dr. Naomi Nevo, a senior anthropologist employed by the Jewish Agency, brought a similar action for an injunction against the employer. The labor courts refused to grant her a judicial remedy. In spite of undisputed evidence of harm to the plaintiff's economic and professional standing, the National Labor Court held, in a majority decision given in 1986, that under the Hazin ruling imposition of early retirement age did not constitute unlawful discrimination. It further held that going on pension was not a "condition of employment" and hence the Hazin ruling was not applicable.[15]

The implications of this ruling were clear and simple: the silence of the Knesset with regard to discrimination in all aspects of employment, including retirement age, showed that its intention was not to prohibit discrimination it in its entirety, but specifically to prohibit in acceptance to employment (the 1981 law) and in payment of wages (the 1964 law). Hence the court concluded: "Where the legislature wished to prevent discrimination (or create absolute equality) it did so specifically; as regards a subject not regulated by an express provision of a statute, the presumption is that the legislature reached the conclusion that the time is not yet ripe for it" (quoted by Raday 1991, 182). This judicial statement, asserting that mandatory early retirement for women was not unlawful discrimination, led to corrective legislation. In 1987, the Equal Retirement Age for Female and Male Employees Law was passed by the Knesset. The law provided that retirement age (65) for men and women was to be equal under collective agreements but that where the agreement itself provided for an earlier retirement age for women, women retained the option of retiring at the earlier age of 60.

The mood of the Knesset was different from that of the previous debate on regaling women's equality in the workplace.

Early retirement age for women was presented as an example of male chauvinism.[16] Gender equality, furthermore, was defined in universal terms ("It is our business as Knesset Members, and not only female Knesset Members").[17] Speakers noted the hurdles facing women wishing to advance in professional life. Yet the bill, while catering to women's predicament, was tailored to their traditional roles. According to one speaker, retaining the option of early retirement was essential for women on the following grounds: "Although at the age of 60 the needs of housekeeping are not as acute as they are in younger age groups, because upon reaching maturity a woman is already a grandmother . . . there is nevertheless a great need at this age to stay home a little more, and to organize time better. This is a present we can give them, these women."[18]

This mood, shared by many other legislators, accentuates the image of the woman, whose main concern is her home—her castle. The law, allowing (though not forcing) women to retire at the same age as men, was approved unanimously by the Knesset on 17 March 1987. Unanimity was encouraged by the financial constraints of the Histadrut-controlled pension funds, wishing to delay, at least temporarily, the withdrawal of funds by retiring women. At the same time, extending the working period for women was disapproved owing to economic hardships arising from widespread dismissals of other workers.[19] The overwhelming majority of women, however, continued to retire at the age of 60.[20] In 1992, the issue reemerged on the public agenda, when full equalization of women's retirement age with men's was called for. At the time of writing, the legal grant of optional early retirement to women remains intact.

Equal Employment Opportunity Law (1988)

The second phase of legislation regarding women in the labor force culminated in the Equal Employment Opportunity Law enacted by the Knesset on 23 February 1988. The law introduced wide-ranging prohibition of discrimination in employment, citing in great detail each and every aspect: acceptance in work, advertisements of offers of employment, conditions of employment, promotion, training and professional study, dismissal and severance pay. The law also included specific prohibition of sexual harassment. Section 7 provides that an employer must not prejudice the employee's work status "by reason of the employee's rejection of a proposal or resistance to an act, of a sexual nature made or done by the employer." The law provides both civil and criminal rights of action against employment discrimination. It further provides that the posing of irrelevant conditions may constitute discrimination, thus allowing an action for indirect discrimination or discriminatory impact (section 2 [6]).

The major innovation of the Equal Employment Opportunity Law lies in the expansion of maternity rights to both parents. As recalled, mothers enjoyed a host of privileges on account of their biological and/or social contribution to reproduction. The 1988 legislation no longer treated women as bearing the sole responsibility for child rearing. It contributed to gender equality by doing justice to fathers. The law acknowledged the entitlement of both parents to absence from work for reason of illness of a child. It is worth noting, however, that this privilege was granted only in cases where the father has sole custody of a child or his wife is an employee and is not absent from work by virtue of the same entitlement. Furthermore, the law entitled the father to compensation if he chose to resign within nine months of his child's birth (on condition that his spouse was employed for at least six consecutive months prior to his resignation. No such condition was applied to the mother). This provision applied also to adopting parents. All in all the law portended a serious commitment, on the part of the state, to gender equality.

To ensure implementation the law places the burden of proof on the employer in civil actions based on its provisions. The plaintiff was allowed six months to present her/his case before expiration. The law bestowed on the labor courts the power to issue enforcement orders and to award damages even if there is no proof of economic injury (section 10). Responsibility for adequate implementation was vested in inspectors, whose major duty was to investigate employers. An advisory public council was nominated to advise the minister of labor on all issues regarding the promotion of equal opportunities in the workplace.

The Knesset debate prior to enactment of the law reflected a deep rift between men and women MKs regarding gender equality. It also demonstrated the growing awareness of gender identity among female politicians. Women MKs insisted that the law was a necessary step toward comprehensive gender equality, in society and the polity at large. The theme underpinning women's contribution to the nation was far less emphasized than in previous deliberations on the issue. Some male MKs paid lip service to the notion of equality, but at the same time clung to the traditional female stereotypes. The minister of welfare and labor (Moshe Katzav, Likud) was particularly concerned with the father's entitlement to "maternity" leave. He said: "One of our society's norms postulates that child caring is vested in the mother. This norm has fundamental roots both in the Jewish tradition and in the cultural heritage of all mankind"[21] Another MK (Amnon Linn, Labor), called upon women "to safeguard the right and duty a Jewish woman has to have a family and raise children. With all our quest for equality, we cannot replace a woman in childbearing."[22] The motion, nevertheless, was widely backed. Even religious MKs stated that the bill constituted an important step toward rectifying injustice prevalent in the Israeli economy. It thus appeared that the winds of equality had blown through the Israeli parliament, which endorsed, by an overwhelming majority, the law ensuring women equality of opportunity in many spheres of the economy.

Although the principle of gender economic equality was widely endorsed some opposition to the provisions of the proposed law were evident, emanating mainly from the business community, concerned about a possible decline in profits. Industrialists were apprehensive about other provisions of the law, besides higher wages for women. While supporting women's equality in principle, they nevertheless feared the prospects of a swelling flow of complaints about sexual harassment and the greater restrictions on their freedom to hire and fire workers, which in their view, should be exclusively their right. Despite their reservations, pronounced mainly behind closed doors (in the deliberations of the appropriate Knesset committee, which are not public), the members of the business community did not openly challenge the idea of women's equal opportunity in the labor market. Explicit and deliberate opposition to such an idea would have been unacceptable in the late 1980s, by which time the idea of gender equality had spread far and wide.

Women's Role in Shaping
Economic (Employment) Policy

The economic woes of women have perennially occupied the political agenda. The scope of legislation enacted to fight inequality reveals serious efforts to tackle the problem and reduce its detrimental effects. The first part of this chapter showed that success was at best partial, but the motivation itself to act in face of injustice deserves credit. It remains unclear, however, if this effort may be attributed to women's pressures. Does it reflect the rising influence of women on the political arena? Have women's associations become committed to push issues pertinent to women's equality? That women's social and political standing is predicated on their economic status is unanimously agreed. Work has been singled out as an essential precondition for the attainment of social equality (Eisenstein 1979; Chafetz 1990). The question nevertheless remains open as to the ability, and willingness, of organized women in Israel to influence the shaping of women's economic equality. A review of the contribution by the women's associations to public discourse and to the legislative process will make possible an evaluation of their influence on policy-making.

In the first phase of labor legislation women's associations played a minor role, both in public discourse and in the policy-making process. They commended, post factum, initiatives taken by other actors, but they themselves were hardly innovative. The Women's Workers Movement, which by virtue of its affiliation to the Histadrut was the natural advocate of women's employment rights, did encourage women to join the labor force. The national theme, however, was loudly stressed, taking precedence over women's rights. In an article entitled "Working Women—A National Requisite,"[23] the principles underlying women's employment were spelled out as follows: "It is a known fact that the increase in the number of women among the breadwinners has been a major factor in the rise of the national income in many countries. . . . This problem of increasing the number of employed women has a special significance in Israel, in view of the specific circumstances of our national economy and in view of our defense needs."

Furthermore, the WWM not only emphasized the advantages of women's employment to the national economy; it also underscored the primacy of maternity functions over outside work. In another article[24] it was specified that women should be encouraged to work only either before they get married or after their children had grown up and left home. Mothers of young children should not be compelled to work. Consequently, it was only natural that a woman was entitled to comprehensive protective legislation "in order to safeguard her health, her position at work, in the family and in society."[25] WWM adamantly opposed a legislative proposal issued by the minister of labor suggesting the abolition of the prohibition on night work by women (in January 1964). Under the headline "Night Shift Harms Women," the movement's secretary-general justified the exclusion of women from working at night by the following argument: "There is a great difference between life styles of a man and a woman. When a man returns home after a night shift, he does not have to deal with any additional work and he can rest as much as needed; when a woman, who is also a mother and a homemaker, comes back from work, she has to deal immediately with home and family chores. . . . [T]his takes a serious toll on her health and well being."[26]

The WWM thus declined to adopt a feminist perspective on problems of women's employment. Nor did it strive to make women equal to men. In fact, the women's association discharged itself from responsibility for women's employment rights, relying on the Histadrut's trade union department to handle women's affairs.

The second phase of legislation presented a different picture, albeit an equivocal one. Women's associations did not play a major role in sparking the legislative process. The sponsor of the first version of the 1981 Equal Opportunity Law, Sarah Doron, who submitted the legislative draft, noted the meagerness of women's influence at that early stage of the policy process:

I blame ourselves. Women do not support one another. We do not give backing, we don't seem able to overlook trivial issues and we fail to become a cohesive pressure group. I am not aware of any sense of "togetherness" among women, or among women's associations. They are doing a wonderful job, all of them . . . but regarding this issue [equal employment opportunity] I am sorry to say that the outcomes are disappointing, and not only the outcomes but also the efforts [of these organizations] are meager.[27]

Naamat declined to take the lead in promoting women's equality in the workplace owing to the political circumstances of the early 1980s. Labor MKs found themselves in the opposition after nearly thirty years in government. Issues regarding women's equality were pushed to the bottom of the list of priorities. Furthermore, the internal rivalry within the Labor Party between the women's department in the Histadrut and Naamat hindered effective action. Naamat, the guardian of working women's interests, showed signs of uneasiness with the ongoing legislative process. Voices were raised against the bill: "This is not the right time to act, when there is deep strife between the Histadrut and the government." At the same time, it was noted: "Obviously, we will not act against the Histadrut, but we must not forget that the Histadrut is not always on our side. . . . We would not like to be the WIZO of the trade union movement."[28] After the law was enacted frustration mounted. Naamat activists did not hide their disappointment: "It is inconceivable that the largest women's movement in the country, which is our movement, will not furnish enduring solutions on the status of the working women."[29]

Women's influence became more noticeable with the passage of time. Some issues got more attention than others. Naamat, for example, faithful to its family orientation, espoused parental rights instead of maternal rights. The issue was placed on the agenda of the Knesset Labor faction as early as 1980, some eight years before legislation. Initially, the proposal to allow men to share parental rights with women encountered vehement opposition, ostensibly in defense of women's rights. Granting fathers the right to take care of their children was a revolutionary idea in a mother-centered society. But toward the late 1980s the legislative arena was ripe for change. In the 1988 legislative process women representatives appeared regularly in the hearings of the Knesset committee, presenting the women's point of view. But their major contribution to policy-making was in presenting amendments to the original draft that widened the scope of the Employment Law and enforced its application. The legal staff of the Women's Network, headed by Frances Raday, a law professor specializing in labor law, was extremely influential in this regard. The prime minister's advisor on women's status, also a legal expert (Nitza Shapira-Liba'i), was likewise instrumental in pushing the bill forward. The law enacted by the Knesset indeed reflects several changes from the original draft submitted by MKs. Three of these are as follows: First, the burden on the employee, that is, the victim, of proving discrimination in the workplace was shifted to the employer, that is the perpetrator, who had to prove there was no discrimination (as was proposed by the original version). Second, the original proposal lacked any provisions for enforcement, which were incorporated in the final version, although in a diluted formula. Third, and perhaps most important, the original draft did not include sexual harassment as a form of job discrimination. This lacuna was filled by the experts of the Women's Network.

Once again, however, the fingerprints of the two larger women's associations—Naamat and WIZO—were not discernible. The former, the women's branch of the Labor Federation, took no part in the important legislation introducing equal retirement age for men and women. In the late 1980s, the problem was no longer political vulnerability, as the Labor Party was part and parcel of the governing coalition, but rather vacillation between feminist advocacy and the commitment to traditional female roles. A prominent female Labor MK stated (in a private interview): "A woman has functions other than working outside her home. We don't have to sacrifice family life for the sake of work. A woman may think she deserves equality at all costs, but she herself pays a heavy toll for attaining it. We cannot enforce gender equality by law, mainly because it is unacceptable and incompatible with the most fundamental values held by a large section of our population."

Naamat, however, faced a more serious constraint that hindered effective lobbying in regard to employment legislation: an encounter with the Histadrut's trade union department. The male-dominated trade union department was opposed to some provisions of the equal opportunity legislation, because of fiscal considerations. Naamat allegedly declined to support the suit against the Jewish Agency (submitted by Naomi Nevo; see above) and refused to grant her either legal or financial assistance.[30] Collective agreements, regulating relations between employers and employees, proved to be more fruitful than the pursuit of women's equality. WIZO, a traditional charity association, was hardly involved in labor legislation as it in fact lay beyond its traditional interests. Likewise, the issue of equality in the workplace has remained outside the concern of feminist groups.

Implementing the Law: Setting Women Aside

The sweeping 1988 legislation did not introduce gender equality and did not eradicate the gender-based economic differentials. Some success is evident in regard to job advertisements, as the proportion of discriminatory publications decreased from 71 percent in 1987 to 40 percent in 1991.[31] With respect to other aspects of equality in the workplace, data continue to reflect the unequal status of women. One of the major reasons for the law's ineffectiveness lies in the reluctance of women to sue employers. The psychological and financial burdens entailed in filing a complaint have deterred the majority of women, who are unwilling to take the economic risks entailed in confronting their employers. Lack of implementation may be attributed also to financial factors. While the Knesset was willing to incorporate the principle of equality in employment in a legal provision, it has not been prepared to pay a fiscal price for its commitment. The 1988 law does not provide a budget for any enforcement agency. Legislators underwrote the principle of equality largely because it was free of charge.

That implementation of the Equal Employment Opportunity Law has been less than desired is evident also from a survey taken two years after the law was enacted (in 1990). Some 60 percent of the respondents were of the opinion that women were discriminated against in the workplace, in both their employment and their promotion opportunities. Men's prospects for being hired were considered better even than these of single, childless women. When asked to explain the unequal treatment, the majority (some 75 percent of the respondents) were of the opinion that women could devote less time and energy than men to outside work; furthermore, it was assumed that women tended to be absent from work more than men (this impression is not substantiated by statistical data on absenteeism: the average weekly absence among women was 11.7 hours in 1992; among men it was 14.4 hours—Statistical Abstracts 1994, 364). Some two-thirds of the respondents attributed discrimination against women in the workplace to the fact that "most employers are men." The survey further confirmed the low awareness of the law. Less than half stated they knew such a law was ever enacted.[32] The survey conducted specifically for this study yielded no better results. Respondents were asked, in an open question, to name the laws dealing with gender equality. Among the 1,163 respondents, only 25 mentioned the law specifically (14 men and 11 women); two respondents were aware of legislation regarding advertisements of job opportunities; two respondents mentioned "labor laws" in general, with no specification. Only one respondent (a woman) was aware of legislation banning sexual harassment. The results of the sweeping legislation in terms of public awareness, are thus extremely disappointing.

The law's ineffectiveness may also have been caused by the fact that those mostly involved, that is, women's representatives, were not partners to its implementation. While women's associations did their best to disseminate information on the Equal Employment Law, they were left out when it came to implementation. Objection to their involvement in enforcement was already evident in the Knesset committee's deliberations. Even one of the most ardent proponents of the bill, the chairperson of the Knesset committee debating the issue (Ora Namir), noted that "we have a problem with women's associations. There are at least fifteen registered women's associations in the country, the majority of which focus on *political* activity" (emphasis mine).[33] Namir's objection to the involvement of women's associations in implementing the law was buttressed by the legal advisor in the Ministry of Justice, who said: "A representative workers' organization is a responsible body that uses its authority with discretion. . . . Women's associations, however, are not genuinely representative. We should not grant authority to irresponsible bodies, or to unrepresentative ones. What these organizations do is incompatible with their members' wishes; in fact, their activities may often be against the workers' best judgment. Authority in this regard can be granted only to a *responsible* body" (emphasis mine).[34]

This statement constitutes a grand delegitimation of women's associations by a senior public official. It also shows that even those organizations that wished to speak on behalf of women on the particular issue of employment equality were denied recognition. Knesset members wondering about this indiscriminate denial were answered with the remark: "[Individual women do not need patronizing. If they have problems they can speak out for themselves."[35] As this view was widespread among legislators, women's associations were practically barred from executing the law. A "Public Council," consisting of representatives of the employees (the trade union department of the Labor Federation), the employers (the Manufacturers' Association), government agencies, and "public representatives," was mandated to carry out the legal provisions. The last-named constituted no more than 10 percent of the council's total membership. The major functions of the council were limited to disseminating the message of equality and to raise public awareness of the law's provisions. The call of the Women's Network for setting up a public council staffed by female experts to handle complaints was rejected by lawmakers. Examination of the council's records reveals that its activities are, at best, symbolic, and that its composition has been determined on a party basis. By establishing the council in its present form, the legislators have tacitly recognized vested interests by handing over implementation to an agency that has been severely handicapped (on a similar pattern in the United States and Great Britain, see Randall 1987, 312). Women's associations have attempted to spread the idea of equal employment opportunity and have called upon women to act against discrimination in the workplace. This activity, however, has yielded only limited results. Women associations have clearly failed to establish a network between themselves and government agencies responsible for promoting gender economic equality.

Conclusion

Israel has joined other Western nations in providing women equal opportunity in the workplace (Randall 1987, 309–14). The state has moved from protecting women, perceived as dainty and frail human beings, to guaranteeing them legal equal rights. Some steps, albeit limited, have been taken toward introducing genuine equality between the sexes, irrespective of the woman's biological uniqueness, as maternal leave for the purpose of early child-rearing and care of sick children has been augmented by paternal leave. As the first part of this chapter demonstrated, however, much of this policy has failed to achieve its stated objective: the eradication of inequality between men and women in the workplace. Unrelenting vertical and horizontal job segregation and the persistent income differentials indicate that women have remained unequal to men in regard to one of the most important ventures of modern life: employment and career. This is not because the state declined to produce public policy aimed at eliminating the economic gap between men and women. Nor did the equalizing legal measures encounter serious opposition. In fact, although they did jeopardize some economic interests of the business community, they posed no threat to the existing political and social order. The major obstacles to their utility are to be found in images of women in the workplace and in the lack of effective implementation machinery.

Policy aimed at promoting gender equality appears to have been more lip service paid to the egalitarian mood than a forceful commitment. Despite the fact that Israel has not experienced severe unemployment problems, the state has been unwilling to seriously tackle the problem of gender economic inequality. Commentators have noted the lack of provisions for enforcement agencies to implement its principles through the courts (Raday 1991a, 186). This stands in sharp contrast to other countries. In France, for example, employers are required to produce annual reports on the comparative positions of male and female employees. An equal opportunities commission was established in many European countries (in Sweden an equal opportunities ombudsman was named in 1979) to monitor adherence to the equalizing laws and to bring employment law into line with EEC requirements (Randall 1987, 312–13). Note, though, that despite serious efforts taken to implement equalizing legislation, results have been disappointing in other countries as well (Vallance and Davies 1986).

The second barrier to economic equality, and not less important, are the attitudes involved in implementing the law. Both legislators and the courts have tended to accept the stereotypes of women as needing protection. Employment legislation was not perceived as the key to the feminist revolution but rather as a measure enabling women to acquire legal rights—without altering fundamental social norms. Initially, women's groups operating from within succumbed to these norms. Since the late 1980s, however, they have increasingly attempted to use employment as the vanguard for equality, showing greater concern about work discrimination. Yet, as in other Western countries, equal opportunities were legislated without active feminist pressure (Randall 1987, 311). Furthermore, gender equality has in many instances remained a matter of choice, as women have retained legal prerogatives to forego opportunities for equality. They *could*, if they wished, refuse to work night shifts; they *could*, if they wished, receive their pension at the age of 60. Parental rights have been indeed guaranteed by law, but they were not applied to collective labor agreements, which grant mothers, but not fathers, the right to work fewer hours. These facts, concludes Izraeli (1991, 175), reveal the ambivalence of the women themselves regarding their equal status in the workplace. When the figures are studied regarding the distribution of women among occupations, and the high incidence of part-time employment, the ambiguity is even more striking. The major cause of this ambivalence is the perception of women as a secondary breadwinner and, above all, the unyielding view of children as the mother's offspring. "Women do not opt for managerial positions because they raise children," asserted the secretary-general of the Histadrut.[36]

Women's associations, for their part, were also ambivalent toward employment opportunities. Naamat, the putative major proponent of women's rights in the labor market, was situated between the hammer—its women members suffering from discrimination and inequality—and the anvil—the powerful trade union with whom it maintained a close political relationship. The case of the equal retirement age, as well as other issues of public policy, have exposed the organizational vulnerability of Naamat, unable to deny its commitment to the cause of women's equality and unable to sever its relations with the male-dominated trade union department. Consequently, no pressures for affirmative action in the economy have ever been exerted. These would have made impossible the mobilization of the trade union to support equalizing legislation. Equality in the workplace has remained a "distributive" issue rather than a fundamental problem of women's rights.

Working from within the establishment to promote women's economic rights has proven futile. However, the growing awareness by individual women of their professional needs on the one hand, and the increased politicization of women's lobbying activity on the other, portend a continuous movement toward equality. It is crucial, though, that the self-imposed shackles on women regarding their central role in the family be loosened, if not completely removed.

CHAPTER 7

Family Policy:
Patriarchy in the Jewish State

In March 1993 a spokeswoman for Naamat stated, at a widely publicized press conference, that the theme chosen for that year's Women's Status Month, was "Family Values."[1] The slogan amply illustrated the centrality of family in organized women's activity in the country. "The family means something special to me," exclaimed the spokeswoman. The theme, she explained, was in line with the UN International Year of the Family. The Israeli scene provided extremely fertile soil for accentuating the subject.

The family is both the woman's province and her prison. There she can fulfill herself, be appreciated for what she does, and find herself a proper place in society. In her family, the woman is queen and ruler (unless she is subject to violence, which is often the case). In the realm of her family the woman can express her feminine attributes: she can be warm and sensitive, sentimental and caring. In short, she can be her real self, or to put it more accurately, she can fit the image portrayed of her from time immemorial. The family is also her prison, distancing and removing her from the outside world, confining her to the private domain. By virtue of her family affiliation, the woman is fettered to her domestic responsibilities and is denied the opportunities available to men in the public domain. By fulfilling her family duties, the Israeli woman, however, can subscribe to the national goals and show her allegiance to the flag. This chapter will show that in Israel the state has consolidated the linkage between women and the family. Some legal provisions, mainly those regarding personal matters, have been unfavorable to women's status. On other issues, for example, economic relations in the family and the protection of women against violence, the state has shown more favor to gender equality.

Centrality of Family in Israeli Life

The centrality of family in social life has been acknowledged by many political theorists from the early Greek period to the present and has been embodied in many legal documents. Good examples are the Canadian Charter of Rights, the Italian Constitution, the Universal Declaration on Human Rights (1948), the European Charter on Human Rights (1950), and the International Charter on Economic, Social, and Cultural Rights (1966). Many states have framed specific constitutional clauses regulating the family and its internal relations. In Switzerland, for example, a particular constitutional provision governs family names, requiring a wife to carry her husband's surname. Until several years ago the Swiss law determined that the division of labor within the family obliges women to be responsible for housekeeping (Senti 1992). The Constitution of the Republic of Ireland provides another example of state interference in family affairs. According to Irish law, a woman's place is in her home, and only there. Only rarely does the state forego its interest in the family and leave the individual leeway to organize his or her life as he or she see fit.

Why have states troubled to go into such details regarding what is considered the private domain? The answer to this question is grounded in the important role families play in social life. The state has customarily shown a great interest in the family, perceiving it as a bulwark of social and political stability. As Randall (1987, 203) has put it: "The family has an important socializing function, transmitting, if not attitudes of positive support for the existing regime, at least a tendency to accept authority and to adhere conservatively to the way things are as normal." A stable family system also helps to ensure that children, the elderly, the sick and the handicapped are cared for, relieving the state of its commitments. The answer lies also in the perception of the family as a reproductive unit whose integrity and well-being are crucial for ensuring a nation's future. Whether the state encourages a higher birth rate or wishes to reduce fertility, whether it aims at economic growth or at economic restraint, the key to achieving these goals, conceivably, is with the family.

The political salience of the family, however, has not been reflected in the history of political thought. In fact, family was not regarded as falling within the political realm at all. Family was considered to be women's private domain, remote from the public world of men. In her seminal work on justice, gender, and the family (1989), Susan Moller-Okin explores in detail perceptions of family in political theory. She shows how the great political philosophers thought the family was centrally important; she also certifies that all defended the existing hierarchical marital structures. They all claimed that the rules applicable to family life are love, altruism, and generosity. Justice belongs to the public realm, from which women are mostly excluded.

In postmodern societies the varieties of family life have perhaps made the traditional nuclear family obsolete. Yet many Western states have witnessed trends of "return to the family" and its hallowed values. The breakup of the nuclear family, the abundance of divorces, the fact that a substantial proportion of children no longer grow up with both their parents, have generated a yearning among some segments of the population for a more traditional pattern, characterized by the endurance and stability of family life. Adoption of "family values" has emerged as a major campaign issue in both the United States and the United Kingdom. In Israel this strategy is superfluous, as the family has been, and still remains, a major component of social life.

The centrality of the family in Israeli society has been widely acknowledged by social scientists (e.g., Shrift 1982; Katz and Peres 1986; Izraeli and Tabory 1988; Safir 1991). The importance of the family is demonstrated in demographic data and in value orientations: only two states (Iraq and Tunisia) show stronger family characteristics than Israel, when judged by three central criteria. All Western societies (including societies in Eastern Europe) portray lower family standards than Israel. The divorce rates in the country (1.4 per 1000 in 1992) are similar to those in traditional and agrarian societies. Fertility rate is also far higher than in other industrialized countries. Total fertility rate in Israel was 2.9 (in 1989), even higher than Catholic countries like Ireland (2.2) and Spain (1.4) (World Development 1991, 257). The percentage of out-of-wedlock births, although growing, was 1.1 in 1986, compared with 7.6 in Germany and 42.0 (!) in Sweden (United Nations 1986, 160, 165).

The importance of family is confirmed by attitudes exhibited in public opinion studies. A survey conducted in 1990 has revealed that in response to a question regarding the preferred life style, the overwhelming majority of the respondents gave marriage priority over every other type of sexual relationship. Had they had other options and alternative life styles, the interviewees stated, they would have nonetheless chosen the path of marriage. Conversely, the unmarried individuals (including widowed, divorced, and single) were less satisfied with their lives. They, in fact, also preferred marriage over any alternative life style (Milbauer and Tzemach 1991, 16). These attitudes were pervasive among both sexes but particularly among women, who viewed marriage as their ultimate goal in life. A poll taken in 1984 revealed that 85 percent of the both men and women, respondents in a national sample, were of the opinion that men preferred women for whom family was a central objective. According to this poll, women for whom work was central, were more likely to be divorced than their home-centered counterparts.[2] The idea so widespread in Western societies about choices made by each individual regarding his or her sexual or social relationship garnered little support in Israel. Marriage is *the* choice made by well-adjusted people; celibacy could be interpreted only in terms of lack of choice. A thriving industry has developed around the marriage ceremony—from beauty parlors that take care of the bride's needs to huge public and private halls that cater the wedding.

Furthermore, marriage is extremely important, but getting married alone is not enough. A marriage without children is not considered a family and the childless couple elicit pity. As noted by Safir (1991, 58), there are periodic news items in all the media of new breakthroughs in fertility treatments. Israel presents the highest ratio per population in the world of IVF (in-vitro-fertilization) clinics. A report issued by the World Health Organization revealed that in 1992 there were 708 IVF units worldwide, eighteen of which (2.5 percent) operated in Israel and were publicly funded. Women from a small outlying town whose hospital had no IVF clinic, staged a protest demonstration in Jerusalem, yelling: "We want a child!"[3] In an article entitled "Anything for a Baby" Alison Solomon (1991) describes the stress of being childless in Israel. Families who fail to reproduce opt for adoption almost at any cost. Every once in a while a story about a couple smuggling a child from a foreign country becomes a news item.

In reality, however, the garden of marriage is often strewn with thorns, as marriage is not nearly as positive an experience for women as it is for men. Actually, for many women marriage seems to be a health hazard (Shrift 1982). Wives experience more stress and strain than their husbands partly because they are typically the ones who are expected to adapt to their husband's lives and not the reverse.[4] Wives were observed to lose their self-esteem and sense of personal identity because they conformed to their husbands' needs (Hazleton 1978). Data consistently confirm the unequal division of labor between men and women in the family. In Western societies the rise of the "house-husband" has been widely acknowledged.[5] In Israel the phenomenon is unknown. Women are responsible for and typically perform most of the child (and elderly) care and housekeeping. They spend approximately twice the time at these tasks as men, regardless of whether they are employed outside the home or are full-time housewives (Izraeli 1988b).[6] Tending to family affairs does not end for women as their children grow up, for they typically acquire new, no less demanding, family commitments. The story of the Israeli adult woman has been vividly painted by Azmon and Izraeli (1993, 3):

> When sons and daughters begin compulsory military service at eighteen, parenting can be more intense than

previously. Soldiers' families are encouraged by the army to play active support roles, such as attending "open days" and military ceremonies, paying weekend visits to the army base, and pampering the soldiers during their weekends and furloughs at home. Care for aging parents, more often the daily responsibility of daughters than sons, is another demanding aspect of family life, especially for middle-aged women. The frequency of visits to elderly parents in Israel is higher than that in other Western countries. . . . A comparison of Israeli career women to American career women at mid-life shows that Israeli women also expressed greater concern for elderly parents and for sons and daughters serving in the army whereas American women were more concerned about career achievements.

The overarching significance of family life has been visible in one of the last bastions of equality in Western society, the Israeli kibbutz. In her study on kibbutz women, Michal Palgi (1993) describes the dramatic changes that have taken place in this form of life. The kibbutz has tried to build a different society, one organized on principles of equality for all. In terms of parity between men and women, however, the kibbutz has had only limited success. While men have been urged to spend time with their children, and to take an active role in looking after their daily needs, raising children has remained largely the woman's business. Even though feeding and educational systems were set up in a way that would grant women freedom from household chores and economic dependence on men, women's first priority was home, children, and family. This was more true for second, third, and fourth generations of kibbutz-born women than for their pioneer mothers, who toiled on the land and dried the swamps, shoulder to shoulder with their men folk. Women insisted on reducing their working hours and on having their children sleeping in the family home instead of in a communal children's house.

Strong patriarchal values and institutions have thus characterized Israeli society. The scope of public policy regarding family matters reflects this pattern.

Marital Status: State-Religion Partnership

Public authorities in Israel have taken a keen interest in family affairs, acting to strengthen the patriarchal nuclear family. But the state has not monopolized regulation of family life; rather, it shares its power with religious authorities. While Israel has been characterized as a Westernized liberal democracy, often referred to as the one and only democracy in the Middle East, strong religious influences can be discerned in both public and private life. Religious traditions find expression in binding legislation and in widespread attitudes and mores. Although Israel has no established religion, nor any provisions in its laws requiring a particular religious affiliation, belief, or commitment as a requirement for holding office, religion does play a an ever-present role in Israeli politics. Israel's society and policy are permeated by religion, as the state explicitly defined itself, in the Declaration of Independence, as *Jewish*. Although many of the founders of Israel were secular, they saw the state as Jewish in the national sense of the term, which in Judaism is equivalent to the religious term (Elazar 1986; Liebman and Don-Yehiya 1987). Underlying all religious commitments in Israel is this inherent intertwining of the religious and the national dimensions of Judaism. This ancient linkage bears far-reaching implications: fundamental national symbols incorporate ancient religious myths and religious holidays, including the Sabbath, are celebrated as national holidays. Announcements in the daily press, issued at the time of writing, reminds the readers that selling products that are not kosher-for-Passover during the eight days of the festival is an illegal act.

Imposition of religious tenets is not confined to a minority of zealots but applies to the population at large. It has been asserted that the "religious establishment has imposed a certain degree of adherence to Jewish law on all Jews living in Israel" (Swirski and Safir 1991, 11). This alleged encumbrance dates back to 1947, when an agreement (known as the status quo agreement) was signed between David Ben Gurion, Mapai's leader, and religious factions, chief among them the ultra-orthodox Agudat Israel. In his attempt to secure their consent for the establishment of the state, Ben Gurion committed his party to four religious arrangements: first, making Saturday the legal day of rest, on which there was to be no public transportation and no entertainment; second, that every institutional kitchen observe the Jewish dietary laws; third, the separateness and autonomy of the religious school systems; and fourth—most pertinent to this discussion—granting rabbinical courts jurisdiction over laws governing what has been termed as "personal matters."

The justification for the incorporation of religious personal law into Israeli legislation has been that to do otherwise would have "split the people." But these concessions have been sustained throughout statehood for two main reasons: the disproportionate power of religious parties and the dissemination of religious mores. Regarding the first, no party in Israel has ever secured an absolute parliamentary majority, so the relatively flexible stances of the religious parties on foreign policy issues have made them convenient bedfellows in government coalitions. The historical concessions anchored in the status quo agreements have been worthwhile politically. Even a cursory glance at Israel's political history reveals that religious parties have remained outside the coalition only for short periods of time. Even when this has been the case (as it is at the time of writing), the prospects for their inclusion militate against rejection of the status quo arrangements.

Regarding the second reason, this is equally important in inhibiting violation of traditional norms, as the significance of religion in Israeli society emanates not just from calculated agreements between political elites. The Jewish characteristics of the state of Israel have never been seriously challenged. An overwhelming majority of the Jewish population, including ardent socialists and avowed atheists, spurn the solution to the Palestinian-Israel conflict offered by some Palestinian factions, namely, to establish a "democratic secular state" in lieu of Israel. Such a "secular" state would necessarily erase the national-religious nexus prevailing in the country. As noted by Arian (1985, 326) the clamor to separate religion from state is alien both to Jewish history and to the experience of the nations of the Middle East. The religious-national nexus has far-reaching implications for political culture. Religious focus on the individual is a modern

Western notion, prevailing in countries where the majority of the population is Christian. Religion in its traditional form has been a *community* concern. Individuals have been identified through their membership of, or affiliation with, this community. The Jewish faith, for example, discourages prayer in solitude but instead prescribes the formation of a mini-community—a quorum of at least ten male adult Jews.

A majority of Israeli Jews, though far from being orthodox in the conduct of their daily life, have largely absorbed the values of their traditional faith. A recent study (Levi et al. 1993) shows a very high incidence of accommodation with religious norms and practices that can hardly be attributed to any form of legal coercion or political calculation: some four-fifths of the Jews in Israel uphold, to a greater or smaller extent, religious tenets. Traditionalism, as being individually defined, is not linked to age, sex, or length of residence in the country, although it is more prevalent among the less educated. Data reveal a very high proportion of people who celebrate religious holidays: nearly 80 percent "always" participate in a Passover Seder, more than 70 percent light Hanukkah candles and fast on Yom Kippur. When it comes to rituals of the life cycle, the proportion conducting themselves in keeping with religious tradition is preponderant. Circumcision is endorsed by 92 percent of the Jews in Israel, religious burial and mourning, by 91 percent; and finally, and most pertinent here, religious marriage is supported and adhered to by 87 percent of the population. Concern for religious values in not confined to individuals, as the state heavily relied on tradition in justifying the Zionist endeavor. This combination of political exigency and historical heritage, coupled with contemporary mores prevailing among the Israeli public, explains the decisive influence of religious institutions over personal status regulating family matters.

The Regulation of Personal Status

In the formative period of the state, when fundamental norms were established and structures were forged, the state resolved to delegate complete authority in dealing with personal status—

marriage and divorce—to orthodox rabbinical courts. The Marriage and Divorce Law, enacted in 1953, made men and women unequal before the law. Although the Women's Equal Rights Law, passed two years earlier in 1951, entitled women to complete legal equality, the 1953 law explicitly excluded matters of personal status, namely, all issues relating to "prohibition and permission to marry and divorce." The fact that these matters became the exclusive domain of religious jurisdiction has had an adverse effect on women, as the Halakha (Jewish religious law) does not treat men and women as equal human beings. Under the Halakha, the man predominates, having rights superior to those of a woman. Women are described as prattles, irresponsible, light-minded, and frivolous. When a woman is praised, she is described as a good homemaker, and a devoted mother (of sons!). Every morning at prayer the orthodox Jew thanks God for not creating him a woman. The following illustrate the unequal status of women in religious tradition: Only men are counted for the *minyan* (the quorum necessary for prayer); a woman cannot be a member of a rabbinical court, nor can she testify before this court; a woman is not expected to speak at all in public. These measures of inequality do not reflect the original intentions of the religious authorities. For the era in which it was promulgated, religious law exhibited a considerably advanced sensitivity to the need to protect women against male exploitation of their property during marriage or loss of it upon divorce (Raday 1991a, 19). Furthermore, Jewish religion does not prohibit divorce; a divorcee and a widow are allowed, even encouraged, to remarry. In the tenth century a ruling was issued forbidding (Ashkenazi) men to marry more than one wife. Throughout the ages there have been ups and downs in Jewish women's status. All in all, however, the Jewish woman's position in the family, as defined by religious percepts, has considerably deteriorated.

Inequality is evident at the very start of the marriage ceremony. The basic concept of the marriage is "purchase" of the woman by the husband, who takes her as his wife in a unilateral ceremony. A Jewish woman cannot receive a divorce without the consent of her husband, even if she is battered or her husband is missing or insane. Until the husband declares that he is willing to divorce his wife, there is no way in which she may be released from the marriage bond.[7] While a man cannot divorce a woman without her consent either, there are special conditions under which men may remarry, or take a second wife. Religious courts discriminate against women in other ways as well. For example, a man can commit adultery and eventually marry his lover, while a married woman is forbidden ever to marry her lover, and any children born from an extramarital relationship are considered bastards (*mamzerim*). In Judaism a bastard is a pariah. He or she cannot marry unless the potential spouse is also a bastard. Neither can a bastard in Israel marry out of the faith as the exclusive control of marriage by the religious authorities precludes such a possibility. Another infringement on women's rights caused by religious law is the levirate marriage: a woman whose husband dies leaving her childless must be released from her deceased husband's unmarried brother in a ceremony carried out in rabbinical court. Often extortion payments may be involved before she gets her release (Swirski and Safir 1991, 14). Widows of war casualties, often childless young women, have occasionally become trapped in this bizarre situation. Inequality has thus been inscribed both in tradition and in legal regulations. How have women coped with this inequality?

Women's Associations and Personal Status

The Knesset has witnessed several attempts to challenge the orthodox monopoly over personal status. Legislative proposals regarding civil marriage have occasionally been initiated, presented, however, by members of political parties advocating separation of state and religion rather than by members of more established parties. The Civil Rights Movement, in all its parliamentary versions, and the left-wing Mapam have scored high in these attempts. The reason for challenging the status quo was more to combat the violation of "individual liberties" that were subject to the allegedly archaic religious law, than to alleviate women's plight. Proposals to allow civil marriage *beside* the religious ceremony have been rejected outright by the political authorities, first and foremost, because of the threat to coalition stability. Being the apple of the religious parties' eye, control of personal status could not have been compromised to assuage liberal demands. The option of a civil matrimonial ceremony, at least to those individuals ineligible for religious marriage, was also ruled out on grounds of a profound reluctance, on the part of many Israelis, including their legislative representatives, to violate ancient, deeply rooted, norms linking the Jews to their heritage and their community.

Knesset deliberations clearly reflected this mood. Those who took part in debates on the issue, not only orthodox MKs but secular members as well, emphasized the fact that religious marriage and divorce were "the key to the unity of the People of Israel. . . . [D]eep in the heart every person knows that if these [religious] laws will be shaken, Israeli society will be profoundly shaken as well."[8] Knesset members took the opportunity to remind their audience that the family is a pivotal institution. A senior government minister, responding to a legislative proposal aimed at weakening the grip of religious laws over personal status, responded by praising "the sanctity of the family cell, its strength and contribution to the consolidation of Israeli society. The bolts that hold Israeli society are constructed from the robustness of family units."[9] Attempts were also made to trivialize the issue and simply remove it from the public agenda. This mood was reflected in the reaction of the justice minister to a proposal to reformulate regulation of personal status as follows: "I cannot understand the heated controversy. I believe there are problems more important and difficult calling for solution. Israel has more serious challenges to cope with. Believe me, this issue, is not numbered among them."[10] Apparently, a majority of Knesset representatives endorsed existing arrangements authorizing orthodox rabbis to monopolize marriage ceremonies and the granting of divorce. Solutions to individual distress caused by religious statutes, so it was stated, were to be sought within the rabbinical establishment without breaching institutional arrangements nurtured by profound and comprehensive norms.

These circumstances placed severe obstacles before women's ability to influence policy regarding family matters. Women's associations were well aware of the difficulties involved in attacking the issue, buttressed by solid opposition to change. At the same time, the prevailing arrangements, anchored in legal regulations and daily use, constituted a clear violation of women's rights. To reiterate just a few: a woman could not testify in rabbinical courts and was deprived of the basic right to present her case (currently a woman may appear before a rabbinical court but her testimony carries less weight than that of a man); a man is entitled to marry a second wife under specific circumstances (e.g., if his wife is sterile or if she bears only daughters), while no parallel right is granted to a woman; a man's adultery is overlooked, a woman's extramarital affair is severely reprimanded.

Women's associations were between Scylla and Charybdis. On the one hand, they were part and parcel of the very values and norms that upheld the application of religious law to matters of personal status in Israel. On the other, they could not acquiesce to serious violations of women's rights. Consequently, women's groups have attempted to reconcile their striving for women's equality with due respect for the Jewish faith. The strategy they adopted was to fight from within, that is, to cooperate with rabbinical authorities rather than challenge them, in order to reform regulation of personal status. Therefore, women have not contested exclusive rabbinical jurisdiction over marriage and divorce but have insisted on making women equal to men within the confines of this jurisdiction.

Practical steps toward reforming the regulation of personal matters were taken in the early 1980s. Responding to Naamat's pressures and to urging by the prime minister's advisor on women's status, in 1982 the minister of justice nominated a committee, headed by Judge Yaacov Scheinbaum (the Committee for Examining the Implementation of Family Laws), whose goal was to examine legal arrangements regarding all family matters, including alimony, injunctions, child custody, property allotment, and so forth. The declared reason for setting up of the committee was compatible with traditional norms: the suffering of children owing to the cumbersome and lingering processes in the rabbinical courts in dealing with divorce cases.[11] Evidence was presented indicating that on the average litigation between the spouses lasted three years. Feminism, that is, the quest for gender equality, was not even mentioned. One woman—representing WIZO—was among the eight committee members. She was chosen first, because of the close association between WIZO and the Likud's premier, but more importantly, because this women's association, a typical nonfeminist group, was not expected to challenge traditional values regarding personal matters.

In its final report (submitted in March 1987), the Scheinbaum committee recommended, inter alia, the creation of family courts that would operate under the auspices of the district state courts to handle a wide range of domestic personal issues, including child custody, support obligations, and even family violence. Marriage and divorce were, however, to remain the exclusive domain of rabbinical authority. This recommendation aimed at rectifying the division of authority over these issues among the judges of the district, youth, and criminal courts. It was directed more toward administrative reform than to eradicating discrimination against women under religious jurisdiction. It was not a gospel of women's liberation from the shackles of unjust orthodox laws.

The committee's report incorporated principles set forth by Naamat, which was emerging as the major proponent of reforming family laws. Declining to endorse a feminist revolutionary posture, Naamat placed the issue of personal matters at the head of its agenda. Family remained a central theme in Naamat's advocacies because it enabled the association to remain faithful to women's traditional roles while at the same time providing an opportunity to promote women's equality. The match between these goals was perfect for a group that vacillated between two objectives: preserving prevailing political and social structures, on the one hand, and promoting egalitarian principles by advancing women's rights on the other. Mobilization efforts might also profit from the centrality of family in Naamat's advocacies, as the majority of Israeli women, as already noted, do appreciate traditional family values and do practice them, to a greater or lesser extent, in their daily life.

The call to establish family courts was not revolutionary in nature. Setting up these judicial institutions would shorten litigation and would enable women to negotiate more vigorously for their rights. Furthermore, people would still have the option of resorting to religious authorities in all family matters, albeit with the consent of both spouses. The new court system was also geared to enable couples to receive marriage counseling, psychological guidance, and mediation before beginning adversarial proceedings, in the hope of getting them to reconcile, or at least to part amicably.[12] Establishing family courts was thus defined as a means to intensify the role of family in society rather than to release women from its chains. Naamat emphasized that the proposed family courts would not replace the rabbinical courts but supplement them. It further stressed that the proposed change did not constitute a backhanded attempt to introduce civil divorce. To prove these points the association added that the proposal to set up a family court was supported by orthodox individuals because of its conciliatory potential on the one hand, and the suffering and foot-dragging, often caused by multiple judicial processes, on the other. In a document entitled "Letter to the Member," the Naamat secretary-general reemphasized the group's adherence to traditional norms: "We in Naamat believe that the majority of the Jewish population in the country is not detached from Jewish tradition, and is ready to accept traditional values regarding marriage and divorce, as well as in other life domains."[13]

Despite the traditional overtones embedded in the proposal to establish a family court, and despite the fact that it was endorsed by a committee comprising traditional and even orthodox members, and appointed by a conservative government, the recommendations have remained a dead letter and have never been implemented. When a motion of order was raised in the Knesset, inquiring what had become of the committee's recommendations,[14] the justice minister replied that he had appointed another committee to devise means for implementation. Repeated appeals by Naamat to the minister have been abortive. No steps have ever been taken to carry out the intention to establish family courts. Insisting on raising the issue on the Knesset agenda, a woman MK, who previously served as Naamat's secretary-general, tabled ten bills designed to implement the Scheinbaum committee's report.[15] These proposals vanished into thin air as no further legislative action was taken. Apparently the subject was shelved and dropped from the agenda. In 1993 Naamat attempted to revive the issue by adopting it as a major theme of "Women's Status Month." Its efforts were hampered by a judicial decision. The Supreme Court, dealing with the issue in response to a religious plaintiff, disqualified Naamat's proposal, asserting that the demand to establish family courts could undermine the authority of the rabbinical judicial system.[16] The entry into office of new chief rabbis in September 1993 reopened a window for reforming family jurisdiction, as a joint rabbinate–women's associations committee was established. The incoming chief rabbi stated that "concerning *agunot* [singular *aguna*, a woman whose husband has disappeared without divorcing her] and those refused divorce there are no two sides. I am willing to protest with the women and carry the placard."[17]

Notwithstanding this public statement, the chief rabbi was not seen in demonstrations protesting women's disability in family law. Other women's associations did join the campaign, evincing unprecedented unity. WIZO was a natural partner as family matters have always been prominent on its agenda. The position of the Women's Network was more equivocal. Initially, the association was reluctant to take a clear stand on the issue of family matters. When asked to delegate members to a forum on rabbinical courts, the WN recommended that members of Naamat and WIZO be included and not its own members.[18] Subsequently, however, the network took firm measures to establish its presence in the campaign to reform family laws. A special subcommittee for personal matters was formed (in June 1988), which seemed resolved to establish an alliance with other women's associations, including, among others, Naamat, WIZO, and Emuna. It further decided to focus on the problem of *agunot*.

The plight of these women captured wide public attention. Being innocent victims, totally dependent on the whims of obstinate and often cruel, inconsiderate husbands, these deserted women aroused compassion and sympathy. The suffering of *agunot* has been widely acknowledged, even penetrating to some rabbinical circles. Women's associations might save these victims of gender discrimination. Centering its activity on the problem of *agunot* enabled the Women's Network to escape internal controversy. As a home base for ardent proponents of civil rights as well as for the zealously orthodox, WN did not challenge outright religious jurisdiction over personal matters and declined to adopt a strict feminist stance. It even refused to include the option of civil marriage in its agenda. Network activists emphasized that attempts to solve the problem of *agunot* absolutely did not contradict, or compete with, Jewish religious law. The WN, however, demanded, that justice be done to women subject to the inequity of rigid religious ruling. The wide agreement on the plight of the *agunot* made possible the formation (in January 1993) of a wall-to-wall coalition, Ikar (a Hebrew word meaning "the most important matter"), including all kinds of women's associations. Among the activists in Ikar were feminist grassroots movements, religious women's associations (Emuna) and of course the major women's associations. This comprehensive mobilization was based on the agreement to "cooperate with the rabbinical institutions in order to forge possible solutions" and to confine demands for legislation to matters outside the jurisdiction of religious law.

Bearing in mind the wide consensus around the issue, the major strategy was to expand support. Several steps were taken to this effect. First, a Knesset lobby, headed by a law professor, MK David Libai, was established to press for legislation.[19] Second, an attempt was made to incorporate rabbinical authorities in the search for a just solution to the misery of *agunot*. As the goal was not to impose new rules on religious authorities but to persuade them to accommodate existing ones to alleviate women's distress, two measures were proposed. First, to introduce a legislative amendment declaring desertion of wives a criminal offense, and second, to establish a rabbinical court specially to deal with *agunot*. This proposal (submitted by Etya Simha, the prime minister's advisor on women's status) was rejected by women's associations, unwilling to grant the rabbinical judicial system the authority it failed to apply justly in the past. Instead, it was proposed that the District Court be authorized to declare a person "marriage hindered,"[20] a proposal supported by both the government and rabbinical authorities.[21] The former favored such legislation because it would correct to a serious injustice; the latter, because it would enhance and widen the authority of rabbinical courts, as in the existing situation the only recourse against those refusing to

grant a divorce was imprisonment. The expansion of legal penalties would not infringe religious law but in fact strengthen it.

Together with the problem of *agunot*, other malpractice by
the rabbinical judicial system were challenged. Calls for sweeping reform were voiced loud and clear. Taking disciplinary
measures against inefficiency and foot-dragging, including
women among the judges and allowing women a wider access
to deliberations were part of the demanded reforms. At the time
of writing no legislative or other practical steps have been taken
to solve the problem of *agunot* or other inequities involved in
orthodox jurisdiction over personal matters.

A heated controversy over family matters recently erupted in
the wider context of civil rights in Israel. In 1992 attempt was
made to anchor civil liberties in a Basic Law amounting to a
comprehensive bill of rights.[22] One article (21a), however, violated
these rights by perpetuating religious jurisdiction over personal
status. A wall-to-wall coalition of women's associations presented
solid opposition to the proposed bill, asserting that "There are no
human [Adam's] rights without Eve's rights." "A Magna Carta
for civil liberties in Israel cannot exclude half the population."
The slogans captured wide support among women. Although the
law did not suggest regulations cutting down existing women's
rights (or rather wrongs), it nevertheless threatened to confirm
the odious status quo. In their opposition to the civil rights law,
the women's associations had strange bedfellows: orthodox parties opposed all legislation thwarting the Jewish character of the
state.[23] Adoption of a comprehensive civil rights law could, and
probably would, reduce religious influence on political and social
life in Israel. Coalition politics took its toll, this time to the advantage of women, as the government yielded to pressures opposing
the adoption of the civil rights law and removed it, perhaps temporarily, off the legislative agenda.

Economic Aspects: Women as Family Heads

Family life styles acquire particular importance in regard to state
supported income, as the norms regulating allowances are not
equal for men and women.[24] Twice, however, women's disad-

vantage has been rectified regarding alimony and support for women heading single-parent families. In both cases women were portrayed as intimidated individuals, meriting state protection. In both cases women's associations played a leading role in triggering public policy.

The Alimony Law (1971)

Although the rate of divorce in Israel is lower compared to that common in other Western societies, many women who are still legally married suffer severe economic disadvantages. The situation is aggravated when the husband does not fulfill his duty to pay the alimony imposed by the court. Reportedly, a high proportion of married men failed to support their families before divorce was granted or after legal proceedings were completed. Often a husband would stop payment, secure in the knowledge that it would take a long time before the police would act and possibly years before the courts ruled. Since the penalties for breach of promise are relatively light, it was also not unusual for a husband to opt for a short prison term rather than pay his former wife a sizable portion of his monthly income.

On 1 October 1971 a law was passed (Alimony Law [Security Payment]—1971) whose purpose was to ensure that a divorced woman should receive her alimony through the National Insurance Institute from the moment the husband reneged. The state agency was vested with two powers: first, to pay the woman the sum she was entitled to; second, to take legal action against the recalcitrant husband. In the Knesset debate, a woman's right to equality was mentioned, but the emphasis was on her vulnerability, and on the advantage taken by an inconsiderate husband of his former wife's feebleness. Likewise, women were depicted as facing difficulties in dealing with the Executor Office, in charge of forcing the husband to comply. As on previous occasions, the discussion centered on the harm done to children, having to witness their parents entangled in legal battles and potentially violent confrontations. The state undertook not only to ensure women minimum economic subsistence, but also to represent them in court and to mediate between them and law-enforcing agencies.

One women's association, WIZO, played a crucial role in initiating the law and pushing it forward to legislation and implementation. Presenting the bill in the Knesset, the justice minister (Yaacov Shimshon Shapira) reminded his audience, at some length, that it was WIZO's Family Council Bureau that supplied the version upon which the law was drafted. Two previous attempts to advance the bill through the mediation of women MKs (in 1966 and in 1968) had not been productive. Party rivalry might have contributed to stalling the legislative process. Evidently, women's interests did not take precedence in the women MKs' political agenda. Only when the association approached the Justice Ministry directly, without the mediation of parliamentary representatives, was the proposal placed on the legislative track.[25] Despite its acknowledged contribution to drafting the law, WIZO's request for representation on the Labor Court whose jurisdiction covered alimony was denied outright.[26]

WIZO did not disguise its legislative campaign in traditional arguments, but clearly perceived the alimony issue as a lever for the promotion of women's status. In a memorandum presenting the draft of the bill, the association emphasized that alimony "is a right, not an indulgence." Further attempts to deprive women whose husbands did not have the means to pay alimony of the law's protection were met by fierce, and united, opposition by women's associations.

Single-Parent Families

Gender inequality is prominent in regard to single parent families, which until recently were anathema to public authorities. A "single-parent family" is defined as a situation where one parent raises a child in his or her home. These include widows, divorcees, unwed mothers, and *agunot*. The proportion of the households characterized as single-parent families, albeit on the increase, is smaller than in other Western societies. According to recent data, only five percent of households in Israel are headed by one parent, 85 percent of these, however, by the mother. About half of the single-parent families are headed by a divorcee; about a quarter by widows; the remaining quarter consists women who have never married. In contrast with the United States, where 20 percent of all births are out of wedlock, only 1.6 percent of all women who gave birth in 1992 were unmarried (Statistical Abstracts 1993, 141). The incidence of single-parent families is high among immigrants from the former Soviet Union, only part of whom have yet been included in official statistics.

Women who head a family face several difficulties.[27] In addition to the hardship involved in raising "fatherless" children, they generally suffer from low social and economic status. Many, especially divorced wives, encounter economic losses. It has been reported that 78 percent of single-parent families live on an income lower than the average.[28] Others, while more affluent, still suffer from social deprivation. The centrality of family in Israeli society takes its toll on single-parent families, whose heads are often alienated and suffer from a sense of lesser worth. Many heads of single-parent families experience anger, frustration, and helplessness in view of their new, often unplanned status.

On 17 March 1992 the Knesset adopted the Single-Parent Families Law, providing benefits such as priority in vocational training; priority in acceptance to daycare facilities; an enlarged state loan for housing. A single parent (of a child younger than seven) is also entitled to 40 percent of the average income and a schooling grant (at a rate 18 percent of the average wage) for every child between the ages of six and eleven. Women's associations played a leading role in formulating the bill. Senior civil servants were very supportive, but the legislative process was sparked by Naamat. Attention was drawn to the problem by a *father* whose wife died in childbirth. Naamat responded by establishing a subassociation catering to the needs of single-parent families. Opposition to the move was waged by religious circles, who objected only to one provision: the entitlement of *agunot* and unwed mothers to the law's benefits. The National Insurance Institute attempted to overestimate the financial rewards to the women of the proposed law. All these controversies were settled, however, prior to the legislative process. The law supporting single-parent families, that is, mothers in distress, was passed unanimously by the Knesset, bearing the distinct fingerprints of the women's associations.

Violence in the Family

The term "violence in the family" has been used as a code word for wife-battering, a common practice that cuts across geographical, cultural, economic, and political boundaries. No accurate data are available regarding the scope of violence in the family in Israel. It has been estimated, however, that every seventh woman in the country is subject, in the course of her life, to physical violence of one sort or another. Yet not until the late 1980s did the subject attract serious political attention. Violence in the family may serve as a good example for the "mobilization of bias," described by Bachrach and Baratz (1962), occurring when dominant values, myths, and established political institutions inhibit the processing of an issue and its formulation into policy guidelines. Violence in the family was hushed up because it was incompatible with the family halo. As noted by Freedman (1991, 101), "the walls of denial are especially thick around family concerns." This was particularly true of violence, the shameful secrets of family life, secrets that Israel has a vested interest in disguising.

The first public mention of wife-battering in Israel occurred in 1962, when the secretary-general of the Women Workers' Movement, MK Beba Idelson, put a parliamentary question to the police minister, inquiring if his ministry was aware of the phenomenon.[29] The minister attempted to assuage women by asserting that the police were coping with the problem and that he saw no need for any further action. Smoothed over in these reassuring terms, the issue was shelved, and was not resubmitted to the parliamentary agenda for some fifteen years. In 1976 Marcia Freedman, the feminist MK, presented a motion of order before the Knesset's plenum on wife-battering. According to her testimony, even the feminist leader of her own party, the Civil Rights Movement, opposed bringing it up. The latter's office, Freedman charged, had a standard reply to letters from battered women: "We do not interfere in matters between him and her" (Freedman 1990, 101). Nobody wanted to hear about wife-beating. The common notion was that "Jews do not beat their wives." Treating it as a private family affair, police authorities did not intervene; political authorities paid no heed. In reply to

Freedman's motion, the police minister said: "I cannot say that there is a specific issue of violence inflicted by men against their wives." For him, beating women was like pushing and shoving to get on the bus. There was no need for authoritative intervention.[30] In fact, wife-battering was subject to ridicule: "Why this discrimination? Why aren't we discussing women who beat their husbands?" asked an MK. A woman MK castigated Freedman for not talking about "spousal" abuse. The issue triggered emotional reactions, as the heckling never stopped throughout Freedman's speech. In view of the wide opposition, the issue was expected to be struck from the Knesset agenda. However, in a rare breach of party discipline, all women MKs had voted against killing the motion. The downfall of the Labor Party ended the deliberation process, which never took off anyway.[31]

In the early 1980s the definition of wife-battering was still compatible with traditional images. Social agencies tended to view it as part of "the dynamics of interaction" between spouses, and to blame the woman for not satisfying her husband's needs. Women were advised to "take tranquilizers" and were granted welfare payments. Even when men were summoned to a police station, the investigation took the form of a "man to man" talk, and the husband understood he had nothing to fear; the police would not prosecute. In the few cases in which the police did open a criminal file on the husband, little effort was made to bring the case to trial (Swirski 1991, 322–23).

Toward the late 1980s the veil of silence was broken. Women's associations contributed to the airing of the violence issue in four different ways. First (chronologically), legal counseling was given to women subject to violence; WIZO was the first association to operate legal bureaus (Freedman 1990, 102).[32] Other women's groups followed suit. Second, women decided to act rather than to talk. The Feminist Movement paved the way by creating a shelter for battered women in Haifa in 1977. Subsequently, other shelters were established by local feminists.[33] This pioneering activity had repercussions: (*a*) the issue of violence against women became a focal point for feminist activity, with spin-offs in the form of centers combating all types of violence against women; (*b*) the shelters won the issue official recognition and legitimacy. The Ministry of Welfare provided funds without awaiting for legislation. Working with other ministries, welfare authorities obtained housing subsidies, counseling services, and medical insurance for battered women. Raising public consciousness had an impact on the police as well, as new procedures for dealing with complaints were instituted. There was a considerable rise in the number of husbands arrested on charges of violence against their wives. A study of shelters has shown that they also helped to reduce wife-battering among violence-prone families (Epstein and Marder 1986). Naamat, faithful to its traditional perceptions, defined the issue in sociopsychological terms. It demanded in a letter addressed to the minister of justice (dated 11 August 1986) that violent husbands be compelled to see a therapist, and that police personnel be granted the status of probation officers acting as social workers' surrogates. Education was thus deemed a major means for curbing violence rather than a legal penalty. In April 1983 a Center for Counseling on Violence in the Family, headed by a criminologist, was established at Naamat's headquarters with great fanfare. All these efforts were widely acknowledged by an official document issued by a Knesset subcommittee on violence in the family. The subcommittee appealed to women to increase their activity, and to the Welfare Ministry to assist them.[34]

The third contribution to the problem of battered wives centered on the provision of information. Naamat was also engaged in a comprehensive fact-finding effort collecting data on the scope of the problem. The results were incorporated in a motion of order presented by MK Ora Namir (Labor), which caused commotion among Knesset members. The survey, conducted among a national sample of Jewish Israelis, revealed how widespread the problem was. Apparently wife-battering was not confined to marginal citizens with origins in less developed countries. In fact, nearly half of the battered wives were born in Israel; 17.3 percent held academic degrees; some 22 percent were professionals. One of the significant findings was that a majority of beaten wives (63.4 percent) never filed a complaint; in 60 percent of the cases no legal measures were taken against the perpetrator of violence. The study also revealed that more than a third of the respondents did not deem wife-battering to be a legal offense.[35] Although a large proportion of the population (some 80 percent) did not vindicate such behavior; yet only one in five thought some circumstances justified wife-beating. Legislators were influenced by these facts. A direct encounter of members of the Knesset's Committee on Labor and Welfare with battered women finding refuge in a public shelter precipitated the legislative process.

Finally, the women's movement, particularly WN, played a leading role in providing legal assistance to state authorities and clearing the way for formulating public policy. In February 1988 the Women's Network set up a subcommittee to recommend legislation. While advocating stringent legal measures against perpetrators, the most important of which would make it mandatory for the violent husband to leave his home, it expanded the issue, seeking support in the Civil Rights Association. WN prompted the Justice Ministry to appoint a committee, headed by a senior attorney (the Karp committee), instructed to formulate legislation on violence in the family. The establishment in 1988 of Bat Adam (Hebrew for Adam's daughter), a coalition of women's associations joining forces "in order to produce effective communication, power, public awareness, and cooperation among the 25 associations active in this field," consolidated efforts on behalf of battered women and gave the issue the visibility required for public policy-making. The bane of battered wives made possible the formation of a wall-to-wall coalition, the first in the history of women's political activity in Israel.

On 19 March 1991 the first reading of the law for the prevention of violence in the family took place in the Knesset. The debate reflected an all-round consensus and a scrupulous desire to bring the legislation to a successful conclusion. The proposer (Avraham Burg, Labor) commended the "thoroughness, serenity, speed, business-like attitude, and active participation of the Knesset committee members."[36] Even religious MKs, who invariably opposed any legislation aimed at women's equality, demonstrated supportive stances. Their endorsement of the law was made possible by the definition of the matter stated by a religious MK: "The status of the battered wife is vulnerable both in the family in society at large. The woman is deeply anxious and fears for the physical and mental well-being of herself and her children. As she is usually dependent on her husband for her living expenses and caring for her children, her resistance to violence is seriously hampered, and her sense of helplessness rises."[37]

The description of women as weak, lesser human beings struck a responsive chord in the Israeli legislators. In one of debates devoted to the issue an ultra-orthodox MK proposed to establish "work camps" and the enforced abandonment by men of violence. Furthermore, the issue was removed from the domain of women and was given a wider definition in terms of "family welfare." It was cloaked in "ancient Jewish values" and presented as a matter of compassion rather than one of fundamental human justice.

The embodiment of these images made possible both the inclusion of women's associations in the legislative process and the relatively smooth processing of the bill combating violence in the family. The law approved by the Knesset accurately meets women's demands. It extends the definition of violence from physical brutality to mental or sexual abuse. The perpetrator of violence may be removed by a court order from his residence and is forbidden to trouble the subject of violence in any way. *Locus standi* is granted to a legal advisor, a family member, and a welfare worker. Although the demand of the women's associations for their own recognition as legal representatives was again rejected, a wide opening was made for them to take part in implementation. A Council for Battered Women was established by the Welfare Ministry, in which women's groups are amply represented. In addition, these groups continue to provide legal aid to individual women and to administer public shelters, to train volunteers, and to operate emergency lines. Being directly involved in the battle against violence, women's groups (particularly the Women's Network) also have drawn attention to obstacles in the way of implementation.[38]

In conclusion, all parties involved claimed copyright on the legislative initiative. Naamat issued a press statement recalling its role in the process; the Women's Network insisted that its team was responsible for phrasing the law's provisions; Judith Karp, a senior attorney in the Justice Ministry and chairperson of the committee that gave the final impetus to the law, stated (in a private communication) that it was she who drew the minister's attention to the problem; and MK Avraham Burg, who submitted the issue to the Knesset, claimed that combating violence against women had always been part and parcel of his political agenda. With so many eager parents it is little wonder that the problem of wife-battering has not remained an orphan. Instead it has been formulated, albeit belatedly, into comprehensive public policy. That violence against women has been subject to policy deliberation does not imply that the problem has been resolved as wife-battering (and even killing) continues to be reported.[39] Yet the problem is no longer subject to bias, which for some three decades obviated state attention.

Conclusion

Public policy regarding the family has centered on three major issues: personal status, that is, matrimonial situation, economic issues, and violence in the family. These, however, were differently regulated. The state surrendered to the rabbinical courts all jurisdiction over marriage and divorce. It has held steadfast to its alliance with the religious authorities regarding personal status not only because of coalition considerations but mainly because any change would have jeopardized the delicate balance that has been achieved in Israel between the orthodox and the secular. Furthermore, the issue of personal status touches on one of the most sensitive nerves of Israeli society, the national-religious nexus.

Women have not seriously challenged the devolution of power to religious institutions concerning marital status. Some efforts have been made to make life easier for some women, subject to severe and unmistakable injustice, but these have not matched, in their scope and intensity, those made on behalf of other issues. The flag on which the Jewish heritage is inscribed overrode the feminist banner. Women have attempted to ally with establishment forces and persuade them from within to change the course of family policy, but so far with little success. Had women's rights taken precedence over religious mores imbued in national sentiments, women would have grappled with the issue of personal affairs much more relentlessly. Division of family property, though also regulated by religious ruling, was not sanctified as an overarching principle. Its reformation involved no threat to the integrity and wholeness of the Jewish people. Already in the early 1970s a radical legislative change was introduced, enabling women to enjoy the economic fruits of a marriage.

The case of violence against women has revealed both the vulnerability and the fortunes of women's associations in Israel. The issue demonstrated how the presentation of women as frail and lesser individuals may pave the way for state intervention on their behalf. Patriarchal practices were unmistakably evident. But turning the personal into the political was made possible precisely when the process did not harbor feminist messages. Assaulting women was defined in negative terms because it is detrimental to the fulfillment of their traditional roles as homemakers and child bearers. Women's associations showed that concerted lobbying activity can be extremely effective if and when it does not challenge fundamental social norms.

CHAPTER 8

Body Politics: The Right to Life and Its Challengers

In a family-centered society like Israel, the question of the right to life could never have remained a private matter, but was bound to become subject to public regulation. As noted, an overwhelming majority of Israelis, women and men, favor granting women the right to decide whether to carry the fetus to birth or to terminate pregnancy. This view is not reflected in public policy regulating abortion. The problem of abortion exemplifies the most profound values of Israeli society. It highlights the clash of ideologies between the major political parties, Labor and Likud; it displays the decisive impact of religious norms and institutions on issues pertaining mostly to the secular population; it presents demographic and economic aspects of Israeli society in a period of rapid social change. In short, the abortion issue throws into relief many facets of politics and society, with one glaring exception: the status of women regarding their reproductive freedom.

The abortion issue has risen high on the political agenda of Western democracies in the twenty past years. Interest groups have mushroomed, crowds have been mobilized, public campaigns launched, and political authorities prodded to take action and expand reproductive choices. Almost irrespective of the political environment, the demand to repeal restrictions on abortion has resounded in many societies. The comment has been made that "equality, emancipation or improvement in women's conditions became empty words when something apparently as trivial as a contraceptive mishap could totally ruin a women's future" (Outshoorn 1988, 207). Imposing the absolute duty of maternity on a woman was seen as denying her free will and judgment in matters affecting her own life. A woman's right to decide to terminate her pregnancy has turned into a symbol of women's liberation and its clash with the male political establishment. The debate over women's control of their own bodies has come to be seen as a one over the place and role of women in society. Although not all women seek "freedom," a substantial proportion of women in Western societies have regarded the issue of reproductive choice as grounded in a "right to bodily self-determination." Abortion, as one of the leading feminists has phrased it, "is the fulcrum of a much broader ideological struggle in which the very meaning of the family, the state, motherhood, and young woman's sexuality are contested" (Petchesky 1990, 295). Reproductive choice has been perceived as "the definitive issue of contemporary feminism" (Randall 1987, 263).

The feminist definition, however, is not the only one qualifying the issue of abortion. At least five additional perspectives may be discerned, each bearing on the question from its own distinct angle. First, the social perspective defines abortion in terms of entitlements granted under the auspices of the welfare state. Countries committed to their citizens' welfare tend to adopt a social outlook that regards abortion as a service supplied by the state within the context of its broad social undertaking (Heckscher 1985, 49–50). The right to terminate pregnancy is akin to the right to health care and other welfare entitlements. Second, the religious definition of the issue derives from theological arguments that conception is the beginning of life, and abortion constitutes a form of infanticide (Schwarz 1990). The proponents of a religious definition oppose abortion not because it is harmful to a woman but because it is incompatible with their fundamental beliefs about life and death. Third, the libertarian perspective sees abortion in terms of human rights, that is, the liberty of all individuals to act as they wish and to make their own choices within the confines of the law. That the citizens affected by abortion policy happen to be women is irrelevant. The fourth perspective is the medical one. Termination of pregnancy requires an invasive medical procedure. It may be justified or not, depending on the woman's medical record. As a health-connected issue, abortion has to be allowed and performed on the basis of medical considerations only, and in compliance with strict medical standards, regardless of any other social or ideological stipulations. The fifth, and final, perceptive is the demographic one. When abortion is defined in terms of demographic needs, it becomes a tool of population policy. Faced with population decline, for example, nations tend to restrict abortion. The Rumanian experience shows how a government can use abortion regulations as a means of encouraging a higher birth rate. The People's Republic of China demonstrated the opposite, as abortion has served as a means for population control: it is mandatory for any woman who already has one child. Which of these six perspectives, including the feminist one, has been adopted by state authorities and by the women themselves?

Public policy regarding abortion reflects authoritative attitudes toward two aspects of the issue: individual choice and the state's commitment to allowing this choice. The first aspect concerns the academic degree of reproductive freedom available to a woman. Some measure of freedom is allowed in a majority of countries around the world, though the extent is often predicated on a set of conditions, such as fetal age, the woman's age, genetic considerations, and the woman's health (Tietze and Henshaw 1986, 12–14). The greatest degree of freedom, in the present context, allows a woman to terminate her pregnancy strictly on the basis of subjective considerations. Examples range from wishing to postpone childbearing in order to obtain an academic degree to the simple desire not to be pregnant at a given time. The second aspect regards the extent to which the state is committed, through funding and health care facilities, to implementing individual choice by making abortion available to all women, regardless of economic level. At stake is the state's disposition to facilitate abortion, not merely to permit it. Both aspects embody normative considerations about human relations; both reflect principles shaped by fundamental social values.

The combined application of the choice and commitment aspects to a state's abortion policy yields four basic types of public policy: first, facilitation, when the state grants freedom of choice and also provides the means to implement this choice. Sweden provides a good example of a country in which the facilitation principle was gradually introduced. In that country abortion is available on demand. As termination of pregnancy is conducted within the framework of the comprehensive national health care services, the state has full responsibility for granting access (Sundstrom-Feigenberg 1988). The second type of public policy is restriction. This is the case where the state both denies private discretion and discourages implementation. Under restrictive circumstances the state has monopolistic control of the articulation of the demand of its execution. The most striking example of restrictive policy in democratic societies is provided by the Republic of Ireland, where abortion is banned even when a woman's life is endangered by her pregnancy (Randall 1986). The third type of policy, hindering, is evident when the state grants individual choice but provides no facilities for implementation. The United States presents a vivid illustration of a hindering abortion policy as the state has acknowledged the right of a private person to make her own reproductive decisions, but at the same time has not committed itself to assisting the woman to act upon this decision (Rubin 1987; Tribe 1990).

The fourth and final type of abortion policy is intrusion. This is the case where the state limits individual discretion but is committed to implementing authorized (that is, legal) abortions. An intrusive policy is more likely to evolve in a country where the government tends to patronize citizens and to meddle in their private affairs by subjecting individual choice to authoritative scrutiny and approval. Israel neatly fits this category (Yishai 1993b). The following discussion will set out the forms of state intrusion into reproductive freedom and women's reaction to it. It will show that even though Israeli public opinion has been supportive of liberalizing abortion, women's associations were initially reluctant to endorse a comprehensive stance supporting freedom of choice. In the second phase of the abortion policy-making, however, women did challenge attempts made by the state to intrude into individual discretion by hindering abortion further.

Liberalization of Abortion

Until the 1970s abortion was regulated by paragraphs 175 and 177 of the Criminal Code Ordinance of 1936 in the legislation Mandatory Palestine, based on a British anti-abortion law of 1861. Under this law procurement of an abortion was defined as a criminal offense for both the operator and the woman undergoing the operation. When health was at stake, the attitude was more lax. Although the conditions under which abortion might be allowed—safeguarding the woman's life or health—were not spelled out in the law, in practice such considerations were not unlawful. In 1966 an amendment was made clarifying that a woman who procured her own miscarriage was not criminally liable. In practice, the prohibition against abortions was a dead letter as they were extensively performed, and prosecutions were not brought, in accordance with the declared policy of the then attorney general Haim Cohen (Raday 1991b, 27). Significantly, although abortion constituted a criminal act, it was doubtless employed extensively as a method of birth control (Friedlander 1974). The operation was performed at public health institutions and at private clinics (Peled and Bakman 1978) with a tacit consent of health authorities.

For more than two decades after the establishment of the state of Israel abortion remained illegal but was practiced. This changed in the early 1970s, when termination of pregnancy became a political issue. In June 1971, Uri Avneri, the sole MK representing a marginal radical party (Haolam Haze),[1] submitted to the Knesset a private member's bill aimed at allowing the minister of health to issue regulations governing abortion, which would be elective. In his Knesset speech the initiator adopted the medical perspective. A week before he submitted the bill, a woman had died after an unsuccessful abortion. Although the operation was performed in a hospital, medical treatment was inadequate. The physician performing the abortion was unable to convince the court he acted to save the woman's life and was sentenced to one year's imprisonment. The court criticized the existing legal sanctions, suggesting that "legislative institutions should consider the provisions dealing with abortions and should adjust them to suit reality and current circumstances in order to prevent disastrous consequences." Avneri was inspired by this verdict, claiming that by removing abortions from the realm of illegal darkness and by granting them full legal acknowledgment such accidents could be avoided. Avneri elaborated on the theme of reproductive choice but did not insist that this formulation be adopted by the Knesset. He urged the legislature to consider his proposal allowing abortion on medical grounds. His definition of this, though, was comprehensive, including "physical, psychological, and social welfare."[2]

The proposal to liberalize abortion on medical grounds encountered wall-to-wall opposition. The minister of health, himself a member of a radical socialist party (Mapam), highlighted the national theme. After acknowledging the medical aspects of abortion, he remarked: "Nevertheless, Members of Knesset, a question ought to be asked: Is seeking abortion only the woman's private affair or that of her family? Does not this issue bear implications for society at large? I indeed think it is a major problem. So when we are asked to determine our position all aspects of the issue and its consequences should be taken into consideration."[3] To drive home his words the minister quoted a story from the French *L'Expres* revealing the great remorse and humiliation a woman had experienced after aborting her eighth child. Repeal of abortion liberalization in Rumania sustained his arguments opposing a radical legal change. Concluding that abortion ought to reflect the unique social reality and national imperatives of the country in question, the minister proposed the establishment of a ministerial committee composed of experts and public figures to study the issue. Note that not one single female voice was heard during this Knesset debate, which proceeded intermittently in 1971 and 1972.

Actually, "study" was not the sole purpose for the appointment at the committee, since by selecting people of various backgrounds whose views were publicly known the minister anticipated its conclusions, which would have cleared the way for appropriate legislation (Yishai 1978a). Within two years the committee submitted its report, which served as the basis for the government's legislative proposal regarding the liberalization of abortion. But the government proposal was not the only one put on the Knesset agenda. A second version, submitted in the form of a private member's bill, was submitted as well. The difference between the two proposals was remarkable. The first, a state-sponsored motion, reflected deeply rooted social norms; the privately sponsored bill expressed a feminist mood. The government version stipulated that abortions would continue to be illegal unless seven specified conditions were fulfilled:

a. The woman was under the legal age of marriage (17) or over 40;

b. The pregnancy resulted from a non-marital relationship or an illicit act;

c. The fetus was suspected to be malformed;

d. Continuing the pregnancy may endanger the woman's life or health;

e. Family or social conditions (economic conditions of the woman or her family, presence of numerous or very young children, etc.) dictated an abortion;

f. A committee, consisting of an obstetrician-gynecologist, a second doctor (psychiatrist or internist) and a social worker (on December 1979 it was decided that at least one member of every abortion committee must be a woman), approved the request for abortion;

g. The abortion would be performed in a recognized, state authorized medical institution. (Falk 1978; Sabatello and Yaffe 1988)

The second, feminist proposal cited "the basic human right of deciding whether or not to bring a child into the world." Accordingly, any woman would have the right to ask her physician to terminate her pregnancy within the first twelve weeks.[4]

The two legislative proposals were thus diametrically opposed: whereas the first, official version suggested strict state control over who may terminate pregnancy (intrusive policy), the second espoused freedom of choice, within the first trimester of pregnancy (facilitation policy). The government proposal viewed the matter primarily from the demographic perspective; the proposal tabled privately adopted the fledgling feminist perspective.

Demography has acquired a salient position on Israel's political agenda. Unlike many other new countries, Israel did not encounter a problem of excessive population growth. In fact, increasing the size of the Jewish population and establishing a decisive Jewish majority was considered to be vital to the country's political future. Surrounded by millions of Arabs, it was deemed essential to increase the Jewish presence in the area. The influx of Jews to their ancient homeland could have mitigated the demographic problem. Immigration was not only the *raison d'être* of the Zionist endeavor but a major source of Jewish population growth. The state's high regard for immigration was manifested in a variety of public policies: one of the first laws passed by the Knesset was the Law of Return, encouraging every Jew to settle in Israel with the assistance of the state. The law gave formal expression to public sentiment and provided a legal basis for a pro-immigration policy. The impact of immigration on population growth in the first years of statehood was indeed impressive (Ben Porath 1986), but the influx of Jews has gradually dwindled over the years. Consequently, parents were called on to fulfill their "demographic duty" to the nation and to increase the size of their families (Friedlander 1974, 53). Even left-wing parties were sympathetic to the idea. In his memoirs David Ben Gurion, the Labor Party's leader and the founding father of the state, asserted that "every Jewish mother can and must understand that the unique situation of the Jewish people, not only in Israel but throughout the world . . . imposes on her a sacred duty to do her utmost for the nation's rapid growth. One of the conditions for growth is that every family have at least four sons and daughters—and the more the better" (Ben Gurion 1971, 839). This mood generated a public policy. A Natality Committee appointed by the prime minister recommended (in 1966) a series of measures to encourage fertility. In 1968 the government established a Demographic Center whose main objective was "to produce an atmosphere and conditions to encourage fertility." In 1987 a foundation of millions of dollars was created to encourage Jews to have more children.[5] The positive attitude toward fertility culminated in a statement made by a senior politician, at the opening of the National Conference of the Family Planning Association whose purpose was to encourage fertility: "This conference is about those who are unable to fulfill the supreme command given to humanity" (quoted in Solomon 1991, 103). A cardinal commandment in Judaism is "Be fruitful and multiply" (Genesis 1, 28). According to Jewish law a woman's infertility justifies divorce and a childless woman may find herself a social outcast. The pro-natal outlook has thus been sustained by a wide set of sociopolitical conditions. The opportunities afforded women to have babies (including reproductive technology) have widely expanded.

Indiscriminatory incentives for population growth, however, could lead to the aggravation of another social problem: high birth rates among the poor. Among Ashkenazi women of European origin family size was on the order of 2.5 children per woman between 1965 and 1969. In the same period the fertility rate for Jewish women of Afro-Asian origin was far higher, namely, 4.4 children per woman (Statistical Abstracts 1989, 131–32). The large family had already been identified as a social risk group in the 1960s. While such families represented only 10 percent of all Jewish households, they raised some 40 percent of Israel's children, frequently under conditions of poverty and distress. In the early 1970s the country was stunned by violent demonstrations by a group identifying itself as the "Black Panthers." Comprising young people of Moroccan origin living in distress neighborhoods, the demonstrators, at one fell swoop, placed the issue of poverty, until them pushed aside, on the political agenda. The authorities responded by appointing a public committee, the Prime Minister's Committee for Youth in Distress, to look into the problems of the underprivileged.

The committee's report confirmed the association between family size and distress. It recommended that immediate measures be taken to prevent unwanted pregnancies, and to limit the size of families whose fertility had proven to be a social burden by allowing legal abortions. The committee also revealed a linkage between ethnic origin and social deprivation. Most of the poor people had come to Israel from Afro-Asian countries. They were caught in a vicious cycle of poverty, low education and income levels, and overcrowded and dilapidated housing conditions (Roter and Shmai 1971). The children's chances of escaping from the poverty cycle were slight, given their depressed living standards. This reality stood in sharp contrast to the pro-birth policy professed by the state. The association between family size and distress was perceived to threaten the quality of future generations with possible grave effects on the development of the state. So although the importance of a higher birth rate for the Jewish people as a whole was consistently invoked, no less important was the need to encourage population control among the less privileged sectors of the Jewish community. The official version of public policy on abortion reflected this demographic imperative. In the presentation of the abortion bill, the social theme was widely expounded. What the country needed most, it was stated, was to bridge the social gap. Family planning was presented as a vital social requirement which need not necessarily decrease natality. The two arguments—pro-fertility and anti-deprivation—were thus merged to form the basis of abortion policy.

The other version of the abortion bill noted above was modeled on the *Roe v. Wade* decision, centered on women's liberties. This second version was presented to the Knesset by Marcia Freedman, the feminist member of the fledging Civil Rights party (previously the Civil Rights Movement). In her speech she said: "Why is abortion so important that women across the globe protest and organize against its limitation? Because control of pregnancy is a necessary condition for a woman to determine her life as a human being. Her body does not belong to the homeland, to the state, to the Ministry of Health, to the physician, to a medical committee, to her spouse or to her children, but to her and only to her"[6] Shulamit Aloni, a co-member in the Civil Rights party and an ardent proponent of women's rights, also emphasized the feminist theme. Summarizing the debate she said: "What the male MKs who have spoken here proposed is that a woman should abdicate her body for the sake of the people, for the sake of the army, and for national purposes. They suggested she deprive it of her own liberal discretion as a human being."[7]

These two women MKs were supported by some of their more liberal colleagues. Women, however, were not numbered among them. Female MKs, both on the left and the right of the political spectrum, endorsed the national theme. Ora Namir (Labor) stated that "the sacredness of the human being, the sacredness of the family, and the sacredness of society serve as our bedrock."[8] Geula Cohen, a fervent nationalist, challenged the "egoistic attitude" centered on the self. For her, national considerations, namely, increased Jewish fertility, surpassed all other arguments. Even Haika Grossman, a socialist and the chairperson of the Knesset committee processing the law, identified with the principles of the official version.

Notwithstanding the government's decision to grant coalition members a free vote on the issue, two-thirds of Knesset representatives supported the government's bill. Religious MKs, opposing the liberalization of abortion, left the chamber to join a protest being held outside the House.[9] These religious groups launched a feverish campaign to halt the bill. Haika Grossman, a Holocaust survivor and famous for her role in the Warsaw ghetto uprising, was branded as incarnation of Hitler. Placard in street demonstrations blared out the message: "Too bad your mother did not abort you." The protest against the bill was not confined to small groups of religious zealots but was joined by prominent figures such as the two chief rabbis of Israel, who demanded that the "bill of murder" be abolished (Yishai 1978a). Opposition to liberalizing abortions was evident among secular politicians as well. In her memoirs Marcia Freedman describes the antifeminist atmosphere in which the law was deliberated:

> Sex was on everyone's mind throughout the months and years of committee hearings on abortion. The committee room was often filled with jokes and lewd remarks, guffaws, and snickers. Sexual matters were the focus of most of our discussions—incest, rape, teenage pregnancy, menopause. It made everyone nervous. The member who sat next to me on my right . . . leaned toward me tittering, "Before a woman needs an abortion, there's something else she has to do first." He thought it was so funny he could hardly stop laughing. (Freedman 1990, 96)

The Israeli political establishment, then, including most of its female members, were inhospitable to the idea of women's liberation. What they decided, in liberalizing abortion, was to vest in the state the authority to determine who may be granted the right to terminate pregnancy. Abortion policy has proven to be intrusive on four grounds: First, as abortion remains a criminal offense unless it is authorized under the specified conditions, the law is restrictive in nature. Second, only the "social clause" was based on subjective indicators, determined at the woman's own discretion; and when this clause was subsequently repealed (see below), nothing was left to individual choice. Third, the woman is obliged to undergo a complicated process of examinations and interrogations before approval for an abortion is granted. The process concludes with a written consent document, explaining the danger of sterility after an abortion, which the woman must sign. A study of decision-making in the abortion committees showed that the doctors (overwhelmingly men) display paternalistic and manipulative attitudes. The women, for their part, behave apologetically, expressing a deep sense of guilt and shame. They feel uncomfortable rebelling against their maternal role, even when it is incompatible with their desire for individual freedom (Laron et al. 1980). Finally, only authorized hospitals are allowed to set up abortion committees. This regulation further curtails freedom of choice.

Once committee approval has been won, however, the Israeli state provides a woman with the necessary facilities to terminate her pregnancy. She pays a sum equivalent to the cost of one day's hospitalization, but even that is often reimbursed by the public health authorities. Being under strict state supervision, abortion is highly medicalized and performed only by certified doctors. Women are kept hospitalized under medical surveillance for at least twenty-four hours. The state is thus committed to providing women with adequate access to abortion facilities, but only after it has ensured a comprehensive control of the authorization process.

How have women fared in this process? Lay women have never been asked. Public opinion surveys focus on vital security issues regarding the occupied territories not on "trivial" issues such as abortion. Only the Feminist Movement (FM) displayed a militant pro-choice stance. It captured media headlines by staging a demonstration in June 1976 inside the Hilton hotel in Tel Aviv, where the Israel Association of Obstetricians and Gynecologists, opposing liberalization of abortion, was holding its annual conference (Freedman 1990, 94–96). Lacking organizational resources and public legitimacy, FM was not able to push forward its feminist version of the abortion bill. Naamat endorsed the official view, reiterating the national theme in the following words: "We should not forget that the question of abortion is embedded in deep moral considerations regarding both religion and tradition. Just as the present situation lags behind reality, so can radical change be diametrically opposed to traditional values."[10] In fact, at stake were not "traditional values" but the future political careers of the Labor MKs. As reported by Marcia Freedman: "Informally, but in a way that bound them all, they [Labor women] were asked to unite around the [official] recommendations. For any one of them to have refused the request would have meant courting disfavor in the party leaders' eyes and the possible end of their political careers." Regardless of their personal views on the issues, "they were all equally committed to one proposition: the survival of the coalition—and their own political survival—took precedence over the interests of women, whatever they believed them to be" (1990, 90–91). These considerations applied to Naamat's leadership as well. Reined in by its party affiliation, the largest women's association in the country either kept silent (leafing through the issues of its monthly publication during the period of the Knesset debate on abortion reveals absolutely no hint that it was taking place) or endorsed the government's position.

Constriction of Abortion

In its second phase (1979 onwards) abortion policy aroused widespread mobilization of women. In May 1977 the Israeli polity experienced a political upheaval, when the thirty-year rule of Labor was replaced by a right-wing coalition led by Likud. One of the first victims of this debacle was the abortion law. On 12 November 1979 the government presented a bill to repeal clause

5 of the abortion law, which allowed the abortion committees to authorize termination of pregnancy on social grounds. A 54-54 tie in the Knesset vote defeated the motion on its first reading. The Likud thereupon took an extreme and unusual step in order to mobilize a majority for the abortion law amendment. The upcoming vote on the second reading was declared a vote of confidence, which by virtue of "collective responsibility" legally binds coalition members to support the government (Yaacobi 1982, 130). This legal measure both reflects and sustains party discipline, often essential for the smooth operation of the conflict-ridden Israeli parliament.[11] By taking this unusual measure even recalcitrant coalition MKs were persuaded to support the amendment. Consequently, on 11 December 1979 the social clause was finally repealed by a small margin (55-50). Israeli women could no longer claim the right to abortion on grounds other than those established by professional authorities.

The policy shift took place for two reasons, one overt, the other tacit. The obvious and straightforward reason was the need to maintain the ruling coalition. The tacit reason was to increase the Jewish population in the country. Winning the elections in Israel means that a party has secured a relative majority that enables it to negotiate with potential coalition partners. Coalition bargaining provides ample opportunity for minor parties to extort concessions from the leading party and obtain benefits for their constituencies. Agudat Israel, an ultra-orthodox party and the major proponent of the legislative amendment, was one of the Likud's potential coalition partners. Although numbering only four Knesset representatives in 1977, the party wielded disproportionate power because without its support the coalition would have been left with only 61 seats in the 120-seat Knesset, a precarious majority of one.

Agudat Israel's major concern was to minimize violations of religious tenets and to enhance observance of orthodox norms in Israeli law and practice. Religious demands touch on many issues including, among others, public transportation on the Sabbath, dietary regulations, employment on holy days, and, primarily, the problem of "Who is a Jew?" But in the 1977 coalition negotiations, Agudat Israel concentrated its efforts on two major items: exemption of religious women from military service and repeal of the social clause in the abortion law. The first largely meant implementing a regulation enacted during Labor's control of government. Although it did cause some ferment, exemption of both religious men and women from compulsory service in the armed forces was already an accepted (though not necessarily welcome) routine. But the second item, the demand to repeal the social clause, marked a striking change from former practice. During the Labor Party's rule, negotiations with religious parties had centered on particular demands of their constituencies. The abortion law clause, however, pertained to the population at large, that is, mainly to secular individuals (Schiff 1990, 285). Agudat Israel was intent on prohibiting abortions on social grounds because, in its view, these were anathema from a religious point of view.

Unlike the Catholic faith, the Jewish tradition is equivocal about termination of pregnancy. Judaism does not ban abortions. In the eyes of ancient Jewish law the fetus has no legal status since it is deemed part of its mother rather than an independent entity. The underlying Jewish principle further asserts that abortion is not murder, although it may amount to killing. The difference between the two lies in the circumstances. Killing is allowed in self-defense, when the victim is not innocent but is considered an "aggressor." But fetus may only be regarded as an aggressor when the mother's health is endangered. The woman's interests, when health considerations are at stake, override those of the fetus. Even though Judaism recognizes "the sanctity of life,"[12] it permits abortion under certain circumstances (Feldman 1986). This attitude was hardly reflected in the pronunciations of religious MK, who vehemently opposed all proposals to liberalize abortion. Termination of pregnancy was defined as "murder and nothing but murder."[13] Following the approval of the abortion law, Agudat Israel was willy-nilly obliged to acknowledge the need to terminate pregnancy on account of health risks to the mother of the fetus, in any case, this principle did not violate Jewish tradition. It also halfheartedly acceded to the other provisions of the 1977 law regarding the woman's age and the nature of the sexual relations resulting in pregnancy. This orthodox party, however, totally rejected justification of abortion on social grounds.

Likud yielded not only because of coalition integrity but also because restricting abortion was compatible with its vision of Greater Israel inhabited by a growing Jewish population. The national anti-abortion argument was bruited by Likud speakers already in 1977. Rejecting the women's "selfish considerations," the right-wing MKs criticized the support lent to the "continued decline in the national growth of the Jewish people residing in Zion." Liberalization of abortion was further perceived as "a serious blow to Jewish fertility rate in the country."[14] Concerns about Jewish majority loomed large in the renewed deliberation of the abortion issue. Demographic figures were indeed a cause for concern as the fertility differentials between Jews and the Arabs persisted and threatened to jeopardize future Jewish claims on the country. The severity of the demographic problem was reflected in data population growth among the Arab Muslims (comprising, between 1955 and 1984, some 77.5 percent of the total non-Jewish population) and the Jews in Israel. The rate of natural increase among Arab Muslims is striking. Although this rate has declined since the mid-1960s, it was more than three times the rate of the Jews in 1979. It was feared that by the year 2000 the Arab population (including the inhabitants of the occupied territories) would constitute a majority in Greater Israel (Soffer 1988).

The capture of territory in the Six Day War of June 1967 aggravated the situation by adding some 1.5 million non-Jews to the 300,000 living in Israel already then. Although the lion's share of the territories remained a separate political entity and were not legally annexed to Israel, the demographic danger loomed larger than ever. In the late 1970s, it became abundantly clear that without a serious increment to Israel's Jewish population the prospects of retaining the territories, a goal adopted by the ruling Likud Party, were extremely dim. Signing a peace treaty with Egypt did not mean that Israeli administration, headed by the pro-retention Likud, was willing to negotiate the West Bank and the Gaza Strip. On the contrary, commentators noted that withdrawing from the Sinai Peninsula was aimed at enhancing Israel's claim to the disputed territories (Sella and Yishai 1986). In the absence of mass immigration of Jews from abroad, an active pro-natal policy was a core issue on the government's agenda. Restricting abortion was perceived as a means for the achieving of broader national objectives.

Likud, with its ultra-religious coalition allies, did not settle for the 1979 amendment that repealed the social clause, but made further attempts to constrain abortion and decrease its scope. Three years after the repeal of the social clause, it became evident that it had not curtailed abortions. Official data, pertaining only to authorized abortions, revealed that despite the elimination of the social clause in 1979, the number of abortions increased.[15] In 1979, furthermore, 39.7 percent of approvals were granted on the basis of the famous clause 5. Following its repeal, the percentage of those granted permission to abort on health grounds increased fivefold compared with 1979 (from 1,299 to 5,796). Clearly, social circumstances were being disguised in the health clause. Following a parliamentary debate on abortion in 1982, a Knesset committee on labor and welfare, headed by an orthodox MK (Menahem Porush, Agudat Israel) issued recommendations regarding abortion (21 March 1983). These recommendations reflected the conservative mood of the day: a woman undergoing unauthorized abortion would incur a serious penalty; it was proposed to abrogate the clause granting women older than forty permission to abort; recommendations were made to impose severe punishments on physicians performing uncertified abortions, to issue a precise list of medical indicators justifying abortions, and finally, to establish a special department in the Ministry of Health to supervise the implementation of the abortion law. To assuage the nonorthodox pro-life constituency, another committee was appointed, headed by Joseph Shenkar, a prominent gynecologist known for his anti-abortion positions.[16] The thrust of the Shenkar report, according to its members, was to establish a uniform pattern for the whole country which would allow only those abortions in line with the abortion law's provisions, and these abortions would be performed efficiently and on the quiet.[17] The report, however, included two important additional provisions: first, to disseminate more information to women seeking abortion on the possible (and, according to the committee's view, probable) damage involved in the interruption of pregnancy; second, to limit the operation of abortion committees to public hospitals only.

This last recommendation generated another wave of abortion restriction which swept the country in 1990. The minister of health submitted a legislative amendment (on 28 May 1990), on the advice of Professor Shenkar: he proposed confining abortion committees to public and government hospitals. The other recommendations were incorporated in administrative directives, which infuriated the proponents of abortion. The reason for the amendment, its initiators claimed, was concern over women's health. Public institutions were conceived as maintaining high medical standards. Publicly employed physicians were presumably less tempted by possible remuneration deriving from the operation. The death of a young woman caused by an abortion performed in a private clinic triggered the amendment. There were also strong political incentives: Although Likud won the 1988 election (by a marginal majority) a national unity government was established, headed by Yitzhak Shamir. But the possibility of an alliance of Agudat Israel with Labor in exchange for religious concessions hovered over Likud. As before, the survival of the coalition government headed by Shamir hinged on orthodox support. The precarious government stability amplified religious anti-abortion pressures. The threat to Likud became more serious when Labor withdrew from the government following the mounting international pressure for reconciliation with the Palestinians. In early 1990 James Baker, then the U.S. secretary of state, initiated a peace campaign involving the Palestinians. More than ever before it was important for Likud to establish a clear Jewish majority in Greater Israel. This goal was compatible with restricting abortions. More than ever before Likud apprehended a possible alliance between Agudat Israel and Labor. Commentators noted that the orthodox party predicated its membership of the Likud-led coalition on restricting abortions. Presumably, this demand constituted another step toward the nationalization of the Israeli woman's womb and using her as an instrument for the production of soldiers.

Women's Mobilization against Abortion Restriction

The intention to repeal the social clause sparked determined opposition. At first, the Israeli public rallied behind the opponents. Data on public attitudes toward abortion revealed massive rejection of the positions adopted by the Likud-led government and endorsed by the Knesset. A public survey taken in 1978 showed wide support of abortion on socioeconomic grounds among all Israelis. Among secular men and women the majority in favor was overwhelming: 99 percent and 96 percent, respectively, but even among those who reported that "they observe most religious commandments" support for the controversial clause was widespread—49 percent of men and 59 percent of women.[18] Respondents in a national sample were further requested to express their opinions regarding the authority to decide on interruption of pregnancy. The results were striking. Only a fraction of all respondents, including observant men, were of the opinion that "every pregnancy should be continued," that is, they opposed abortion under any circumstances. A surprising proportion of both orthodox men and women (about one-third) stated that it was a woman's prerogative to determine the interruption of pregnancy. Approval of abortion by a professional (medical) committee was more popular among the religious respondents than among their secular counterparts, but in no case did the need to obtain the committee's clearance secure wide support. Thus a solid majority of Israelis were far more liberal than their government regarding the performance of abortion.

The Israeli medical community, too, joined the opponents to the legislative amendment. In the first phase of the political debate on the issue, physicians had opposed any liberalization of abortion. The Association of Obstetricians and Gynecologists warned in press advertisements that its members would refuse to cooperate with pro-choice abortion legislation on the grounds that it was unsafe and because they had "real concern for the health and future fertility of the Israeli woman."[19] The association rescinded its objections when the moderate version of the abortion law became legally binding, as it placed the decision to approve abortions in the physicians' hands. In 1979, however, the gynecologists vehemently opposed the annulment of the social clause.

The most relentless objection to the repeal of the social clause in the abortion law emerged from women's associations. It was not surprising that the Feminist Movement launched an aggressive campaign against the legislative amendment, but more conservative women's organizations, including WIZO and Naamat, also joined the public strife. The arguments brought against the repeal were varied: above all, the social implications of the amendment were glaringly exposed. If executed to the letter, the abrogation of clause 5 of the abortion law would have been disastrous for poor women—precisely those who were originally intended to be the main benefactors. It was assumed that affluent women could obtain abortion in the private market without requesting a committee's approval.

Moreover, the significance of the social consequences of repealing clause 5 was magnified in view of the Likud's political milieu. The advent of Likud to power had become possible through a belated rejection of socialist mores, by the corruption of the long-time ruling elite, by a growing impatience with Israel's unsolved foreign and domestic problems, but primarily through the defection of the Sephardi community from Labor (Yishai 1982). From 1969 Jews from Afro-Asian origin abandoned Labor en masse, and cast their ballot for Likud. They were prompted by a complex set of motivations: a deep sense of resentment against what they considered their unsuccessful absorption in the state of Israel, identification with the religious themes embedded in the Likud's ideology, and a hawkish position on issues of security.[20] By 1979 the association between Likud and what has been termed the "second Israel," comprising residents of development towns and distress urban neighborhoods, was already an established fact. Women's associations wondered why Likud was aiming to hurt precisely the constituency that brought it to power.

Women's associations used a variety of strategies to combat the proposed amendment. Press conferences were held; personal letters were sent to MKs and ministers; meetings were held with influential politicians; petitions were signed; meetings were convened; and a large protest demonstration was staged (14 March 1979). One line of advance was manifestly absent from the strategy: women's associations, as well as other public organizations, including the Israel Medical Association and the Union of Social Workers, were not invited to take part in the Knesset committee's deliberations preceding legislation. A member of the Labor and Welfare Committee testified in the Knesset to the refusal of the chairperson to invite experts to the committee's hearings. Women's groups were simply denied access to the policy-making process.[21]

When the repeal of the social clause became a fait accompli, women's associations (Naamat and WIZO) adopted a positive instead of a critical stance. They urged the state to initiate and implement a family planning policy. In Israel women's access to contraception is rather limited. Even Labor, with more liberal attitudes to abortion than its rival Likud, did very little to encourage birth control. The Labor-controlled General Sick Fund (Kupat Holim), whose health insurance scheme at the time covered over 80 percent of the Israeli population, did not include among its activities the distribution of birth-control devices. General practitioners, responsible for the health care of the overwhelming majority of Israel's population, did not bring up family planning but waited for the women to raise the subject. Poor women were usually more reluctant than affluent to discuss intimate personal affairs with a (male) physician. The General Sick Fund glossed over family planning not only because of budgetary restraints or an overloaded health system but owing to the pro-natal mood. Public health authorities did not force poor women to have children; however, among the less privileged sectors of society, traditional concerns, a sense of pride in producing babies (especially males) the country so desperately needed, and primarily, ignorance and lack of access to adequate family-planning services promoted childbearing. Women associations called on the government to take charge of the issue. A woman MK (Nava Arad, Labor, a former secretary-general of Naamat) submitted a motion for the agenda indicating the need to adopt a comprehensive family-planning program, and allocating resources for its implementation, but hers remained a lone voice in the wilderness. In face of an unresponsive government, women's associations, likewise, dropped the family-planning issue from their agenda.

Women's recruitment to the cause of abortion resurged in 1990. The proposed amendment, to restrict abortion committees to public hospitals, infuriated women who mobilized to an unprecedented extent, in their opposition to the move.

Eliminating private hospitals from the abortion map was perceived not as a means of ameliorating justice and safety but as a stratagem to limit abortions. Data revealed that in 1988, out of 15,255 abortions performed in Israel, 10,048 (i.e., 65.8 percent!) were performed in private hospitals and clinics.[22] Eliminating this option would have dealt a serious blow to the availability of abortion in Israel. The most important step taken by women's associations was the establishment of a coalition uniting all of them in opposition to the proposed amendment. In 1990 the abortion issue did at last form a focal point for women's mobilization. The chief instigator of the coalition was the Women's Network, whose human, political, and financial resources were dedicated to the pro-abortion struggle.

The 1990 pro-abortion campaign was different from that of 1979 not only in the actors involved but also in strategies. After failing to quietly persuade religious parties to accept an alternative amendment, the following confrontational strategies were employed:

First, both women's associations as well as individuals swamped the authorities with letters disapproving of the government policy. Two years later the minister of health stated that never in his life had he received so many letters as in the two months preceding the meeting with a women's delegation.[23] Letters were sent not only by Israeli individuals but by members of Jewish organizations in the United States. Unlike American citizens, Israelis are not accustomed to writing letters to their representatives. The fact that neither legislators nor ministers are elected directly by the voters but rather by political parties, and that they are not directly accountable to their constituencies, greatly reduces recourse to direct communication. The campaign against restricting abortions, with its mass letter-writing, thus constituted a conspicuously exceptional political strategy rather than routine behavior.

Second, the expansion of an issue has been noted as a major key for political influence (Cobb and Elder 1972). By this criterion the women's campaign proved highly successful. The alliance formed to challenge the proposed amendment to the abortion law was not confined to women. Among its members were gender-neutral associations such as the Association for

Family Planning, the Civil Rights Association, the Movement for Progressive Judaism, and the New Israel Fund. Naturally, women groups also joined the coalition. What was unusual, though, was the partnership created between conservative associations such as WIZO and Naamat on the one hand, and the Feminist Movement and the Union for the Assistance of Rape Victims on the other. All these groups were one in their outrage at the attempt to restrict abortions. They combined because their gender interests were at stake. As one of the coalition leaders put it, "Because no member of the present government was ever pregnant, abortion is not at the top of their priorities, and they do not understand the issue."[24]

Third, the women's coalition, aided by the resources of its member-associations, set up an impressive organization within a relatively short time. It had a title ("The Coalition against Amendment no. 30 to the Criminal Code—Abortion Law"); it printed its letterhead on its stationery, it successfully mobilized support and activated its members; it issued publications, convened press conferences, and held a mass rally (on 27 December 1990) attended by 1,000 demonstrators, including fourteen MKs, one of whom was a Likud member. Unlike 1978, the anti-amendment proponents had obtained wide access to the Knesset Committee on Labor and Welfare.

Fourth, the coalition used one of the common techniques employed by interest groups in their quest for power: data gathering. Women activists presented accurate information on various aspects of abortion. Among the topics researched were the number of weekly hours abortion committees operated; the resort of women immigrants from the former Soviet Union to abortion; and the scope of abortions in the orthodox community.

Finally, the fifth strategy was the holding of a personal meeting with the health minister in which he admitted that he, in fact, was not enthusiastic about the proposed amendment. Although the minister insisted the amendment must be processed, he did so half-heartedly.[25]

The coalition's successful mobilization triggered counter-efforts by the authorities. A conference was convened, under the auspices of the Ministry for Health and the Ministry of Labor and Welfare to discuss abortions in Israel.[26] But the opposition to the proposed amendment was too strong to be ignored. Both parties to the dispute—the coalition on the one hand, and state authorities on the other—presented a compromise proposal. The coalition demanded that abortion committees be set up at the main clinics of the sick funds. A sufficient number of such committees would make it possible to disband them in private hospitals. It would also prevent the terrible consequences of delayed access to an abortion committee. Needless to say, this compromise proposal was rejected by the political authorities. The official compromise was mooted by the prime minister's advisor on women's status, politically affiliated with the Likud. The gist of her proposal, endorsed by Agudat Israel, was to merge the private hospitals' committees with public ones. This proposal was unacceptable to the coalition, which insisted that the spread of committees throughout the hospital network in the country, and the greater opportunity for secrecy in private-located committees, constituted a guarantee against the limitation of abortion. This story has a happy ending from the women's viewpoint. The proposed amendment was dropped from the parliamentary agenda and shelved. The inception of the Gulf War (January 1991) raised other issues to the top of the agenda. In addition, Likud realized that the enormous opposition mounted against the proposed amendment might have been more detrimental to its political assets than a disgruntled religious party. Abortions, in their intrusive Israeli version, continue to be performed unabated.

Conclusion

Abortion continues to be regularly practiced in Israel. Since 1979 the rate per 1,000 women is around 15. Although an overall decline in the number of abortions has been noticed (Sabatello 1994), it is similar to that documented in Scandinavia and the United Kingdom—0.4–0.6 abortions in a woman's life span (Sabatello 1993). In 1991 in Israel there were some 18,000 requests for abortion, which 15,500 were granted. The official publication of these figures demonstrates the shift Israeli authorities made in 1977 on the issue. But the movement was not induced by a sudden fondness for feminism, nor by the acknowledgment of women's right to bodily self-determination. Rather, liberalization of abortion (as well as its restriction) was anchored in national considerations. The formulation of public policy regarding abortion demonstrates two major attributes, ostensibly mutually exclusive, of Israeli politics: the wide consensus over fundamental values on the one hand, and conflictual coalition politics on the other.

The initial legislative measures taken to liberalize abortion were embedded in a comprehensive consensus. This became possible because the issue was defined in terms of social imperatives. The majority of the legislators embraced this definition. There was little controversy over the need to end unwanted pregnancies in those social sectors that could not raise their children properly. The humiliation and fury that swept Israeli society following from the violent demonstrations of the Black Panthers paved the way for the legalization of abortion. Yet coalition politics highlighted the dissonance in Israeli society. Dogged coalition negotiations, coupled with the desire to raise the birth rate among Jews, regardless of the economic or social deprivation caused by large families, set the scene for the restrictions on abortion resulting from the repeal of the social clause. Further attempts to curb abortion, persistently made by consecutive Likud governments, failed. Agreement on the need to allow women to terminate an unwanted pregnancy has proved to be stronger than coalition pressures.

As elaborated in some detail, Israel has adopted a specific form of abortion liberalization. By keeping the procedure under strict and meticulous state supervision, the authorities have given women a certain leeway but at the same time have let it be known who the real boss is. Israeli women were granted permission to terminate pregnancies not because choosing to do so is inscribed among fundamental human rights, but because a state-sponsored committee found that the women's arguments were convincing enough to vindicate the procedure. This intrusive policy manifests the characteristic of Israel as a "guided democracy."

As for the women's role in the process of formulating abortion policy, women as usual remained equivocal, although their equivocation has turned into a clear position in recent years.

That women were torn between their desire to take command of their reproductive organs and their fidelity to the nation is evident from the initial legislative debate. Equivocation, in this case, was not within individual women, but between two distinct groups of women: feminists, who keenly supported the pro-choice version, and other women's associations, who leaned toward the national version. Equivocation gave way to determination when further attempts were made to impose measures deemed to restrict that limited degree of choice granted in 1977. The women's coalition opposing the proposed legislative amendment demonstrated their insistence on their gender interests. In the 1990s women are stating, clearly and loudly, that their womb is no longer political. They have unmistakably opted for the feminist banner over the national flag.

CHAPTER 9

Conclusion: From Integration to Mobilization?

This study has sought to examine the political life of women in Israel, a visionary democracy, where democratic procedures are supplemented (or superseded) by overarching collective national norms. The analysis has delineated the alternative path for women's political affiliation and activity: integration into the prevailing system or mobilization on behalf of the feminist cause. The Israeli case is intriguing not only because the dilemma of acting from "within" or "without" is so critical, but also because of the sharp contrast between vision and reality, between legal promise and its performance. This gap between ground rules for equality and the actual disparity has been another riddle relevant to the political status of Israeli women.

Studies on the women in politics have shown considerable disagreement regarding the type of social system that may be most conducive to women's equality. Some studies, founded on liberal theory, suggest that modernization has removed traditional constraints on women and fosters their equalization. Others, based on Marxist theory, argue that women's emancipation will result from the termination of the class struggle. Studies propagating a feminist perspective argue that neither liberal nor Marxist theory deals adequately with the woman's question, because both treat women as a dependent variable to be determined within the broader sociopolitical environment (Park 1990). This book has been an inquiry into what women themselves chose to do. Exposed to feminist winds long before feminism became a political issue, and simultaneously subjected to deep-penetrating national imperatives, women in Israel have vacillated between the two alternatives: mobilization to the feminist banner or integration with institutions associated with the national flag. Their choices, across time, and the state's reactions to these choices in specific policy issues, have been the major themes of the book.

Political Women in Israel: A Developmental Perspective

The analysis of women's politics in Israel has centered on three main issues: (1) political structures for women's activity; (2) women's input into political life, and (3) policy output regarding women. In all three parameters changes over time have been evident.

Political Structures for Women's Activity

The first research question focused on the structures available to women through which they might exert and direct political power. Two arenas for political action were distinguished: the formal arena of politics and the associational arena. The first comprises the legislature, the government, the local government, civil service, the headquarters of political parties, and the bureaus of economic and professional interest groups. The conclusion reached at in this discussion is unequivocal: women are underrepresented in the locus of power. A comparative perspective, however, may provide grounds for optimism as well as pessimism. When Israel is compared with other Western countries, women do not fare badly. The country lies in the middle of the spectrum, between some European countries and the United States on the one hand, where women's underrepresentation is manifest, and the Scandinavian countries on the other, where women have gained impressive access to governing bodies. But from a diachronic viewpoint there seems to be little cause for joy, as over the years the share of women's representation in decision-making bodies has made a trifling advance. According to this technical criterion, women in Israel are not highly *integrated* into the political elite. Their merely token representation in all forums where critical decisions are taken regarding Israel's future, sidelines them to all intents and purposes.

Women's exclusion from the core of power is particularly evident in the dramatic events of contemporary politics. The inception of the Middle East peace process opened a new page in the history of Israel. The Oslo Israeli-Palestinian accord has revolutionized the political agenda at one fell swoop, as politicians and members of the business community presented far-reaching plans affecting many domains of social life. The end of belligerence portends a startling shift in the country's priorities. Domestic issues, heretofore pushed to a corner, have sprung up, attracting much attention and concern. One aspect of Israeli life, however, has remained unchanged: the peace process, ramifying into a multiplicity of committees, forums, and domains, has remained womenless. Not one woman took part in the long and arduous talks with the Palestinians or with the leaders of the Arab states. The peace arena has remained men's domain. This gloomy picture notwithstanding, women's access to power has been recently enhanced. The fact that two female ministers serve in the present government (1994), and that women are members of the prestigious Knesset Foreign and Security Affairs Committee, may indicate that the era of women's exclusion from the inner circles of power is behind us.

For many years, organized women protested verbally against their being denied entry into the political elite, but calculated the benefits to be derived from their integration into the political system. Four distinct patterns of women's mobilization have been isolated: women's associations branching off from political parties; charity groups; political lobby associations; and feminist organizations. Until only a decade ago the women's movement showed clear symptoms of integration. Working from within manifested itself in elite recruitment, membership mobilization, resource solicitation, and formulation of objectives. The dominant movement on the scene, Naamat (previously the

Working Women's Movement), was a party institution, directed by, and subservient to, party headquarters. The movement, furthermore, subscribed to the collective values advocated by the party whose ethos was associated with the nation's *raison d'être*. The attempt to establish a genuine feminist movement, doing away with patriarchal values cloaked in national slogans, proved unsuccessful. Women's associations derived most of their resources from establishment organizations and not from rank-and-file women; their tactics were "integrative" in the sense they did not resort to protest politics but opted for acting from "within." Here Israel stood in contrast to other countries of the Western world, which have been swept by rising feminist mobilization since the late 1960s.

Since the mid-1980s, however, there have been two harbingers of change. First, a women's association was established independent of the established political structure. Its main purpose was precisely to influence this structure while maintaining its autonomy. Although not totally independent of male-dominated organizations, which provide it with resources required for political action, the Women's Network nevertheless paved the way for a new women's politics in the country. The Women's Network shied away from radical feminism, adopting a more conventional stance. Serving as an umbrella organization for women of all political shades, it has gained the respectability of "integration" essential for political clout in Israeli society. At the same time, it showed signs of autonomy unprecedented on the women's associational scene. The feminist movement, for its part, has almost ceased to be active. It has been replaced, however, by a host of viable self-help groups on nearly all issues of gender concern. This spin-off has had a tremendous effect on women's politics in the country. The veteran women's groups could not rest idle and watch their junior counterparts gather the fruits of political success. By adopting both the objectives and the strategies of the "new" women's movements, they have grown increasingly distant from integration, stressing their adherence to feminism. Joyce Gelb has noted that in Sweden feminism was obtained without feminists; in Israel feminism was endorsed by nonfeminist associations *because of* the feminists.

Coalition among women was noted to be one of the chief attributes of mobilization. Each strand of the women's movement in Israel had different origins and different goals. Despite this diversity, opportunities for cooperation abounded, but in the past they were rarely realized. Collaboration among women could be secured only in matters relating to their status in the family. Common discontent with the plight of women proved insufficient to generate a stable alliance of women's associations. The women's movement in Israel was divided and incoherent. Gradual changes have taken place in this respect, caused both by a turnover in leadership and by the changing political agenda. The veteran leadership of women's associations, whose political maturation took place in political parties or charity associations, has been replaced by younger, professional women who share similar social backgrounds, are moved by similar ideas, and hold similar expectations for the future. These women find it easy and natural to communicate and forge common strategies. Likewise, the controversy over women's role in society has lost its edge. Admittedly, Naamat still places family affairs high on its agenda, and WIZO still encourages women to volunteer on behalf of the indigent, but both associations are deeply concerned with other aspects of inequality: in the workplace, in the economy, and particularly in politics. This shared concern provides fertile soil for concerted women's action.

Women's Input into the Polity

The second research question focused on women's input into the political process, which, if sufficiently great, might serve the women's movement should it choose to act from without. An underlying query was whether women's political participation and identity were like those of men or unique to their own sex. The existence of a gender gap does not necessarily imply that women tend to subscribe to feminism, as women's activity in politics, for example, may signify their adherence to traditional norms that exclude them from the political arena. Whether women are mobilized to participate in politics under the feminist banner, or are integrated into the usual patterns of political participation, is thus a complex question whose answer depends not only on quantitative data but also on qualitative analysis.

Many of the opportunities for women to participate in political life have been limited by past and present political structures. Women's party activities are channeled through the established party system. Their voting preferences are circumscribed by the same set of choices that face all Israelis. Despite repeated attempts, women have failed to offer an alternative to the political organizations that govern the state. It may thus be concluded that women's activity in Israeli politics has been generally confined to traditional modes. In their inferior scores on the conventional scales of political participation, and in their hawkish stances on foreign affairs, women showed that they adhere to the flag far more than to the banner. Yet changes are noticeable here too. Contemporary women show remarkably greater interest in politics than did women in the past; they have gained confidence regarding their ability to affect results by their involvement, and they have increasingly participated as voters. The clearest sign of change, however, is the tendency of the higher strata of women, the natural constituency for organized feminism, to steer clear of modes of participation associated with establishment politics. This documented pattern of behavior expresses an evident tendency toward mobilization. The combination of increased political participation on the one hand and avoidance of conventional party channels on the other may portend the diffusion of a feminist mood, if not organization, among Israeli women. The fact that this inclination is stronger in the more affluent sectors of Israeli women signals that with the rise of educational standards and growing numbers of women entering the labor force the swing to the mobilization might be even greater.

Have women come to constitute a "group" in terms of their identity? To form a distinctive political group, several conditions must be satisfied: forging internal consensus, shaping clear boundaries marking the group off from its environment, and developing membership identification. In many respects women in Israel have fulfilled these three requirements. A wide measure of agreement (around 70 percent) has been evident in eight of the ten items on the scale of gender identity. By and large, women in Israel tend to adhere to views associated with classical feminism to a degree far higher than anticipated. The wide endorsement of free reproductive choice, for example, is most striking. Moreover, the gender gap regarding issues of major concern to women is clear and visible. But it remains an open question if these views have generated "membership identification." As the question juxtaposing gender and national identity showed, the latter takes clear precedence over the former.

Conforming to feminine attitudes, furthermore, may bear little or no political implication (Sears and Huddy 1990). This is the case in Israel, where there is a vast distance between women's views on women's status in society, with their apparently progressive stances regarding gender equality, on the one hand, and their political mobilization for the women's cause on the other. As for awareness of women's movements and their activity, and of specific legislation targeted at women, the ignorance of Israeli women is astonishing. Women (and men) mostly knew about those associations and activities that followed the integrative track. They knew considerably less about the new feminist associations in the country. Here the slogan "feminism without feminists" applies nicely to the Israeli scene. The feminist groups were successful in inculcating feminist values, but they were no match for the established women's movement; the latter, however, responded to their constituency's expectations and changed course. The success of feminism was therefore not through the public being mobilized by their efforts, but through the acceptance by the veteran women's groups of their prophesies on the one hand and growing gender consciousness among ordinary Israeli women on the other. There is another plausible explanation for the gap between ideas and behavior, namely, a simple time lag between the emergence of feminist views and their conversion into political mobilization. Only future studies will show whether Israeli women are distancing themselves from the integrative pattern and mobilizing for a feminist effort; whether gender identity, growing firm among ordinary women, is an antecedent to political mobilization or its substitute.

Policy Output Regarding Women

The third research question focused on the outcomes of women's efforts in terms of public policy centered on women's issues. One factor looms large in the discussion: the space on the political agenda occupied by issues relating to gender has expanded dramatically. There are now some thirty laws safeguarding aspects of women's equality. During the past two years (1993–4), since the incumbency of the present Knesset, fifteen additional legislative proposals have been placed on the legislative agenda. Gender inequality cannot be blamed on insufficient legislation. Steps have constantly been taken to grant women equal rights, as long as these do not clash with the state's fundamental values. It is in public policy on women that the influence of the "flag" is most marked, and it is here that women have gained most influence, because they acted within the framework hammered out by the "vision."

The development of public policy on women in Israel shows that while not responding to feminism the authorities have become increasingly aware of the problems exercising feminists. State agencies were willing to comply with feminist demands as long as these did not violate the traditional order and did not breach basic values. The state has labored to facilitate women's equality in economic life. Initially, it tempered this equality with protective measures, describing women as "equal but different." Subsequently, however, the "difference" was downplayed in favor of genuine equality. The processing of economic policy for women did not encounter much opposition, but neither did it stir much enthusiasm among women's associations. Until the 1980s, the economic sphere was nearly monopolized by the state and its agencies. Only in the middle of that decade did women become involved in economic legislation, and those who took part were not the female branch of the Labor Federation, the watchdog of women's rights in the workplace. A wide consensus prevailed on the right of women to enjoy privileges equal to those of men in the workplace and it was sustained by the fact that no resources were required for implementation. Embracing principles of equality, in this instance, was not a zero-sum game. Women's economic equality, Israeli style, did not subtract from men's privileges as the law contributed very little to changing the unequal reality. Economic legislation has had some educational and legitimizing effect, but implementation lags far behind. Women have usually opted for the integrative course.

The case of family policy is more ambiguous. When personal status was at stake, the force of traditional values was solid and all-encompassing. All those concerned—legislators, political parties, and women's associations—acquiesced in the principles governing personal status. Very rarely were the postulates of the Jewish faith challenged. All strategies were aimed at influencing from "within" rather than confronting the traditional pillars of Judaism. So far, success has been extremely modest and Israeli women continue to be subjected to unequal treatment by religious authorities and continue to suffer through humiliating and antiquated rules.

An opposite picture emerged from the analysis of public policy regarding violence in the family. Wall-to-wall agreement made (belated) legislation possible, followed by fairly effective implementation, combating violence against women. The reason for this broad consensus is clear and simple. When subjected to violence, women conform to their traditional image as vulnerable and weak human beings. It is in this situation especially that they need state protection in general and male guardianship in particular. Furthermore, violence against women is perpetrated at home, where women naturally belong. Even ultra-orthodox groups subscribed to a policy protecting women against undue violence. True, it has taken more than forty years for public authorities to realize that women-battering is not a personal family affair but a public issue. When at last it did appear on the agenda it was treated with speed and facility uncharacteristic of the legislative process. Curbing violence against women did not threaten fundamental values, nor did it jeopardize institutional structures. The perpetrators of violence, being social pariahs, did not mobilize to counter the pro-women legislation.

Public policy took a different approach to the question of abortion. Body politics was the cause of a deep rift. Religious groups were antagonistic to any liberalizing move: the interruption of pregnancy interfered with the will of God. But opposition to the liberalization of abortion went far beyond religious circles. An overwhelming majority of policy-makers, including women members of the elite, kept a safe distance from the essence of feminism, being the free choice of women to fulfill their reproductive function or not. The compromise achieved was nothing of the sort, as it left the state with the authority to decide who was eligible for abortion and who was not. Women have succeeded in preventing further erosion of abortion rights, but the fundamental premise on which these rights are founded has remained intact and unchallenged. Abortion in Israel is still not a matter of a woman's free choice but of state's choice. Public opinion, particularly among women, is more keen than the women's movement to allow women reproductive freedom. This mood, however, has bypassed both organized feminism and the political establishment.

All in all, there are strong indications that Israeli women are moving, gradually and cautiously, from the flag to the banner. The "lower" the political level, the more pronounced this phenomenon is. Among ordinary women there is a wide support of feminist ideas; grassroots associations are also acting from without, relying on sparse resources accumulated through the mobilization of women. Recently, feminism has begun to take hold on the elite level as well, as the established women's organizations and women legislators are starting to think, speak, and even behave like feminists. This picture remains incomplete, however, as feminism stops short of assailing "public ideas" fostered by entrenched norms and institutionalized power structures. These too have prevented the eradication of gender inequality.

Constraints on Women's Equality: The Family Golden Cage

In February 1978, the Commission on the Status of Women presented its report to the Israeli prime minister, Menahem Begin. Of the 241 recommended measures required for the advancement of women, only 36 have been fulfilled so far to the letter; 117 have been partially attended to, and 88 have been totally ignored. Those relating to legislation have been mostly accommodated; those applying to the distribution of both economic and political resources have been mostly overlooked. The major argument of this book has been that the constraints on women's equality are linked to collective values embedded in the process of nation-building. Israel, perennially engaged in a conflict with its Arab neighbors and so always on the brink of war, has developed a male-oriented culture in which women are expected to conform to feminine, rather than feminist, roles. Most women have been socialized into this culture and have sustained it by their occupational choices and daily practices. Society expects it of women to be the soldiers at home, and to form the frontline for ingathering the exiles. These are important functions, though different from those accomplished by men. Women have accepted this destination because they were part and parcel of the collective that shaped their identity. A possible challenge to collective values was deflected by the centrality of women in the family, an institution most cherished in Israeli society. As suggested earlier, the pivotal status of the family has been widely discussed by Israeli social scientists. The political implications of this centrality, however, have been largely evaded. In the wake of feminism, women demanded the conversion of personal into the political, that is, to place so-called "private" issues on the public agenda. In Israel, however, *the personal is political*. The overarching need for personal security, for belonging, and for attachment has been politicized not by extracting personal issues from the realm of private life and placing them in the realm of public life, but by eradicating the boundaries between individuals and society.

Israel has been described as a community-state, where particular bonds take precedence over nonpersonal universalistic interactions (Liebman 1988). An emphasis on the particular aspects of social life has generated a political dilemma. Israel aspires to be a state based on universal democratic values; at the same time it is imbued with particularistic norms, in which the family plays a central role. The impact of particularism has been considerable both on the domestic and on the international scene. It has obstructed the integration of the non-Jewish citizens into Israeli society, and has militated against the application of universal norms in the civil service. Particularism has found its most articulate expression in the emphasis on family life, where women have been the central axis. Why has familism in Israel gained such a prime importance? Eight different explanations have been offered to account for this centrality. These are grounded in the historical legacy of the state of Israel as well as in its contemporary environment, in psychological inner motivations as well as in formal institutional procedures and regulations.

The first explanation relates to the country's precarious security. The fact that Israel is a state under siege, engulfed in frequent defense crises, has contributed to the consolidation of the family and has enhanced the quest for close-knit relations. A continuous state of anxiety has been found to be associated with a yearning for intimacy. Furthermore, the concern for sons and brothers, serving in the army for three to five years of their young adult lives, and for husbands, performing on reserve duty approximately one month a year until they are in their fifties, has generated a need to establish a safe haven, distant from the sound and fury of military life: the caring family. The "crowded nest" syndrome, where the female hovers over the males preoccupied with combating real and imaginary enemies, and attending to their needs, is a typical outcome of these circumstances. The Arab-Israeli conflict was said to contribute to consolidating family life, despite the fact that researchers (Peres and Katz 1980, 16–17) found only a weak relation between wars and three indicators of family strength.

The second explanation for the salience of family in modern Israel relates to religious norms and practices, all revolving around the family. Studies have shown that family life was stronger and more stable among Jews than among non-Jews in the United States (Winch 1968). This fact may be attributed to the importance of the family in Jewish history as a means of assuring individual and communal survival. The family was described as a "portable homeland" (quoted by Baker 1993, 124). For a people who over the years have been forced to wander, who have had to settle in foreign cultures amid different religions, the family has always had a special significance. Jews expected it to provide the solace and security they often lacked outside. Hence, Judaism was described as a religion practiced mostly within the family, a "domestic religion" linking its ethnic experience with family ritual and cultural influences (Baker 1993, 124–25).

These norms have been sustained by contemporary historical circumstances, constituting the third explanation for the family's importance. The majority of the Jewish people residing in Israel have a short family history. Only about a third of the Jews residing in Israel are native-born; the proportion of third-generation Israelis is astonishingly small. This means that most Israeli youngsters have actually not known their grandparents. Israelis lack the sense of continuity that prevails in "normal" countries. They yearn for permanence and stability. To this may be added the traumatic experience of the Holocaust, felt not only among the survivors of the Nazi tyranny and their offspring but in society at large. The fact the many of the survivors lost their closest relatives fueled the flame of family life. The "wandering Jews," finally having a homeland of their own, had a powerful urge for a stable family life.

The fourth explanation takes into consideration the demographic structure of Israeli society. Some 40 percent of Israelis originated in traditional societies in Asia and Africa, where the family constitutes the fundamental social unit. Traditional families, governed by a patriarchal father, constituted both an economic and political unit. The family income consisted of the remuneration of all its members. The family gave a person social standing and determined one's chances for a secure economic position and for education. One of the major crises confronting the immigrants in the early years of Israeli statehood was the shattering of the traditional family structure and the decline of the father's authority. Yet compared with Western societies these families still retain much of the halo they enjoyed abroad. Some of these attributes of traditional families have become incorporated into Israeli society.

The fifth explanation also puts the family in a historical perspective, albeit a more contemporary one. As argued by Bernstein (1992a), family played a central role in pre-state Israel. Socialist Zionists rejected many of the qualities embodied by the Jewish family as it existed in history, as they shunned many other aspects of traditional life. The family, furthermore, was seen as a threat to collective pioneering ideas, reflecting the foundations of bourgeois-capitalist society. Yet within a short time the traditional family reemerged as a basic social unit, involving a traditional division of labor between men and women. The decline of the socialist dream and the exigencies of the labor market contributed to the formation of a family stronger than ever. Family became the embodiment of the collective, rather than an individual refuge.

The sixth explanation attributes the strength of the family to the sociocultural milieu prevailing in contemporary Israel. The breakdown of the traditional family in Western societies was partly caused by decreasing social control. The anonymity of the big urban centers, the fact that each and every individual was expected to "do it alone," legitimized the breakup of nuclear families. Israel presents a different picture. Numerically the size of the population—over five million—matches that of some European countries, for example Norway and Denmark. In the eyes of its citizens, however, Israel has remained a small, vulnerable society. The lack of traditional respect for individual rights, on the one hand, and a pervasive desire for mutual support on the other, have generated pressures toward communality. The intimacy of personal relations among the Israeli (Jewish, and only Jewish) population is based on kinship, common fate, shared historical memories, and deep fraternity. This sense of fraternity was spelled out by a famous Israeli writer in the following words:

> We are a tribe, an extended family, a *hamula* [an extended Arab family including even distant relatives]; often this fact suffocates. I have the urge to run from here to the end of the world so that I can be with myself and not carry, day and night, the burden of this Israeli intimacy. But you cannot escape: at the end of the world some foreign journal will be there, including a news item about an atrocity performed by Israeli soldiers, or about a contemptible Jewish *Gesheft* [Yiddish for "deal"], or about a shooting on the northern border, or about antisemitism on the rise in northern Argentina, all causing an immediate constriction in my throat: here comes more trouble. (Oz 1985, 218)

The family-like cohesion characterizing Israeli society has been noticed by social scientists as well (e.g., Leibman 1989). Israeli citizens, so it was claimed, base their collective identity on a sense of intimacy. They regard themselves as members of an intimate community founded on primordial contacts rather than citizens of a civil society. Every victim of belligerence is a "brother," every soldier on the front a "dear son."

The seventh explanation for the centrality of family in Israeli society may be described in terms of political psychology. The insecurity presumably sensed by many people emanates not only from the chronic conflict with the Arabs but from enduring problems of identity confronted by many Israelis. Studies show that many have abandoned their Jewish identity and have not yet adopted a distinct Israeli image. One of the reasons for the blurred identity is Israel's unresolved problem of political affiliations. In the Middle East the country is still regarded as alien. Despite the successful initiation of the peace process, the country can hardly be labeled "Asiatic." Israel intensely solicits its integration into the European market. One of the justifications for this quest is the recent European heritage of many Jews in Israel. But the fact of the matter is that Israel has failed to integrate with Europe and has been denied entrance to its political institutions. The state has striven to establish close contacts with the Jewish community in the United States, but the gap between Israeli Jews and their brethren across the Atlantic continues to be wide. Ways and means are sought to bridge this regrettable divide, but Israeli Jews, in some way, somehow, thrive on their own precarious identity, detached from that of the Diaspora. At home there is also much to be desired. Horowitz and Lissak (1989) have suggested that Israel has not fulfilled its utopian dreams and has largely failed to meet expectations of sovereignty based on universal political values. Under these confusing circumstances, it is little wonder that the Israeli finds refuge in the family, where he/she can realize his or her identity and focus his or her passions.

The eighth and final explanation relates to the institutional inducements to nurture the family provided by state authorities, noted for their capacity to manipulate the citizenry and inculcate high priority values (Galnoor 1982). Strengthening family ties has always ranked uppermost among these priorities. The reasons for emphasizing the family over other social institutions are varied and complex. The state may have catered to the tacit desires of its people for security and intimacy; it may have wished to use the family as a source of social control. Whatever the case may be, state authorities have perennially encouraged natality, and arranged social life to fit family needs. As noted earlier (chapter 8), David Ben Gurion was a leading proponent of a high birth rate. A series of economic measures was introduced to enhance the importance of family in the lives of Israelis. State subsidies granted, for example, for the procurement of cars and telephones, and housing loans, were made available only to people with families, not to single individuals. Housing policy, indeed, played a major role in enhancing family ties. The overwhelming majority of Israelis own their own homes, although purchasing an apartment involves an investment far above the modest means of the average person. Consequently, a young couple wishing to settle down has to resort to outside financial assistance from parents and/or public and private loans. The reliance on external help sustains family stability, as it militates against divorce, in which case the couple would become embroiled in the confusion of selling the apartment, dividing the proceeds, and repaying the loan.

The centrality of a woman to a stable family life cannot be exaggerated, as long as she fulfilled the expectations attached to her. In the Jewish tradition a woman was likened to a tent, all-encompassing and indispensable. A woman was to provide security, continuity, stability, and shelter. In a famous poem Haim Nachman Bialik, the national poet, called for the woman to be a "safe shelter from all cares. . . . The hiding place of rejected prayers" (Bialik 1924, 13). The image of the woman as a safe shelter and a mother was incorporated into her political entity. In the Knesset debate on the Women's Equal Rights Law (1951), David Ben Gurion justified granting women equality in the following words:

> As I presume that every person has or had a mother, when I speak about my own mother I am referring to any other mother. The first human being that every per-

son contacts is the mother. This is also the person most cherished by every man or woman. My mother passed away in my childhood, when I was ten years old, but I remember her so well as if she were alive now. And I know she was the symbol of purity, of love, of human nobility, and devotion. I am positive that this description is pertinent to the overwhelming majority of mothers. The fact that this dearest mother is not equal to me, generates the utmost desecration of human values. I am deeply hurt, to the bottom of my heart by the fact that I have rights, and she does not have them. . . . No, one cannot comply with such dishonor of a mother, dishonor of the most precious person in life.[1]

Forty-two years later, in a recent (1993) Knesset debate to celebrate International Women's Day, the prime minister, Yitzhak Rabin, reiterated the theme. After praising all governments serving in Israel since independence for promoting women's equality he said:

I will conclude with a tribute, a tribute to the Jewish mother, the Israeli mother, whose days and nights are full of worry and concern, a woman that makes the home, cares for our children, the woman who is inseparable from our personal and national life, and one without whom, as we all know, life is simply impossible. The praise for a woman has no end, for the Jewish mother and the Israeli woman. Let me quote [the poet] Natan Alterman: "I will tell you all good words that I have, that I will have." Thank you, Israeli woman, from the depth of my heart.[2]

The mother-politics nexus was internalized by women. Those running for political office emphasized their family responsibilities or lamented the lack of them. In a public interview, Shoshana Arbelli Almozlino, a veteran Labor activist, apologized for having remained childless. "To my great regret, I was not privileged to have children. . . . What happiness it brings the family when children arrive."[3] Nearly ten years later a Knesset member explained, in a press interview, why she decided to run only six weeks before election day. One of the chief reasons, as expected, was family burden: "Home, family, and children. . . . I do not believe in multiple tasks." The same woman described the difficulties encountered by her husband, having to face social pressures regarding his role in the family: "My husband accepts it [the fact that I have career of my own]. He is ready to help me with the kids in addition to his own work because he knows that I am very busy and that I cannot be home at lunch with the children, but society makes it extremely hard for him. These are my best friends whom I know mean well, and my mother, who no doubt means well, and she constantly nags him: 'You're alone again?' That's why it was extremely important for me to get Danny's [the husband's] approval." [4]

Women were mobilized to the national effort through a variety of strategies. The emotional needs of individuals in a society under siege, whose men are often killed in bloody wars, and the burden of immigrant absorption, coupled with a familial tradition, have exerted strong pressures on women to remain loyal to traditional values, sustained by national norms. Women were expected to produce the "New Jew," the antithesis of the "Diaspora Jew" whose negative image was denounced by the early Zionists. Women were also assigned the role of boundary marker (Yuval-Davis 1989, 102) as a Jew, according to Jewish ruling, is a person born of a Jewish *mother*. The task of being a mother therefore was not perceived as falling within the private domain, but rather as a public mission, carrying national significance. The personal and the political were, in the Israeli case, inseparable entities. Hazleton (1977) noted the impact of the "political womb" on the lives of Israeli women. Motherly functions, in this family-centered society, provided a passport to political life.

Women and the Israeli Polity: What Does the Future Portend?

An understanding of the female's place in any society is critical for understanding the nature and aims of the political life of that particular community (Saxonhouse 1985, 16). What can be learned from this analysis of women's political status about the Israeli polity? The case under discussion highlights some of the more stable characteristics of the political system, as well as some of the changes it has been undergoing. The position of women reflects in a nutshell the high politicization of the country, the collectivist mood, the overriding power of the state, and the homogeneity of Israeli society.

- For at least the first three decades of Israeli statehood, and in some respects up to the present, women's activity was directed through partisan channels. The waxing and waning of political careers was determined at the headquarters of political parties. Public policy on women's equality was also a product of party commitments, rather than a reflection of individual efforts for the benefit of women. Negotiations on behalf of women were conducted in smoke-filled rooms at the party central office.

- That Israel was (and to some extent still is) a collective-oriented society should be clear from the foregoing discussion. The individual was expected literally to sacrifice his/her life for the sake of the nation. A widely quoted saying of one of the early pioneers—"It is good to die for our country"—exemplifies this sentiment. The harnessing of women's lives to the national wagon through the family was one symptom of this attribute.

- Like other peoples engaged in a struggle for national liberation, the Israelis turned their state into a sublime entity. The process of nation-building required a host of individual sacrifices. At the same time it necessitated the development of strong state institutions assiduously disseminating resources and mobilizing support for achieving collective goals. The status of women demonstrated the effectiveness of the national mobilization process, as well as the monopolization by the state of the issue of gender equality.

- Finally, Israel has been characterized as a melting pot. Having absorbed Jews from all corners of the world, and being a home for non-Jewish citizens, it often boasts of its pluralism and heterogeneity. But the fact of the matter is quite different. There is a low level of tolerance in Israel to variance and to being different. Any deviation from the mainstream is severely criticized as detrimental to society and as a threat to national unity. When women interests were articulated in a separatist way, they gained less legitimacy than in other Western countries.

Women's present status mirrors the changes that have swept the country. The advent of a technological economy, the integration of the most of the newcomers into Israeli society, the emergence of a broad middle class, the increased exposure to the outside world through the media and tourism, and primarily the easing of regional tensions and the genesis of the peace process—all have sparked considerable changes in Israel's polity. Currently the country is undergoing processes of depoliticization, personalization, privatization, and diversification. Political parties no longer monopolize, or even dominate, the articulation of interests in Israel, as the power of interest groups and political movements has increased dramatically (Yishai 1991). The growing importance of the individual is evident not only from vague impressions of the political culture, but also from institutional arrangements. Political parties now recruit their legislative representatives through the system of primaries. This measure has increased the personal accountability of the legislators and their reliance on individual voters. The state, for its part, has swayed with the winds of privatization blowing from the industrialized world. A wide-ranging campaign is under way to sell state companies and decrease the government's involvement in corporate affairs. Finally, there has been a growing sense of diversification in Israeli society. In recent years a law banning discrimination against homosexual men and lesbian women was approved by the Knesset, and Ethiopian Jews were allowed to conduct their own wedding ceremonies. These are harbingers of a more liberal spring. If the processes outlined here continue uninterrupted, the face of the Israeli polity is bound to change.

Will women contribute to this change? The answer must wait until women hold a significant share of the senior decision-making positions in the country. The first steps, however, are well advanced. As the final lines of this book were being written, (August 1994) the Ministry of Education announced the adoption of a comprehensive program, formulated by the women's movement, to introduce education in gender equality into the state-controlled school system. The reaction of Alice Shalvi, chairperson of the Women's Network, is indicative of the women's current status in Israel. She said: "Even in the lives of those striving for gender equality, who at times become depressed by the lack of far-reaching social change, there are moments of exhilaration, days when a ray of light signals some change, even small, in the status of women in Israel."[5] This exhilaration is justified by women's growing eagerness to strive for their equality, an eagerness that is expressed by combining mobilization and integration, rather than choosing between them.

NOTES

1. Between the Flag and the Banner

1. *Maariv*, 15 April 1994.

2. In 1988, ten years after the commission's recommendations were presented to the prime minister, the women's movement noted that they were hardly implemented. Major directives remained a dead letter. Yet women's consciousness has leapt forward. Already in 1976 a first center for Women's Studies was established at Ben-Gurion University in Beer Sheba, in the southern part of Israel. Academic units centering on women were also set up in other universities carrying social science studies.

3. The Secretary's Column, *Dvar Hapoelet*, September 1975.

2. Women in the Elite

1. A noted author, compiling data on members of the first five Knessets, ignored the fact that the woman MK represented a women's party, and classified her as "liberal" (Zidon 1965, 386).

2. In June 1994 the Foreign and Security Affairs Committee assigned, for the first time in Israeli history, a woman—Yael Dayan—to chair a subcommittee on the territories. *Haaretz*, 22 June 1994.

3. Meir was nominated foreign minister following a major rift between David Ben Gurion and Meir's predecessor, Moshe Sharet who was known for his moderate views on the Arab-Israeli conflict.

4. Tamar Eshel, *Dvar Hapoelet*, August–September 1977.

5. *Naamat*, November 1976.

6. Shoshana Arbelli-Almozlino, *Naamat*, March–April 1983.

7. Limor Livnat, Broadcast Services, 22 February 1992.

8. Golda Meir, *Dvar Hapoelet*, January 1966.

9. Nava Arad, *Naamat*, July–August 1981.

10. Women's Network, information leaflet, 1994.

11. In an interview with Dafna Sharfman the late Rachel Kagan claimed that among the Israeli members of the WIZO board the vote was split equally between those supporting her Knesset candidacy and those opposing it (Sharfman 1988, 66).

12. The following discussion is based mainly on Sharfman 1988 and Freedman 1990.

13. Independent socialists constituted one component of the peace camp, including also the Panters, Uri Avneri's group, and Moked. These three organizations were not hospitable to women's demands.

14. The Women's Party included a token man among its candidates, indicating it did not run purely as a women's list.

15. In the Labor Party, quotas were granted to women (20 percent), young members (15 percent), and pensioners (7 percent). Any woman, whether young, middle-aged, or elderly, would be counted in the women's quota. Note that the principle of affirmative action, whereby women enjoyed a quota in electoral lists, was harshly criticized by party activists. One activist feared a boomerang effect, working against voting for women who in any case were likely to win a safe seat. Another activist did not challenge the principle but its contents, suggesting that the 20 percent allotted to women was only token, not reflecting women's real power. Avirama Golan, "Women Divided," *Haaretz*, 30 March 1992.

16. Anticipating future partnership with religious parties in a ruling coalition, the party declined to make specific commitments on family policy, being satisfied with the following statement: "The party will act to formulate a comprehensive family policy in Israel, in order to ensure the family's economic security and harmonious functioning. This policy will be formulated through coordination among government ministries dealing with all aspects of the family issue" (provision

6.6, chapter 6). This version deviated widely from Naamat's proposal submitted by the women's section in the party to abolish the exclusive authority of rabbinical courts on family matters.

17. Leadership of the section consists of rabbi's wives rather than women selected on their own merit. *Haaretz,* 7 January 1992.

18. The proportion of women in the Labor Party center was 11 percent; in its secretariat—6.5 percent in 1970. In Herut, the Likud's predecessor, the rates were 5 percent and 3 percent, respectively. Even in Ratz (the Civil Rights Movement) women's representation was not impressive: 30 percent on the council, but only 7 percent on the executive (Yishai 1978, 242).

19. The sample size was as follows: all women in the two highest ranks of the civil service (except one who declined to be interviewed), a total of 39; a sample of 79 senior male civil servants, and a sample of 87 women of middle rank.

20. Among senior women 60.5 percent were married; 82.1 percent had children. Among senior men, 98.7 percent were married, and all of these had children.

21. The Nurses Union, the Paramedics Union, Physiotherapists Union, and the Needle Workers Union.

22. Oaks and Almquist (1993) argue that women's lack of economic power may block their way to decision-making bodies. This aspect is dealt with in chapter 6.

23. *Naamat,* "Editorial," February 1980.

24. *Haaretz,* 7 January 1991.

3. Women's Associations and Movements

1. The decision to establish a separate unit followed the failure to invite a woman representative to the fifth conference of the agricultural union of the Galilee. Women barged in and protested; they also decided to convene their own conference of women agricultural workers (Maimon-Fishman 1929, 52, quoted in Izraeli 1992, 189).

2. The radicals favored direct elections by a general meeting of women workers at the local level without regard to women's party affiliation and free of party intervention. Their major concern was to

establish meaningful ties between the delegates and the women workers. The loyalists advocated that women candidates be nominated by the party functionaries of the local labor council in cooperation with the WWM. They were more concerned about the effectiveness of women representatives, fearing that withdrawal of Histadrut support would be detrimental to women's power (Izraeli 1992, 200–201).

3. *The Saga of a Movement: WIZO 1920–1970.* (WIZO, n.d.), 11.

4. The Representative Assembly ratified the principle of women's suffrage in 1925, then nullified it under pressure of the orthodox, who demanded a referendum on the question. After Agudat Israel, the ultra-orthodox party, announced it would boycott the referendum, the more moderate religious party, the predecessor of the NRP, assented to women's suffrage, which was ratified by the Representative Assembly. Of 221 delegates to the Second Assembly 26 were women (Swirski 1991a, 292–93).

5. The change of title took place as a result of the unification of the WWM's two branches: the Council of Working Women and the Organization of Working Mothers.

6. The law stipulates that the property accumulated by a couple in the course of their marriage be equally divided upon divorce.

7. Beba Idelson, *Dvar Hapoelet*, September–October 1965.

8. Rivka Katzenelson, interview with Beba Idelson, ibid., June 1965.

9. Beba Idelson, "Women's Parliament," ibid., August 1966.

10. Naamat's petition was based on the Declaration of Independence, enacted in 1948. While this declaration serves as a judicial guideline, it carries no constitutional binding power. See Arian 1989.

11. Women are exempt from military service on grounds of being religiously orthodox. They may, however, volunteer for "national service" in civic institutions such as hospitals and schools, thereby fulfilling their national duty without being exposed to secular society.

12. Nava Arad, *Naamat*, April 1981.

13. Masha Lubelsky, "Give Me a Hand?!", ibid., October–November 1984.

14. Editorial. ibid., June–July 1985.

15. Ibid., February 1985.

16. "The Peace of the Galelee," ibid., May 1982.

17. In 1984 WIZO opened its first shelter for battered wives, serving since as the flagship of the association and a point of attraction for contributors from abroad.

18. *The Saga*, 244 n. 3.

19. Helena Glazer, "The Woman's Platform," WIZO pub., 1992.

20. Alice Shalvi, the elected chairperson the association since its inception, in Women's Network, information leaflet, February 1992.

21. Women in Black organized in 1988 around the slogan, "End to the Occupation." The group, comprising between 5 and 250 women demonstrated each Friday until the Oslo agreements were signed. Their title was derived from the fact that all demonstrators wore black clothes while standing in major crossroads. Lili Galili, "250 Weeks in the Town Square," *Haaretz*, 3 January 1994.

22. The formal institutional makeup of Naamat is as follows: A national conference convenes after elections; it selects a National Council of 301 members. This council convenes twice a year to discuss issues decided by the conference. A National Secretariat, consisting of 101 members of the ruling party and its coalition allies, convenes every month. An Active Secretariat is responsible for day-to-day running of the association.

23. In the last elections to the Histadrut, in April 1994, Labor failed, for the first time in the organization's history, to secure a winning majority. In Naamat, however, the Labor list did gain over 50 percent of the vote.

24. The legal committee, composed of attorneys and legal experts, operates to reveal and combat gender discrimination and to draft legislation to erase gender inequality. The political committee, composed of representatives of political parties, is concerned mainly with encouraging women to run for political office while committing them to the feminist cause.

25. *Haaretz*, 14 March 1994.

26. A partial list of feminist subgroups in Israel includes the following: Association for Victims of Sexual Abuse, Claf (Community of Lesbian Feminists), Woman to Woman, Institute for Media Research, Women's Health Information Center, NO—Combat Violence Against Women, Noga (a feminist magazine), rape crisis centers, shelters for

battered women, Shin—The Movement for Equal Representation of Women, and Women against Offensive Publicity. For details, see *Services for Women,* Jerusalem: Israel Women's Network, 1994.

27. Masha Lubelsky, *Naamat,* November 1981.

28. Protocols of Naamat secretariat, 16 November 1983. Naamat Archives.

29. Ibid., 16 November 1983. Naamat Archives.

30. Ibid., 22 May 1989.

31. Nava Arad, *Naamat,* July 1977.

32. Nava Arad, *Naamat,* July–August 1981.

33. A letter from Ronit Lev Ari, head of Naamat's Department for the Prevention and Treatment of Violence in the Family, to Ora Namir, chairperson, the Knesset Committee on Labor and Welfare, 15 July 1991. Naamat Archives.

34. Avirama Golan, *Haaretz,* 8 March 1992.

35. Amira Segev, "The Color of Feminism," *Haaretz,* 20 June 1994.

36. The information for this section is derived from questionnaires distributed by the author to political grassroots movements (including women's movements) in 1992. The findings of the study within which data were collected were summarized in "Challenging Them or Fighting Them: Political Movements in Israel." Paper presented at the annual meeting of the European Consortium for Political Research, Limerick, Ireland 1992.

37. Number of members in the groups ranged between 50 (Coalition of Women and Peace) to 1,500 (Women's Network for Peace),

38. Claf activists stated that the association did not aim at broad social change or exerting pressure on decision-makers, but targeted its efforts at Israeli lesbians in order to raise their consciousness.

39. The fact that the associations were granted legitimacy only on a personal basis is also evident from the answer to a question probing their correspondence with public authorities. Answers varied from "only rarely do authorities answer our letters" to "they never answer."

40. In 1973 a group of Arab women, students and university graduates, began a consciousness-raising activity in Acre, the outcome of which was the creation of Dar e-Tifl el-Arabi, a school teachers' training institute. Swirski 1991, 295.

41. A. Dayan, "Her Father, her Brother, her Husband," *Haaretz*, 13 September 1991.

42. *Jerusalem Post*, 3 January 1991.

43. Erela Shadmi, "Question Marks." *Noga* 26 (Autumn 1993): 23.

44. Ofra Friedman, *Haaretz*, 14 July 1994.

45. Masha Lubelsky, *Naamat*, February 1990.

4. Political Participation

1. The survey, conducted in the winter of 1993 for this study covered a national sample of 1,170 Jewish urban respondents, comprising 529 men and 641 women.

2. Beba Idelson, "In Right and not in Charity," *Dvar Hapoelet*, November 1961.

3. Ofra Friedman, *Naamat*, June 1994.

4. The study of the non-Jewish population was conducted in Shefar'Am, a small Arab town located in the Galilee. The survey, conducted in the spring of 1993, comprised 340 women and 118 men.

5. The proportion of Israelis who read a daily newspaper at least one day per week was 77.8 percent in 1991–92. *Statistical Abstract of Israel* 1993, 748.

6. At the time of writing, June 1994, the Knesset passed a National Health Insurance Law aimed at abolishing the party–health care nexus. It remains to be seen if this law will weaken the grip of parties on social services.

7. The survey was conducted by Asher Arian of Haifa University and Michal Shamir of Tel Aviv University. Some results of this survey were published in Shamir and Arian 1994. The sample included 1,180 respondents—624 women and 556 men.

8. Rachel Adiv, "In the Margins of the Meeting." *Dvar Hapoelet*, March 1962.

9. The 1973 survey, conducted by Asher Arian was based on a national sample of 1,885 Jewish respondents—1,010 women and 875 men.

10. The data presented in tables 4.1 and 4.5 do not match because the former was derived from the survey conducted for this study and the latter from the Shamir-Arian pre-election study.

5. Women's Gender Identity

1. Masha Lubelski, *Naamat* 91 (August 1986).

2. The majority of senior male administrators reported that their wife was responsible for cooking and housework (75.9 percent and 59.5 percent respectively). Among the women the proportion of those stating their spouse performed these jobs was far lower (11.1 percent and 11.5 percent, respectively).

3. The research literature distinguishes between "discrimination," which is the objective dimension of actual unequal treatment, and "deprivation," which is the subjective perception of rewards (Levitin et al. 1971). Another distinction refers to two types of deprivation: one is felt on account of a group's placement within society; the other on account of the individual's placement within the specific group (Runciman 1966). In the present context, the term is used as a subjective concept referring to individuals' own experience.

4. The cutting point for distinguishing between women with a high gender identity and a low gender identity was as follows: Answers to the questions presented in each category—equality in politics, family, and society—ranged on a scale from 1 (highly agree) to 4 (highly disagree). High identity was ranged between those scoring 3–5 points (on a 12-point scale); low 9–12 points.

5. The distinction between high gender identity and low gender identity regarding political orientations and participation was analyzed on the basis of all ten statements with the cutting point as follows: high—10–20; low—30–40, both on a 40-point scale.

6. The exact wording of the question was: "To what extent does it interest you to watch television programs on each of the following subjects?"

7. The following data reveal the low status of Arab women. The proportion of those who have acquired less than eight years of schooling is 54.7 percent compared with 49.7 percent among Arab men and 21.3 percent among Jewish women. The respective figures for those who have acquired higher education (13 years of schooling or more)

are 7.0 percent for Arab women, 10.9 percent for Arab men, and 29.9 percent for Jewish women. Only 35.4 percent of Arab women work outside their home, compared with 41.6 of Jewish women. *Statistical Abstracts* 1992, 335, 341, 362, 364.

8. In 1991 the fertility rate among Moslems in Israel was 4.70, compared with 2.05 among the Jews. *Statistical Abstracts* 1992, 136.

9. A quote from a presentation given by an Arab activist in a symposium on Women and Peace. Haifa, April 1994.

10. Printed in the quarterly *Newsletter*, quoted in *Jerusalem Post*, 3 January 1990.

11. *Jerusalem Post*, 3 January 1991.

12. Quoted in Women's Network, information leaflet, February 1992.

6. Labor Policy

1. *Ha'ir*, 29 January 1993.

2. A woman physician was denied internship in a public hospital by a department head (a man) who was quoted saying: "If I can choose between a man and a woman I will prefer a man. . . . I can't help it, but a woman gets pregnant and bears a child. Men's work is more intensive than women's; they devote themselves to their jobs, their research performance is higher." *Haaretz*, 18 March 1994.

3. Peak participation of women in the labor force is in the 35–44 age group (75.6 percent). In older age groups the rate gradually declines. *Statistical Abstracts* 1993, 12.5

4. The index ranges between 0 (no segregation) to 100 (total segregation). The index score indicates the percentage of men or women who would need to change their occupation in order for the percentage of the sexes in each occupation to equal their respective proportion in the labor force. Cohen et al. 1987, 97.

5. The following data, on women's membership of the boards of directors of economic enterprises, demonstrate the glass ceiling they face in their attempts to ascend to senior economic positions: Egged (the major bus company): 1 woman out of 31 members; Bank Hapoalim (one of the three major banks): 1 out of 31 members; Tnuva (a major

marketing company for agricultural products): 0 women members; Kupat Holim (the major health insurance fund in the country): 14 out of 96 members. *Naamat*, September 1982.

6. *Haaretz*, 30 April 1993.

7. Israeli women are unequal before the law in income tax regulation. A working woman enjoys tax concessions for each of her children younger than 18. Since 1983 a woman has been entitled to information regarding her husband's remuneration. Furthermore, she is entitled to present her own annual report to income tax authorities. However, a married Israeli woman is still unable to have her own tax file. Even if she handles her own report, the final evaluation is made on the basis of her husband's file. Even if she is entitled to concessions, these are credited to her husband's account and usually are not payable.

8. The study of senior women public officials revealed a gender gap in one of the major benefits of the position: a free trip abroad. Among senior women 64.1 percent reported that they had never been given a chance to travel abroad; among senior men the proportion denied this privilege was only 32 percent.

9. In 1989 the Knesset enacted a law prohibiting dismissal of both spouses undergoing fertility treatment.

10. Women were prohibited from working between midnight and 6 a.m. in service industry and commercial jobs, and between midnight and 5 a.m. in agriculture. The law did set forth certain exception to be specified by the minister of labor. These were bound to be "essential to the state and not likely to be especially prejudicial to the health of a woman."

11. France was the last state in Europe to cancel the century-long prohibition against women working night shifts. *Haaretz*, 28 February 1992.

12. [1972/73] 4 Piskei Din (P.D.) 365.

13. *Knesset Minutes*, 15 March 1978, p. 2108.

14. Ibid., p. 2109.

15. *Nevo v. the Jewish Agency*, [1986/87] 18 P.D. 197, 219.

16. Haim Ramon, *Knesset Minutes*, 20 January 1987, p. 1281.

17. Ibid., p. 1282.

18. Ibid., p. 1284.

19. On 5 December 1983, the trade union department of the Histadrut passed a resolution, making extension of retirement age for women conditional on the agreement of every economic enterprise. The Histadrut general conference, however, invalidated this resolution. Haviva Avi-Guy, chairperson of the Department on the Status of Women in Naamat, to Haim Haberfeld, chairman of the trade union department, 29 December 1985. Naamat Archives.

20. *Globes,* 3 November 1992.

21. Moshe Katzav, *Knesset Minutes*, 5 November 1986, p. 114.

22. Amnon Linn, ibid., 20 October 1987, p. 109.

23. *Dvar Hapoelet,* February 1961.

24. "Moetzet Hapoalot—Towards a Mass Integration of Women in the Labor Force," ibid., May 1961.

25. Beba Idelson, "Knesset Comes and Knesset Goes." ibid., June 1961.

26. Ibid., January 1964.

27. Sarah Doron, *Knesset Minutes*, 15 December 1986, p. 106.

28. Naamat Secretariat meeting, 22 November 1982. Naamat Archives.

29. Ibid., 29 November 1983.

30. Shulamit Aloni, *Knesset Minutes*, 13 December 1986, p. 712.

31. The information was given by the Department for the Status of Women in the Ministry for Labor and Welfare.

32. *Work, Welfare and National Insurance.* (Jerusalem: National Insurance Institute, 1990).

33. Ora Namir, Knesset Labor and Welfare Committee, 10 November 1987. Private Archive.

34. Yitzhak Barak, the legal advisor of the Ministry of Work and Welfare, ibid.

35. Beni Shalita (Likud), *Knesset Minutes*, 23 February 1988, p. 1988.

36. *Segol-Maariv*, 10 October 1990.

7. Family Policy

1. *Haaretz,* 8 March 1993.

2. The survey's results were published in *Naamat,* October 1984.

3. *Haaretz,* 23 February 1993.

4. The study of senior state officials has revealed that a quarter of the senior women administrators had foregone occupational opportunities for the sake of their husband's careers. Among the male senior officials, the proportion of those reporting they had to make such concessions was negligible, 1.2 percent. More than 10 percent of the senior women officials stated that their husband's attitudes towards the women's career served as major constraint for their promotion. Only 1.3 percent of the male senior officials perceived their wives' attitudes as a deterrent to their careers.

5. *Financial Times,* 27 July 1992.

6. But when wives' income is equal to or greater than their husbands', the division of labor in the family is more egalitarian (Izraeli and Silman 1992).

7. In her book *Women as Human Beings,* Shulamit Aloni, a minister in Yitzhak Rabin's government (1994), describes cases whereby stubborn husbands were haled before the courts year after year on account of their refusal to grant a divorce. No one, however, could compel them to do so. Aloni 1976, 50–51.

8. Moshe Nissim, justice minister, *Knesset Minutes,* 19 March 1986, p. 2278.

9. Avraham Sharir, justice minister, *Knesset Minutes,* 22 July 1987, p. 3786.

10. Moshe Nissim, justice minister, *Knesset Minutes,* 19 March 1986, p. 2276.

11. *Davar,* 24 January 1983.

12. Masha Lubelski, Naamat's secretary-general, at a press conference, 10 March 1987, Naamat Archives.

13. Masha Lubelski, *Letter to the Member,* 13 November 1988.

14. Nava Arad, *Knesset Minutes,* 7 July 1987.

15. Ibid., 22 July 1987, p. 3785.

16. *Haaretz,* 13 May 1993.

17. Ibid., 28 September 1993.

18. A letter from Alice Shalvi to Prof. Pinhas Shifman, 29 December 1987. WN Archives.

19. The WN included members of many parties: Sara Doron and Yigael Horowitz (Likud); Amnon Rubinstein (Shinui); Menahem Hacohen (Labor).

20. The legal definition of a marriage hinderer was: one who has separated from one's spouse and has lived separately for at least two years with the aim of breaking the marriage bond. "Such a person, i.e., one refusing to grant a divorce or stipulating an unreasonable condition for it, is not entitled to hold an Israeli passport, to leave the country, to possess a driver's license, to be nominated to any position in the civil service, in local government or in the armed forces, or to appeal for judicial welfare." These provisions are cited from the proposed bill on the Prevention of Marriage Hindrance (1989), published by the Women's Network on 20 February 1990.

21. *Haaretz,* 11 November 1992.

22. According to a Knesset decision taken in 1951, the entire body of Basic Laws would add to the state's Constitution.

23. *Haaretz,* 25 November 1992; 1 December 1992.

24. For example, child allowance, is determined on be basis of the man's income, regardless of the earnings of his wife. A man barely passing the means test is entitled to this benefit even though his wife's earnings are double his.

25. *Knesset Minutes,* 18 May 1971. Note the unconditional support for the law of Shoshana Arbelli-Almozlino (Labor), the chairperson of the Welfare Committee.

26. Letter from Tanya Levenfish, the chairperson of WIZO's Council for the Status of Women, to Meir Shamgar, the government's legal advisor, 2 May 1971. WIZO Archives.

27. The only exception is war widows, who enjoy special status and economic benefits in Israeli society. Katz 1993.

28. *Knesset Minutes,* 10 December 1991, p. 1205.

29. Beba Idelson, ibid., 31 January 1962, p. 1123.

30. Shlomo Hillel, ibid., 14 July 1976, p. 3537.

31. In 1979 a woman MK, Tamar Eshel (Labor), raised the issue in the Committee of Interior Affairs, but the discussion yielded no results in terms of policy.

32. In her Knesset speech Freedman commended WIZO for its role in promoting the issue: "Of all the interested parties and bodies to which I applied, this was the only one to prove sensitive to the subject and ready to assist me." *Knesset Minutes*, 14 July 1976, p. 3538.

33. 1978: No to Violence against Women, in Herzliya, a small coastal town near Tel Aviv. 1981: Woman to Woman, in Jerusalem. 1984: WIZO shelter, in Ashdod. 1991: Naamat Shelter, in Tel Aviv.

34. Subcommittee's conclusions, submitted to the Knesset on 9 March 1988.

35. In 1986 Naamat demanded to incorporate in the Penalty Law a provision regarding violence in the family. Penalties were to range from a fine to imprisonment. Letter to Justice Minister Avraham Sharir, 11 August 1986, Naamat Archives.

36. *Knesset Minutes*, 19 March 1991, p. 2869.

37. Rafael Pinhasi (Shas), ibid.

38. The Women's Network, for example, proposed, in a letter to the Ministry of Justice on 8 March 1992, amendments such as abolishing the fee paid for issuing a complaint and introducing uniformity to the judicial treatment of complaints.

39. During 1992–94, 104 women were murdered by their husbands. This figure does not include women who were murdered by their boyfriends. Women MKs complain that the policy still regards wife-battering as a family dispute rather than as a criminal offense. *Haaretz*, 19 September 1994.

8. Body Politics

1. *Haolam Haze* (This World) was the name of a radical weekly of which Avneri was the editor. He ran for the Knesset in order to safeguard freedom of the press and gave his paper's name to his party.

2. Uri Avneri, *Knesset Minutes*, 30 June 1972, pp. 3038–40.

3. Victor Shem-Tov, ibid., p. 3040.

4. The campaign to liberalize abortion was joined by another actor. In 1971 the General Sick Fund (Health Insurance) became involved with abortion politics as a result of two major events: first, in a step without precedent, two of its physicians were prosecuted for performing illegal abortions, one of them committed suicide in the course of the trial, the other was sentenced to one year in prison. Although the case was dropped the situation called for legal clarification. Second, studies of interruptions of pregnancy in the Sick Fund's hospitals revealed that only in a few cases were medical factors the reason for requesting the procedure (Yishai 1978a).

5. *Jerusalem Post*, 23 October 1987.

6. Marcia Freedman, *Knesset Minutes*, 15 January 1975, p. 1320.

7. Shulamit Aloni, ibid., 25 January 1977, p. 1241.

8. Ora Namir, ibid., 27 January 1976, p. 1401.

9. *Jerusalem Post*, 28 January 1977.

10. Naamat, information leaflet, 1974.

11. The law of collective responsibility stipulates that if a party, without prior government consent, votes in favor of a no-confidence motion, or votes against a government confidence motion, the government has a right to decide within seven days if this constitutes a breach of responsibility and if the minister whose party so voted should be treated as though he/she had resigned from the government.

12. According to an ancient Jewish proverb, he who saves one soul saves the entire world.

13. One orthodox MK insisted that permission from the husband ought to be obtained prior to certification of abortion.

14. *Knesset Minutes*, 10 February 1976, p. 1607.

15. The figures are 15,925 abortions in 1979 and 16,829 abortions in 1982. *Israel Statistical Abstracts* 1985, 678.

16. Professor Shenkar served for many years as the medical advisor of Efrat—the Israeli pro-life association.

17. Shenkar report, 4 April 1984, p. 1.

18. *Yediot Ahronot*, 4 December 1979.

19. *Jerusalem Post*, 16 February 1976.

20. According to some scholars, the adoption of militant nationalism followed identification with Likud rather than being caused by it. See Shamir and Arian 1990.

21. *Knesset Minutes*, 25 December 1979, pp. 1125, 1127, 1130.

22. *Israel Statistical Abstracts* 1992, 142.

23. Personal communication from Alice Shalvi, chairperson of the Women's Lobby, 25 July 1993.

24. *Haaretz*, 28 November 1990.

25. Doron Haran, Summary of the meeting, WIZO Archives.

26. Naamat protested vehemently it was not invited to the conference. Letter from Masha Lubelski to the minister of health, Ehud Olmert, and the minister of labor and welfare, David Magen, 10 September 1990.

9. Conclusion

1. David Ben Gurion, *Knesset Minutes*, 2 July 1951, p. 2131.

2. Yitzhak Rabin, ibid., 3 March 1993, p. 3712.

3. Shoshana Arbelli-Almozlino, *Naamat* 62, (March–April 1983).

4. Interview with Dalia Itzik, (Labor), *Hadashot*, 10 April 1992.

5. "The Chairperson Speaks," Israel's Women Network, information leaflet, June 1994.

BIBLIOGRAPHY

Almond, Gabriel A. and Sidney Verba. 1989. *The Civic Culture*. Beverly Hills: Sage.

Alvarez, Sonia E. 1989. "Women's Movements and Gender Politics in the Brazilian Transition." In J. S. Jaquette, ed., *The Women's Movement in Latin America*. London: Unwin Hyman.

———. 1990. *Engendering Democracy in Brazil: Women's Movements in Transition Politics*. Princeton, N.J.: Princeton University Press.

Annual Report 43. 1993. Ministry of Treasury, Civil Service Authority, Jerusalem.

Apter, David. 1965. *The Politics of Modernization*. Chicago: University of Chicago Press.

Arat, Y. 1989. *The Patriarchal Paradox: Women Politicians in Turkey*. Rutherford, N.J.: Fairleigh Dickinson University Press.

Arian, Asher. 1973. *The Choosing People*. Cleveland: Case Western Reserve University Press.

———. 1989. *Politics in Israel: The Second Generation*. 2nd ed. Chatham, N.J.: Chatham House.

Azmon, Yael. 1993 "Women and Politics: The Case of Israel." In Azmon and Izraeli 1993.

Azmon, Yael and Dafna N. Izraeli, eds. 1993. *Women in Israel*. New Brunswick, N.J.: Transaction.

Bachrach, Peter, and Morton Baratz. 1962. "Two Faces of Power." *American Political Science Review* 50: 947–52.

Baker, A. 1993. *The Jewish Woman in Contemporary Society: Transitions and Traditions*. London: Macmillan.

Bar-Yosef, Rivka and Dorit Padan-Eisenstark. 1993. "Role System under Stress: Sex Roles in War." In Azmon and Izraeli 1993.

Barnes, Samuel, Max Kaase, et al., *Political Action: Mass Participation in Five Western Democracies*. Beverly Hills: Sage.

Bashevkin, Sylvia B. 1985. *Toeing the Lines: Women and Party Politics in English Canada*. Toronto: University of Toronto Press.

Baxter, Sandra and Marjorie Lansing. 1983. *Women and Politics: The Visible Majority*. Ann Arbor: University of Michigan Press.

Ben Eliezer, Uri. 1993. "The Meaning of Political Participation in a Nonliberal Democracy: The Israeli Experience." *Comparative Politics* 25: 397–412.

Ben Gurion, David. 1971. *Israel: A Personal History*. New York: Funk and Wagnalls.

Ben Porath, Yoram. 1986. "Patterns and Peculiarities of Economic Growth and Structure." *Jerusalem Quarterly* 38: 43–63.

Bergmann, Barbara. 1986. *The Economic Emergence of Women*. New York: Basic Books.

Bernstein, Deborah S. 1987a. *The Struggle for Equality: Urban Women Workers in Pre-State Israeli Society*. New York: Praeger.

———. 1987b. "The Women Workers' Movement in Pre-State Israel, 1919–1939." *Signs* 12: 454–70.

———. 1991. "Oriental and Ashkenazi Jewish Women in the Labor Market." In Swirski and Safir 1991.

———, ed. 1992a. *Pioneers and Homemakers: Jewish Women in Pre-State Israel*. Albany: SUNY Press.

———. 1992b. "Human Being of Housewife: The Status of Women in the Jewish Working Class Family in Palestine of the 1920s and 1930s." In Bernstein 1992a.

———. 1993. "Economic Growth and Female Labour: The Case of Israel." In Azmon and Izraeli 1993.

Bialik, Hayyim Nahman. 1924. *Poems from the Hebrew.* London: "Hasefer."

Bih-er, C., C. Clark and J. Clark. 1990. *Women in Taiwan Politics: Overcoming Barriers to Women's Participation in a Modernizing Society.* Boulder: Lynne Reinner.

Black, Naomi. 1980. "Feminism and Integration: The European Communities' Surveys 'European Men and Women'." *Journal of European Integration* 4: 83–103.

Boneparth, Ellen and Emily Stoper. 1989. Women, Power and Policy. Toward the Year 2000. 2nd ed. New York: Pergamon.

Bloom, Anne R. 1991. "Women in the Defense Forces." In Swirski and Safir 1991.

Bourque, Susan C., and Jean Grossholtz. 1974. "Politics an Unnatural Practice: Political Science Looks at Female Participation." *Politics and Society* 4: 225–66.

Brichta, Avraham and Yael Brichta. 1994. "The Extent of the Impact of the Electoral System upon the Representation of Women in the Knesset." In J. Zimmerman and Wilma Rule, eds., *The Impact of the Election Systems on Minorities and Women.* Westport, Conn.: Greenwood Press.

Browning, G. K. 1987. *Women and Politics in the USSR: Consciousness Raising and Soviet Women's Groups.* New York: St. Martin's Press.

Bubber-Agassi, Judith. 1991. "How Much Political Power Do Israeli Women Have?" In Swirski and Safir 1991.

Carroll, Susan, J. 1988. "Women's Autonomy and the Gender Gap: 1980 and 1982." In C. M., Mueller, ed., *The Politics of the Gender Gap: The Social Constraints of Political Influence.* Beverly Hills: Sage.

Catt, H. and McLeay E., eds. 1993. *Women and Politics in New Zealand.* Wellington: Victoria University Press.

Chafetz, Janet S. 1990. *Gender Equity.* Newbury Park, Calif.: Sage.

Christy, Carol A. 1987. *Sex Differences in Political Participation: Processes of Change in Fourteen Nations.* New York: Praeger.

Cobb, Roger W. and Charles D. Elder. 1972. *Participation in American Politics: The Dynamics of Agenda-Building.* Baltimore: Johns Hopkins University Press.

Cohen, Yinon, Shlomit Bechar, and Rebecca Reijman. 1987. "Occupational Sex Segregation in Israel, 1972–1983." *Israel Social Science Research* 5: 97–106.

Conover, Pamela Johnston. 1984. "The Influence of Group Identifications on Political Perceptions and Evaluations."*Journal of Politics* 46: 760–85.

———. 1988. "Feminists and the Gender Gap." *Journal of Politics* 50: 985–1010.

Costain, Ann N. 1989. "Representing Women: The Transition from Social Movement to Interest Group." In E. Boneparth Ellen and E. Stoper, eds., *Women, Power and Policy: Toward the Year 2000.* New York: Pergamon.

———. 1992. *Inviting Women's Rebellion: A Political Process Interpretation of the Women's Movement.* Baltimore: Johns Hopkins University Press.

Costain, Ann N. and W. D. Costain. 1987. "Strategy and Tactics of the Women's Movement in the United States: The Role of Political Parties." In Katzenstein and Mueller 1987.

Dalton, Russell J. 1988. *Citizen Politics in Western Democracies.* Chatham, N.J.: Chatham House.

Danez, V. H. *Women and Party Politics in Peninsular Malaysia.* Oxford: Oxford University Press.

Davies, Miranda. 1983. *Third World—Second Sex: Women's Struggles and National Liberation.* London: Sed Books.

De Beauvoir, Simone. 1961. *The Second Sex.* New York: Bantam Books.

DiPalma, Giuseppi. 1970. *Apathy and Participation: Mass Politics in Western Society.* New York: Free Press.

Distribution of Seats between Men and Women in National Parliaments. Statistical Data from 1945 to 30 June 1991. 1991. Geneva: Inter-Parliamentary Union.

Dogan, M. 1975. "The Political Power of the Western Europe Mandarins: Introduction." In M. Dogan, ed., *The Mandarins of Western Europe: The Political Role of Top Civil Servants.* New York: Halstead.

Duverger, Maurice. 1955. *The Political Role of Women.* Paris: UNESCO.

Eduards, Maud L. 1981. "Sweden." In Joni Lovenduski and Jill Hills, eds., *The Politics of the Second Electorate.* London: Routledge and Kegan Paul.

Efroni, Linda. 1980. "Promotion and Wages of Women in Israel." Ph.D. dissertation (Hebrew). Hebrew University, Jerusalem.

Eisenstadt, Shmuel, N. 1985. *The Transformation of Israeli Society*. London: Weidenfeld and Nicolson.

Eisenstein, Zillah R. 1979. "Developing a Theory of Capitalist Patriarchy and Social Feminism." In Z. Eisentein, ed., *Capitalist Patriarchy and the Case of Socialist Feminism*. New York: Monthly Review Press.

Elazar, Daniel. 1986. *Israel: Building a New Society*. Bloomington: Indiana University Press

Elshtain, J. B. 1981. *Public Man/Private Woman*. Princeton, N.J.: Princeton University Press.

Epstein, Cynthia F. and R. Coser, eds. 1981. *Access to Power: Cross-National Studies of Women and Elites*. Boston: George Allen and Unwin.

Epstein, Maxine and Reggi Marder. 1986. *Shalom Bayit: A Follow-Up Study of Battered Women in Israel* (Hebrew). Haifa: Breirot.

Etzioni-Halevi, Eva and Ann Illy. 1993. "Women in Legislatures: Israel in a Comparative Perspective." In Azmon and Izraeli 1993.

Falk, Zeev W. 1978. "The New Abortion Law of Israel." *Israel Law Review* 13: 109–10.

Feldman, D. M. 1986. *Health and Medicine in the Jewish Tradition*. New York: Crossroads.

Firestone, Shulamit. 1972. *The Dialectic of Sex*. New York: Bantam Books.

Freedman, Marcia. 1990. *Exile in the Promised Land: A Memoir*. Ithaca, N.Y. Firebrand Books.

Freeman, Jo. 1975. *The Politics of Women's Liberation*. New York: David McKay.

Friedlander, Dov. 1974. "Israel." In B. Berlson, ed., *Population Policy in Developed Countries*. New York: McGraw-Hill.

Friedman, Menachem. 1977. *Society and Religion: The Non-Zionist Orthodox in Eretz Israel, 1918–1936* (Hebrew). Jerusalem: Yad Yitzhak Ben Zvi.

Fuchs, Victor R. 1988. *Women's Quest for Economic Equality*. Cambridge, Mass.: Harvard University Press.

Galnoor, Itzhak. 1982. *Steering the Polity: Communication and Politics in Israel*. Beverly Hills: Sage.

Gelb, Joyce. 1989. *Feminism and Politics: A Comparative Perspective*. Berkeley: University of California Press.

Gelb, Joyce and Marian Palley. 1987. *Women and Public Policies*. 2nd ed. Princeton: Princeton University Press.

Gellner, W. 1983. *Nations and Nationalism*. Oxford: Blackwell.

Gilligan, Carol. 1977. "In a Different Voice: Women's Conceptions of Self and of Morality." *Harvard Educational Review* 47: 481–517.

Goldberg, Giora. 1982. "The Performance of Women in Legislative Politics: The Israeli Example." *Crossroads* 9: 27–49.

Goot, Murray and Elizabeth Ried. 1984. "Women: If Not Apolitical, Then Conservative." In Janet Siltanen and Michelle Stanworth, eds., *Women and the Public Sphere*. London: Hutchinson.

Gottlieb, Aharon and Ephraim Yuchtman-Yaar. 1983. "Materialism, Post-Materialism, and Public Views on Socioeconomic Policy: The Case of Israel." *Comparative Political Studies* 16: 307–35.

Greenberg, O. and Hanna Herzog. 1978. *A Voluntary Women's Organization in a Society in the Making* (Hebrew). Tel Aviv: Department of Sociology and Anthropology of the Tel Aviv University.

Gurin, Patricia. 1985. "Women's Gender Consciousness." *Public Opinion Quarterly* 49: 143–63.

Haavio-Mannila, E. and T. Skard. 1985. "The Arena for Political Activity: The Position of Women in the Nordic Societies Today." In Elina Haavio-Mannila et. al., *Unfinished Democracy: Women in Nordic Politics*. Oxford: Pergamon Press.

Hartman, Harriet. 1993. "Economic and Familial Roles of Women in Israel." In Azmon and Izraeli 1993.

Hazleton, Leslie. 1977. *Israeli Women: The Reality behind the Myths*. New York: Simon and Schuster.

Heckscher, Gunar. 1985. *The Welfare State and Beyond: Success and Problems in Scandinavia*. Minneapolis: University of Minnesota Press.

Hernes, Helga M. 1989. "Women and the Welfare State: The Transition from Private to Public Dependence." In A. S. Sassoon, ed., *Women and the State*. London: Unwin Hyman.

Herzog, Hanna. 1991. "Profile of the Female Candidate for Local Office." In Swirski and Safir 1991.

———. 1992. "The Fringes of the Margin: Women's Organizations in the Civic Sector of the Yishuv." In Bernstein 1992.

———. 1994. *Realistic Women: Women in Local Politics* (Hebrew). Jerusalem: Jerusalem Institute for Israel Studies.

Horowitz, Dan and Moshe Lissak. 1989. *Trouble in Utopia*. Albany: SUNY Press.

Inglehart, Ronald. 1977. *The Silent Revolution: Changing Values and Political Styles among Western Publics*. Princeton, N.J.: Princeton University Press.

———. 1990. *Culture Shift in Advanced Industrial Society*. Princeton, N.J.: Princeton University Press.

Izraeli, Dafna N. 1979. "The Sex Structure of Occupations—The Israeli Experience." *Sociology of Work and Occupations* 6: 404–29.

———. 1981. "The Zionist Women's Movement in Palestine, 1911–1927: A Sociological Analysis." *Signs* 7: 87–114.

———. 1988a. "Burning Out in Medicine: A Comparison of Husbands and Wives in Dual Career Couples." *Journal of Social Behavior and Personality* 3: 329–46.

———. 1988b. "Women's Movement into Management." In N. Adler and Dafna Izraeli, eds., *Women in Management Worldwide*. New York: M. E. Sharp.

———. 1991. "Women and Work: From Collective to Career." In Swirski and Safir 1991.

———. 1992. "The Women Workers' Movement: First Wave Feminism in Pre-State Israel." In Bernstein 1992.

Izraeli, Dafna N. and Naomi Silman. 1992. "Money Matters: Spoucal Incomes and Family/Work Relations among Physician Couples in Israel." Paper presented at the annual meeting of the American Sociological Associations, Pittsburgh, PA, 20–24 August.

Izraeli, Dafna N. and Ephraim Tabory. 1988. "The Political Context of Feminist Attitudes in Israel." *Gender and Society* 2: 463–81.

Jayawardena, Kumari. 1986. *Feminism and Nationalism in the Third World*. London: Zed Press.

Jones, K.B. 1993. *Compassionate Authority: Democracy and the Participation of Women*. New York: Routledge.

Karmon, Arik. 1994. *Jewish Sovereignty* (Hebrew). Tel Aviv: Hakibbutz Hameucha.

Katz, Richard, S. Peter Mair, et al. 1992. "The Membership of Political Parties in European Democracies, 1960–1990." *European Journal of Political Research* 22: 329–45.

Katz, Ruth. 1993. "Widowhood in a Traditional Segment of Israeli Society: The Case of the Druze War Widows." In Azmon and Izraeli 1993.

Katz, Ruth and Yohanan Peres. 1986. "The Sociology of the Family in Israel: An Outline of its Development from the 1950's." *European Sociological Review* 2: 148–59.

Katzenstein, Mary Fainsod. 1987. "Comparing the Feminist Movements of the United States and Western Europe: An Overview." In Katzenstein and Mueller 1987.

Katzenstein, Mary Fainsod and Carol McClurg Mueller. 1987. *The Women's Movements of the United States and Western Europe*. Philadelphia: Temple University Press.

Kirkpatrick, J. 1974. *Political Woman*. New York: Basic Books.

Klandermands, Bert P. 1990. "Linking the 'Old' and 'New': Movement Networks in the Netherlands." In R. J. Dalton and M. Keuchler, eds., *Challenging the Political Order: New Social and Political Movements in Western Democracies*. New York: Oxford University Press.

Klein, Ethel. 1984. *Gender Politics*. Cambridge, Mass.: Harvard University Press.

Kramer, Ralph. 1981. *Voluntary Agencies in a Welfare State*. Berkeley: University of California Press.

Lane, Robert E. 1961. *Political Life: Why People Get Involved in Politics*. Glencoe, Ill.: Free Press

LaPlombara, Joseph. 1974. *Politics within Nations*. Englewood Cliffs, N.J.: Prentice-Hall.

Lapidus, Gail W. 1978. *Women in Soviet Society*. Berkeley. University of California Press.

Laron, N. B. Maner-Licht, Yaira Rotstein, and N. Voghera. 1980. "Abortion Committees in Israel: A Reflection of Social Dilemma from the Viewpoint of Social Workers" (Hebrew). *Society and Welfare* 3: 334–50.

Lehman-Wilzig, Sam N. 1990. *Stiff-Necked People, Bottle-Necked System.* Bloomington: Indiana University Press.

———. 1992. *Wildfire Grassroots Revolts in Israel in the Post-Socialist Era.* Albany: SUNY Press.

Levi, Shlomit, Hanna Levinson, and Elihu Katz. 1993. *Beliefs, Adherence to Commandments, and Social Relations among Jews in Israel.* Jerusalem: Guttman Institute for Applied Social Research.

Levitin, R., R. P. Quinn and G. L. Staing. 1971. "Sex Discrimination against the American Working Woman." *American Behavioral Scientist* 15: 237–54.

Liebman, Charles S. 1988. "Conception of the 'State' in Israeli Society." *Jerusalem Quarterly* 47: 95–107.

Liebman, Charles S. and Eliezer Don-Yehiya. 1987. *Civil Religion in Israel: Traditional Religion and Political Culture in the Jewish State.* Berkeley: University of California Press.

Lipset, Martin S. 1971. *Political Man.* London: Heinemann.

Lovenduski, Joni. 1986. *Women and European Politics. Contemporary Feminism and Public Policy.* Brighton, Essex: Wheatsheaf Books.

———. 1993. "Introduction: The Dynamics of Gender and Party." In Lovenduski and Norris 1993. Lovenduski, Joni and Pippa Norris, eds. 1993. *Gender and Party Politics.* London: Sage.

Lovenduski, Joni and J. Woodall. 1987. *Politics and Society in Eastern Europe.* Bloomington, Ind: Indiana University Press.

Maimon-Fishman, Ada. 1929. Women Workers in Eretz Israel (1904–1929). Tel Aviv: The Central Committee of Hapoel Hatzair (Hebrew).

Mansbridge, Jane. 1986. *Why We Lost the ERA.* Chicago: University of Chicago Press.

Mar'i, Mariam M. and Sami K. Mar'i. 1991. "The Role of Women as Change Agents in Arab Society in Israel." In Swirski and Safir 1991.

Medding, Peter Y. 1972. *Mapai in Israel: Political Organisation and Government in a New Society.* Cambridge: Cambridge University Press.

Meir, Golda. 1975. *My Life.* Jerusalem: Steimatzky.

Milbauer, Varda and Mina Tzemach. 1991. *Zug O Peret?* (Hebrew). Tel Aviv: Am Oved.

Milbrath, Lester W. 1968. *Political Participation*. Chicago: Rand McNally.

Milbrath, Lester W. and M. L. Goel. 1977. *Political Participation. How and Why do People Get Involved in Politics?* 2nd ed. Chicago: Rand McNally.

Molyneaux, M. 1985. "Mobilization without Emancipation? Women's Interest, the State, and Revolution in Nicaragua." *Feminist Studies* 11: 227–54.

Moncrief, Gart, Joel Thomson, Robert Schuhmann. 1991. "Gender, Race, and the State Legislature: A Research Note on the Double Disadvantage Hypothesis." *The Social Science Journal* 28: 481–87.

Mosher, F. 1968. *Democracy and the Public Service*. New York: University Press.

Mueller, Carol McClurg, ed. 1988a. *The Politics of the Gender Gap: The Social Constriction of Political Influence*. Beverly Hills: Sage.

———. 1988b. "The Empowerment of Women: Polling and the Women's Voting Bloc." In Meuller 1988a.

Mumtaz, K. and F. Shaheed, eds., 1987. *Women of Pakistan: Two Steps Forward, One Step Back?* London: Zed Books.

Norris, Pippa. 1987. *Politics and Sexual Equality: The Comparative Position of Women in Western Democracies*. Boulder, Colo.: Rienner.

———. 1991. "Gender Differences in Political Participation in Britain: Traditional, Radical and Revisionist Models." *Government and Opposition* 26: 56–74.

Oakes, A. and E. Almquist. 1993. "Women in National Legislatores. A Cross-National Test of Macrostructural Gender Theories." *Population Research and Policy Review* 12: 71–81.

Okin, Susan M. 1979. *Women in Western Political Thought*. Princeton: Princeton University Press.

———. 1991. *Justice, Gender and Family*. New York: Basic Books.

Outshoorn, Joyce. 1988. "Abortion Law Reform: A Woman's Right to Choose?" In M. Buckley and M. Anderson, eds., *Women, Equality and Europe*. London: Macmillan.

Oz, Amos. 1979. *Under this Blazing Light* (Hebrew). Tel Aviv: Sifriat Poalim.

Palgi, Michal. 1993. "Kibbutz Women: Gender Roles and Status." *Israel Social Science Research* 8: 108–21.

Panda, S. 1990. *Determinants of Political Participation: Women and Public Activity*. Delhi: Ajanta Publications.

Park, Ae Kyong. 1990. "Women and Revolution in China: The Sources and Constraints on Women's Liberation." *Korea and World Affairs* 14: 747–74

Participation of Women in the Political and Social Life. European Regional Seminar of UNESCO, Bonn, 24–26 October 1982.

Pateman, Carol. 1989. *The Disorder of Women: Democracy, Feminism and Political Theory*. Stanford: Stanford University Press.

Peled, Ziona and N. Bakman. 1978. *Planned Abortions in Israel: A Behavioral Study of Appeals to Abortion Committees*. Jerusalem: Institute for Applied Social Research.

Peres, Yohanan and Ruth Katz. 1980. "Stability and Centrality: The Nuclear Family in Modern Israel" (Hebrew). *Megamot*, 26:37–55.

Petchesky, Rosalind, P. 1990. *Abortion and Women's Choice*. Rev. ed. Boston: South End Press.

Peterson, V. Spike and Ann Sisson Runyan. 1993. *Global Gender Issues*. Boulder, Colo: Westview Press.

Pharr, S. J. 1981. *Political Women in Japan*. Berkeley: University of California Press.

Pomper, Gerald. 1975. *Voters' Choice: Varieties of American Electoral Behavior*. New York: Dodd, Mead.

Pope, Juliet J. 1991. "Conflict of Interests: A Case Study of Naamat." In Swirski and Safir 1991.

Raday, Frances. 1983. "Equality of Women under Israeli Law." *Jerusalem Quarterly* 27: 81–87.

———. 1989. "Labour Law and Relations—Trends and Directions, 1988." *Israeli Law Journal* 1 (Hebrew).

———. 1991a. "Women, Work and the Law." In Swirski and Safir 1991.

———. 1991b. "The Concept of Gender Equality in a Jewish State." In Swirski and Safir 1991.

Ram, Uri. 1993. "Emerging Modalities of Feminist Sociology in Israel." *Israel Social Science Research* 8: 51–76.

Randall, Vicky. 1987. *Women and Politics: An International Perspective*. Chicago: University of Chicago Press.

Rinehart, Sue Tolleson. 1992. *Gender Consciousness and Politics*. New York: Routledge.

Robinson, Robert V. 1983. "Explaining Perceptions of Class and Racial Inequality in England and the United States of America." *British Journal of Sociology* 35: 344–66.

Rokkan, Stein. 1970. *Citizens, Elections, Parties: Approaches to the Comparative Study of the Processes of Development*. New York: David McKay.

Roter, Rafi and Nira Shamai. 1990. "Social Security and Income Maintenance Policy." In M. Sanbar, ed., *Economic and Social Policy in Israel: The First Generation*. New York: Latham.

Rubin, E. 1987. *Abortion, Politics and the Courts*. Westport, Conn.: Greenwood Press.

Runciman, W. G. 1966. *Relative Deprivation and Social Justice*. Berkeley: University of California Press.

Rusciano, Frank L., 1992. "Rethinking the Gender Gap: The Case of West German Elections, 1949–1987." *Comparative Politics* 24: 335–57.

Sabatello, Eitan F. 1993. "The Impact of Induced Abortion on Fertility in Israel." *Social Science and Medicine* 36: 703–7.

———. 1994. "Short-Range Changes in Fertility and Abortion Patterns among Female Immigrants from the USSR to Israel." *Social Security* 41: 48–56 (Hebrew).

Sabatello, Eitan F. and N. Yaffe. 1988. "Israel." In P. Sachdev, ed., *International Handbook on Abortion*. Westport, Conn.: Greenwood Press.

Safir, Marilyn. 1991. "Religion, Tradition and Public Policy Give Family First Priority." In Swirski and Safir 1991.

Sanbar, Moshe. 1990. "The Political Economy of Israel, 1948–1982." In M. Sanbar, ed., *Economic and Social Policy in Israel: The First Generation*. Lanham, Md.: University Press of America.

Sapiro, Virginia. 1983. *The Political Integration of Women*. Urbana, Ill.: University of Illinois Press.

Saxonhouse, A. 1985. *Women in the History of Western Political Thought: Ancient Greece to Machiavelli*. New York: Praeger.

Schiff, G. S. 1990. "Recent Developments in Israeli Religious Parties." In G. S. Mahler, ed., *Israel after Begin*. Albany: SUNY Press.

Schneider, Anne and Helen Ingram. 1993. "Social Construction of Target Populations: Implications for Politics and Policy." *American Political Science Review* 87: 334–47.

Schwarz, S. D. 1990. *The Moral Question of Abortion*. Chicago: Loyola University Press.

Sears, D. O. and L. Huddy. 1990. "On the Origins of Political Disunity among Women." In L. A. Tilly and P. Gurin, eds., *Women, Politics and Change*. New York: Russell Sage.

Sella, Amnon and Yael Yishai. 1986. *Israel: The Peaceful Belligerent, 1967–1989*. London: Macmillan.

Semyonov, Moshe and Vered Kraus. 1993. "Gender, Ethnicity, and Income Inequality." In Azmon and Izraeli 1993.

Senti, M. 1992. "Equality and Difference in the Political Decision-Result: The Implementation of Women-Rights in Switzerland." A paper presented at the ECPR Joint Sessions in Limerick, Ireland, April.

Seton-Watson Hugh. 1977. *Nations and States: An Inquiry into the Origins of Nations and the Politics of Nationalism*. Boulder, Colo.: Westview Press.

Shamir, Michal and Asher Arian. 1994. "Comparing Values and Policy Choices: Israeli Public Opinion on Foriegn and Security Affairs." *British Journal of Political Science* 24: 249–71.

Shapira, Rina, Eva Etzioni-Halevi, and Shira Chopp-Tibbon. 1978. "Occupational Choice among Female Academicians—The Israeli Case." *Journal of Comparative Family Studies* 9: 65–82.

Sharfman, Dafna. 1988. *Women and Politics* (Hebrew). Haifa: Tamar.

Sharkansky, Ira. 1988. "Too Much of the Wrong Things." *Jerusalem Quarterly* 45: 3–26.

Shenhav, Yehuda A. and Yitzchak Haberfeld. 1988. "Scientists in Organizations: Discrimination Processes in and Internal Labor Market." *The Sociological Quarterly* 29: 451–62.

Shreiner, Olive. 1914. *Women and War*. New York: Frederick and Stokes.

Shrift, Ruth. 1982. "Marriage: Option or Trap." In A. Fruednabm, Ruth Shrift, and Dafna N. Izraeli, eds., *The Double Bind: Women in Israel* (Hebrew). Tel Aviv: Hakibbutz Hameuchad.

Siim, Birte. 1988. "Towards a Feminist Rethinking of the Welfare State." In K. B. Jones and A. G. Jonasdottir, eds., *The Political Interests of Gender.* London: Sage.

———. 1991. "Welfare State, Gender Politics and Equality Policies: Women's Citizenship in the Scandinavian Welfare States." In Elizabeth Meehan and Selma Sevenhuijsen, eds., *Equality Politics and Gender.* London: Sage.

Smith, Antony D. 1986. *The Ethnic Origins of Nations.* Oxford: Blackwell.

———. 1991. *National Identity.* London: Penguin.

Smooha, Sammy. 1989. *Arabs and Jews in Israel: Conflicting and Shared Attitudes in a Divided Society.* Boulder, Colo.: Westview Press.

Soffer, Arnon. 1988. "Population Projection for the Land of Israel." *Middle East Review* 20: 43–49.

Solomon, Alison. 1991. "Anything for a Baby: Reproductive Technology in Israel." In Swirski and Safir 1991.

Statistical Abstract of Israel. Jerusalem: Central Bureau of Statistics.

Stiel, Isaac E. 1992. *Speeches from the Knesset* (Hebrew). Tel Aviv: Acro.

Sullivan E. L. 1986. *Women in Egyptian Public Life.* Syracuse: Syracuse University Press.

Sundstrom-Feigenber, K. 1988. "Sweden." In P. Sachdev, ed., *International Handbook on Abortion.* New York: Greenwood.

Swirski, Barbara. 1991a. "Israeli Feminism New and Old." In Swirski and Safir 1991.

———. 1991b. "Jews Don't Batter their Wives: Another Myth Bites the Dust." In Swirski and Safir 1991.

Swirski, Barbara and Marilyn P. Safir, eds. 1991. *Calling the Equality Bluff: Women in Israel.* New York: Pergamon.

Tietze, C. and S. K. Henshaw. 1986. *Induced Abortion: A World Review.* 6th ed. New York: The Alan Guttmacher Institute.

Tiger, Lionel and Joseph Shepher. 1975. *Women in the Kibbutz.* New York: Harcourt, Brace Jovanowich.

Togeby, Lise. 1992. "The Nature of Declining Party Membership in Denmark: Cases and Consequences." *Scandinavian Political Studies* 15: 1–19.

Toren, Nina. 1993. "The Status of Women in Academia." In Azmon and Izraeli 1993.

Tribe, L. H. 1990. *Abortion: The Clash of Absolutes*. New York: Norton.

Tzemach, Tamar and Tziona Peled. 1983. *The Status of Women in the Public Eye*. Jerusalem: Institute for Applied Social Research.

Vallance, E. and Davies E. 1986. *Women of Europe, Women MEP's and Equality Policy*. Cambridge: Cambridge University Press.

Verba, Sidney, Norman Nie, and J. Kim. 1980. *Participation and Political Equality*. Cambridge: Cambridge University Press.

Waintrater, Regine. 1991. "Living in a State of Siege." In Swirski and Safir 1991.

Walby, Sylvia. 1991. "Women and Nation." *International Journal of Comparative Sociology* 33: 81–100.

Walker, Jack L., Jr. 1991. *Mobilizing Interest Groups in America: Patrons, Professions, and Social Movements*. Ann Arbor: University of Michigan Press.

Welsh, Susan. 1980. "Sex Differences in Political Activity in Britain." *Women and Politics* 1: 29–46.

Winch, R. 1968. "Some Observations on Extended Familism in the U.S." In R. Winch and W. Goodman, eds., *Selected Studies in Mariage and the Family*, 3rd ed. New York: Holt, Rinehart and Winston.

Wolfsfeld, Gadi. 1988. *The Politics of Provocation: Participation and Protest in Israel*. Albany: SUNY Press.

Wolkinson, Benjamin, Gedaliahu H. Harel, and Dafna N. Izraeli. 1982. "Employment Discrimination against Women: The Israeli Experience." *Employee Relations Law Journal* 7: 466–89.

World Development Report 1991: The Challenge of Development. Oxford: Oxford University Press.

Yaacobi, Gad. 1982. *The Government of Israel*. New York: Praeger.

Yishai, Yael. 1978a. "Abortion in Israel: Social Demand and Political Responses." *Policy Studies Journal* 7: 270–89.

———. 1978b. "Women's Political Representation in Israeli Parties." *Megamot* 24: 238–51 (Hebrew).

———. 1982. "Israel's Right-Wing Proletariat." *Jewish Journal of Sociology* 24: 87–98.

———. 1984. "Responses to Ethnic Demands. The Case of Israel." *Ethnic and Racial Studies* 11: 283–306.

———. 1985. "Women and War: The Case of Israel." *Journal of Social, Political and Economic Studies* 10: 195–214.

———. 1991. *Land of Paradoxes: Interest Politics in Israel*. Albany: SUNY Press.

———. 1993a. "The Hidden Agenda: Abortion Politics in Israel." *Journal of Social Policy* 22: 193–212.

———. 1993b. "Public Ideas and Public Policy: Abortion Politics in Four Democracies." *Comparative Politics* 25: 207–28.

———. 1994. "Interest Parties: The Thin Line between Groups and Parties in the Israeli Electoral Process." In K. Lawson, ed., *How Political Parties Work: Perspectives from Within*. New York: Praeger.

———. 1995. "Equal but Different? The Gender Gap in Israel's 1992 Elections." In Asher Arian and Michal Shamir, eds., *The Elections in Israel 1992*. Albany: SUNY Press.

Yuval-Davis, Nira. 1985. "Front and Rear: The Sexual Division of Labour in the Israeli Army." *Feminist Studies* 11: 649–76.

———. 1989. "National Reproduction and 'the Demographic Race' in Israel." In N. Yuval-Davis and F. Anthias, eds., *Woman—Nation—State*. New York: St. Martin's Press.

Zidon, Asher. 1965. *The Knesset—Israel's Parliament* (Hebrew). Jerusalem: Achiasaf.

INDEX

285